THE
ARCHANGEL
MICHAEL

THE ARCHANGEL MICHAEL

His Mission and Ours

Selected Lectures and Writings
edited by Christopher Bamford

RUDOLF STEINER

✑ Anthroposophic Press

ACKNOWLEDGMENTS: Rudolf Steiner Nachlassverwaltung for permission to translate *Früheste ausführliche Nachschrift von Rudolf Steiner's Darstellungen des Michael-Ereignisses im Jahre 1879*, contained in *Beiträge zur Rudolf Steiner Gesamtausgabe, Nr. 67/68*; Rudolf Steiner Verlag (Rudolf Steiner Nachlassverwaltung) for permission to translate the first six lectures of *Die Sendung Michaels* [The Mission of Michael], which is volume number 194 in the Complete Works (Gesamtausgabe) of Rudolf Steiner, translated by Marjorie Spock. Also Rudolf Steiner Press for permission to reprint the following: *Foundations of Esotericism*, Lecture XXIX, pp. 234–35; *Guidance in Esoteric Training*, p. 84; *The Mission of the Individual Folk Souls*, pp. 31–36, 45–46; *Occult Science and Occult Development. Christ at the Time of the Mystery of Golgotha and Christ in the Twentieth Century*, pp. 21ff; *The Festivals and their Meaning*, pp. 359–66, 376–79; *The Four Seasons and the Archangels*, pp. 9–23; *Rosicrucianism and Modern Initiation*, pp. 83–98; *Karmic Relationships (Esoteric Studies)*, Volume VI, pp. 142–163; *Karmic Relationships (Esoteric Studies)*, Volume III, pp. 119–130; *True and False Paths in Spiritual Investigation*, pp. 33–37; *Karmic Relationships (Esoteric Studies)*, Volume VIII, pp. 31–45; *The Last Address*, pp. 17–19. For further bibliographical information see the references at the back of the book.

Published in the United States by Anthroposophic Press
P.O. Box 799, Gt. Barrington, MA 01230

www.anthropress.org

LIBRARY OF CONGRESS CATALOGING-IN-PUBLICATION-DATA

Steiner, Rudolf, 1861–1925.
  [Selections. English. 1994]
  The Archangel Michael : his mission and ours : selected lectures and writings / Rudolf Steiner : edited by Christopher Bamford.
    p. cm.
  Includes bibliographical references.
  ISBN 0-88010-378-7
  1. Anthroposophy. 2. Michael (Archangel) I. Bamford, Christopher.
II. Title.
BP595.S894E5
299'.935—dc20   94–25045
                                                CIP

10 9 8 7 6 5

CONTENTS

INTRODUCTION by Christopher Bamford .... page 9

PROLOGUE: Intimations of the Archangel Michael
in Different Traditions .... page 11

PART ONE

1. RUDOLF STEINER'S EARLY ACCOUNTS OF THE MICHAEL EVENT OF 1879
Berlin, *November 3, 1905* and *October 9, 1907;*
Münich, *December 5, 1907*..page 30

2. THE INTEGRATION OF HUMANITY INTO THE RANKS OF THE HIERARCHIES
Düsseldorf, *April 15, 1909;* Oslo, *June 7 and 8, 1910*............ page 34

3. MICHAEL, THE MESSENGER OF CHRIST
London, *May 2, 1913* .... page 43

4. THE ARCHANGEL MICHAEL: THE TIME SPIRIT
Stuttgart, *May 18, 1913* .... page 53

5. MICHAEL AND THE BUDDHA
Stuttgart, *May 20, 1913* .... page 60

6. BEHIND THE SCENES OF EXTERNAL HAPPENINGS: THE FALL OF THE SPIRITS OF DARKNESS
Zürich, *November 6 and 13, 1917* .... page 64

7. SIGNS OF THE TIMES: MICHAEL'S WAR IN HEAVEN
AND ITS REFLECTION ON THE EARTH

Münich, *February 17, 1918* ....page 77

PART TWO

THE MISSION OF
THE ARCHANGEL MICHAEL

Revelation of Essential Secrets of the Human Being

LECTURE 1

The contrast between the evolution of the head and the rest of the organism—Triad and duality in the world and human understanding—The abolition of the tripartite human being at the Eighth Ecumenical Council of Constantinople of 869—The Christ-Impulse as the balance between Lucifer and Ahriman

Dornach, *November 21, 1919* .... page 99

LECTURE 2

The head as retrogressive, the rest of the organism as progressive —Pre-Christian Revelations: Day Revelations through the head (Lucifer), Night Revelations through the rest of the organism (Jahve)—Michael, the Countenance of Jahve—The transformation of Michael from Night Spirit to Day Spirit—Michael's Task in the past and the future: The Word becomes flesh and the flesh becomes Spirit

Dornach, *November 22, 1919*...page 112

LECTURE 3

Luciferic and Ahrimanic influences—Michaelic thinking—The true concept of evolution—Progressive and regressive evolution—Beauty in art and the battle between beauty and ugliness

Dornach, *November 23, 1919*...page 127

LECTURE 4

The Mystery of Golgotha, the central point in earthly evolution, prepared for in Greek thinking, the last remnant of ancient Mystery culture—Scholasticism, the continuation of Greek thinking— Since the fifteenth century: the preparation of a new Mystery culture—The need to penetrate the heart organization with the Christ-Impulse (to balance Lucifer penetrating the head and Ahriman working in the limbs)

Dornach, *November 28, 1919* .... page 143

LECTURE 5

The evolution of the human soul—The problem of necessity and human freedom—The evolution of the God concept from the fourth to the sixteenth centuries—Michael's deed influence as the counterpole to Ahriman—The necessity of the Christ-Impulse

Dornach, *November 29, 1919* .... page 160

LECTURE 6

The ancient yoga culture and the new yoga will—The achievement of a new knowledge of pre-existence as Michael culture in the future

Dornach, *November 30, 1919* .... page 175

PART THREE

1. MICHAEL'S MISSION: THE SPIRITUALIZATION
OF THE KNOWLEDGE OF SPACE

Dornach, *December 17, 1922* .... page 193

2. MICHAEL, THE DRAGON, AND THE HUMAN SOUL
OR GEMÜT

Vienna, *September 27, 1923* .... page 201

3. THE MICHAEL IMAGINATION

Dornach, *October 5, 1923* .... page 214

4. THE TASKS OF THE MICHAEL AGE

Dornach, *January 13, 1924* .... page 225

5. FROM THE GABRIEL TO THE MICHAEL AGE

Arnhem, *July 19, 1924* .... page 239

6. THE MICHAEL IMPULSE: TO READ IN THE BOOK
OF NATURE

Dornach, *August 1, 1924* .... page 258

7. MICHAEL, SOPHIA, AND MARDUK

Torquay, *August 11, 1924* .... page 267

8. MICHAEL, ARTHUR, AND THE GRAIL
Torquay, *August 21, 1924* ....page 269

9. FROM RUDOLF STEINER'S LAST ADDRESS
Dornach, *September 28, Michaelmas Eve, 1924* ....page 282

10. FROM: *THE MICHAEL LETTERS*
August 17 and *31, 1924;*

November 9 and *16, 1924* ....page 284

APPENDIX: JOHANNES TRITHEMIUS. A Treatise on the Seven Secondary Causes: A Little Book or MYSTICAL CHRONOLOGY, Containing within a Short Compass Marvellous Secrets Worthy of Interest .... page 299

BIBLIOGRAPHY .... page 317

INTRODUCTION

Under different names, from the moment the idea of humanity was born in the Divine Mind, the spiritual Being known as Michael has ✓ accompanied humanity on its journey through the cosmos.

This Being or divine-cosmic Presence was most important to Rudolf Steiner. Every aspect of Steiner's life and work is permeated by service to Michael's evolutionary task.

This task—Michael's mission—is closely related to that of the Christ and hence also to that of the Earth, whose meaning Christ is, as well as to that of Sophia, the Divine Wisdom or Cosmic Intelligence, upon whose concrete, human realization God's vision of the universe hangs.

Thus Michael's task depends in turn upon what human beings are called upon to do. Michael cannot fulfill his mission without humanity's cosmic vocation of freedom, individuality, and love. Human beings, too, depend on Michael for the fulfillment of *their* task.

But Michael stands ready on the other side of the threshold. His joy is helping those who of their own free deed enter the ranks of those collaborating in the great work of the invisible.

Since 1879, this has been his special province. Since then, too, extraordinarily powerful spirits of darkness have been shifted into the human realm—making the issue of right orientation central in all psycho-spiritual endeavor.

Yet to turn and find Michael we need only orient ourselves in earnest to the business of transforming our ways of thinking and perceiving. Then the Spirit, present everywhere—in all things and places, realms and peoples—can begin to awaken and become conscious in and through our activity.

This work of mutation is the next evolutionary moment. It contains the promise of a new art of science and religion that, transforming space and matter, will reconnect us with the cosmos, the divine, and ourselves.

The essence of this path is creativity. To participate in it—to create anew in every moment—requires courage, patience, and selfless dedication.

It is a cosmopolitan path, asking us to penetrate beyond differences of language and discourse to a new sphere where living thinking becomes cosmic feeling. And cosmic feeling becomes primal will, which is creative, originary Love.

From 1894, when he published *The Philosophy of Freedom*—the first truly Michaelic work—to 1925 when, on his death bed, he composed the so-called *Michael Letters,* Rudolf Steiner dedicated his entire being to the task of helping human beings fulfill their cosmic role as Michael's helpers. In this book we have gathered together a representative sampling of his lectures and writings dealing with this theme.

May those who read this work find themselves also to be "Michael's helpers," "pupils" in Michael's school.

In the words of a meditation Rudolf Steiner gave in 1922:

> The soul's true home
> is the spirit's sphere
> and we shall surely reach it
> if we go the way of true thinking,
> choosing the heart's powers of love
> as our strong leader
> and opening our inner soul senses
> to the script
> which we can always find
> and which everywhere
> reveals itself in world existence,
> heralding the spirit's presence
> in all that lives and, living, acts
> and in all that lifeless
> extends itself in space
> and in all that passes
> in time's stream of becoming.[1]

CHRISTOPHER BAMFORD

---

1. Cf. Rudolf Steiner, *Verses and Meditations*, p. 139.

Intimations of the Archangel Michael
in Different Traditions

INDIAN

FROM THE *Rig Veda*:

Let me now sing the heroic deeds of Indra, the first that the thunderbolt-wielder performed. He killed the Dragon and pierced an opening for the waters; he split open the bellies of mountains.

He killed the Dragon who lay upon the mountain; Tvastr fashioned the roaring thunderbolt for him. Like lowing cows, the flowing waters rushed straight down to the sea.

Wildly excited like a bull, he took the Soma for himself and drank the extract from the three bowls in the three-day Soma ceremony. Indra, the generous, seized his thunderbolt to hurl it as a weapon: he killed the first-born of Dragons.

Indra, when you killed the first-born of Dragons, and overcame by your magic the magic of the magicians, at that very moment, you brought forth the sun, the sky, and dawn. Since then, you have found no enemy to conquer you.

With his great weapon, the thunderbolt, Indra killed the shoulderless Vrtra, his greatest enemy. Like the trunk of a tree, whose branches have been lopped off by an axe, the Dragon lies flat upon the ground.

For, muddled by drunkenness like one who is no soldier, Vrtra challenged the great hero who had overcome the mighty and who drank the Soma to the dregs. Unable to withstand the onslaught of his weapons, he found Indra an enemy to conquer him and was shattered, his nose crushed.

Without feet or hands, he fought against Indra, who struck him on the nape of the neck with his thunderbolt. The steer, who wished to become the equal of the bull bursting with seed, Vrtra lay broken in many places.

Over him, as he lay there like a broken reed, the swelling waters flowed for human beings. Those waters that Vrtra had enclosed within his power—the dragon now lay at their feet....

In the midst of the channels of the waters, which never stood still or rested, the body was hidden. The waters flow over Vrtra's secret place: he who found Indra an enemy to conquer him sank into long darkness.[1]

* * *

PERSIAN

FROM THE *Denkard*:

It is thus manifest that, after the passing of the thirtieth year from his birth, Zardusht went at dawn to the bank of the river Daiti, to make the hom-libation.

When he came up from the water, he saw Vahman, the Amahraspand,[2] in the shape of a man, fair, bright, and radiant. Vahman wore a garment like silk, which was as light itself. And he was nine times taller than Zardusht. He questioned Zardusht: "Who are you? Whose are you? What is your chief desire? In what are you diligent?"

And Zardusht answered: "I am Spitaman Zardusht. My chief desire, in both existences, is righteousness. And my wish is to become aware of the aim of the two existences. And I shall practice as much righteousness as they show me in the pure existence."

And Vahman bade Zardusht: "Go forward to the Assembly of Divine Beings."

1. *Rig Veda* 1,32. Adapted from the translation by Wendy O'Flaherty (Penguin Books, 1981).
2. Vahman=Vohu Mana=Good Mind, Wisdom; Amahraspand=one of the Seven Bounteous Immortals.

Zardusht took ninety steps to the nine steps of Vahman. And when he had taken ninety steps, he saw the Assembly of the Seven Amahraspands. And when he came to within twenty-four feet of the Amahraspands, he no longer saw his own shadow on the ground, because of the great light of the Amahraspands.

Zardusht paid homage. And he said: "Homage to Ohrmazd! Homage to the Amahraspands!" And we went forward and sat in the place of the seekers after enlightenment. . . .[3]

* * *

CHALDEAN
(Babylonian)

FROM THE *Babylonian Epic of Creation*:

"Thou, Marduk, art most honored of the great gods,
thy decree is unrivaled, thy word is Anu.
From this day unchangeable shall be thy pronouncement.
To raise or bring low—these shall be in thy hand.
Thy utterance shall be true, thy command shall be
     unimpeachable.
No one among the gods shall transgress thy bounds. . . .

O Marduk, thou art indeed our avenger.
We have granted thee kingship over the universe entire.
When in Assembly thou sittest, thy word shall be supreme.
Thy weapons shall not fail; they shall smash thy foes!
O lord, spare the life of him who trusts thee,
but pour out the life of the God who seized evil."

Having placed in their midst a piece of cloth,
they addressed themselves to Marduk, their first-born.

---

3. Adapted from *Textual Sources for the Study of Zoroastrianism*, edited and translated by Mary Boyce (Totowa, N.J.: Barnes and Noble, 1984).

"Lord, truly thy decree is first among gods.
Say but to wreck or create; it shall be.
Open thy mouth and the cloth will vanish!
Speak again, and the cloth shall be whole."
At the word of his mouth the cloth vanished.
He spoke again and the cloth was restored.
When the Gods, his fathers, saw the fruit of his word,
joyfully they did homage: "Marduk is King!"
They conferred on him scepter, throne, and vestment;
they give him matchless weapons that ward off foes:
"Go and cut off the life of Tiamat.
May the winds bear her blood to places undisclosed.". . .

Then Tiamat and Marduk, wisest of Gods, joined issue.
They strove in single combat, locked in battle.
Marduk, the lord, spread out his net to enfold her,
the evil wind that followed behind he let loose in her face.
When Tiamat opened her mouth to consume him,
he drove in the evil wind that she close not her lips.
As the fierce winds charged her belly,
her body was distended, and her mouth was wide open.
He released the arrow, it tore her belly,
it cut through her insides, splitting the heart.
Having thus subdued her, he extinguished her life.
He cast down her carcass to stand upon it.
After he had slain Tiamat, the leader,
her band was shattered, her troupe broken up. . . .

When Marduk hears the words of the gods,
his heart prompts him to fashion artful works.
Opening his mouth, he addresses Ea
to impart the plan he had conceived in his heart:
"Blood will I mass and cause bones to be.
I will establish a savage, 'humanity' shall be its name.
Verily, savage-humanity I will create.
It shall be charged with the service of the gods

—that they might be at ease!..."
Ea answered him, speaking a word to him,
giving him another plan for the relief of the gods:
"Let but one of their brothers be handed over;
he alone shall perish that humanity may be fashioned...."

Marduk summoned the great Gods to Assembly:...
"Who was it that contrived the uprising
and made Tiamat rebel, and joined battle?
Let him be handed over who contrived the uprising...."
The Igigi, the great gods, replied to him:...
"It was Kingu who contrived the uprising,
and made Tiamat rebel, and joined battle."
They bound Kingu, holding him before Ea.
They imposed on him his guilt, and severed his blood.
Out of his blood they fashioned humanity....

After Ea, the wise, had created humanity,
had imposed upon it the service of the gods—
that work beyond comprehension;
artfully planned by Marduk, created by Nudimmud—
Marduk the king of the gods divided
all the celestial gods above and below....[4]

* * *

GREEK

I

FROM THE *Homeric Hymn to Apollo*:
... Phoebus Apollo laid out the foundations [of Delphi],
broad and long from beginning to end; and on them

---

4. Adapted from the *Enuma elis*, "When on high," Tablets IV and VI in *The Ancient Near East, An Anthology of Texts and Pictures*, vol. 1, translated by E. A. Speiser (Princeton: Princeton University Press, 1958).

the sons of Erginos, Trophonios, and Agamedes,
dear to the immortal gods, placed a threshold of stone.
And numberless races of humanity built the temple all around
with hewn stones, to be a theme of song forever.
Near it there was a fair-flowing stream, where the lord,
son of Zeus, with his mighty bow, slew a She-Dragon,
a great, glutted, and fierce monster, which afflicted
many evils on the people of the land—many on them and many on
their slender-shanked sheep: for she was bloodthirsty.
And once from golden-throned Hera she received and reared
dreadful and baneful Typhaon, a scourge for mortals.
Hera bore him in anger at father Zeus. . . .

. . . Cow-eyed, mighty Hera took him and, piling evil
upon evil, she commended him to the care of the She-Dragon.
He worked many evils on the glorious races of humanity,
and she brought their day of doom to those who met her, until the
lord, far-shooting Apollo, shot her
with a mighty arrow. Rent with insufferable pains
she lay panting fiercely and writhing on the ground.
The din was ineffably awesome, and throughout the forest
she was rapidly thrusting her coils hither and thither; with a gasp
she breathed out her gory soul, while Phoebus Apollo boasted:
"Rot now right here on the earth that nourishes human beings;
you shall not ever again be an evil bane for those who live
and eat the fruit of earth that nourishes many . . . but right here
the black earth and the flaming sun will make you rot."
Thus he spoke boasting and darkness covered the Dragon's eyes
and the holy fury of Helios made her rot away;
hence the place is now called Pytho, and people
call the Lord by the name of Pytheios, because on that spot
the fury of piercing Helios made the monster rot away. . . .[5]

---

5. Adapted from the "Homeric Hymn to Apollo" in *The Homeric Hymns*, translated by Apostolos N. Athanassakis (Baltimore: The Johns Hopkins University Press, 1976).

II

FROM THE *Orphic Hymn to Apollo*:

... Slayer of Pytho, Delphic diviner,
you are a wild, light-bringing and lovable god, O glorious youth.
You shoot your arrows from afar, lead the Muses into dance,
and, O Holy One, you are Bacchos, Didymeus, and Loxias, too.
Lord of Delos, eye that sees all and brings light to mortals,
golden is your hair, and clear your oracular utterance.
You gaze upon all the ethereal vastness,
and upon the rich earth you look through the twilight.
In the quiet darkness of a night lit with stars
you see the earth's roots below, and you hold the bounds
of the whole world. You, too, are the beginning and the end.
You make everything bloom, and with your versatile lyre
you harmonize the poles....[6]

*   *   *

HEBREW

FROM THE *Book of Enoch*:

I

These are the names of the holy Angels who watch.
Uriel, who is over the world and over Tartarus. [7]
Raphael, who is over the spirits of human beings.
Raguel, who takes vengeance on the world of the luminaries.[8]
Michael, one of the holy Angels, to wit, he who is set over the best
part of humanity and over chaos.[9]
Saraqael, who is set over the spirits who sin in the spirit.

---

6. Adapted from the "Orphic Hymn to Apollo" in *The Orphic Hymns*, translated by
Apostolos N. Athanassakis (Missoula, Montana: Scholars Press, 1977).
7. Or: "who presides over clamor and terror."
8. Or: "who inflicts punishment on the world and the luminaries."
9. Or: "who, presiding over human virtue, commands the nations."

Gabriel, who is over Paradise and the serpents and the Cherubim.

Remiel, one of the holy Angels, whom God set over those who rise....[10]

II

And I saw thousands of thousands, and ten thousand times ten thousand. I saw a multitude beyond number and reckoning, who stood before the Lord of Spirits.

And, on the four sides of the Lord of Spirits, I saw four Presences, different from those that sleep not.

And I learned their names: for the Angel who went with me made known to me their names and showed me all the hidden things.

And I heard the voices of those four Presences as they uttered praises before the Lord of glory:

—the first, blessing the Lord of Spirits for ever and ever;

—the second, blessing the Elect One and the elect ones who suffer on account of the Lord of Spirits;

—the third, praying and interceding for those who dwell on the earth and supplicate the name of the Lord of Spirits;

—and the fourth, fending off the Satans and forbidding them to come before the Lord of Spirits to accuse them who dwell on the earth.

Then I asked the Angel of Peace, who went with me and showed me everything that is hidden: "Who are these four presences which I have seen, whose words I have heard and written down?"

And he said to me: "The first is *Michael,* the merciful and long-suffering;[11]

—and the second, who is set over all the diseases and all the wounds of the children of humanity is *Raphael;*

—and the third, who is set over all the powers is *Gabriel;*

—and the fourth, who is set over the repentance unto hope of those who inherit eternal life, is named *Phanuel.*"

---

10. From the Book of Enoch, XX.

11. Compare the prayer of Rabbi Eleazar Kalir: "Michael, prince of mercy, pray for Israel, that it may rule in the heights, in the light of the countenance of the King who sits there on his throne of mercy."

These are the four Angels of the Lord of Spirits and the four voices
I heard in those days....[12]

III

And after that it came to pass that my spirit was translated
And it ascended into the heavens
And I saw the Holy Sons of God.

They were stepping on flames of fire:
Their garments were white,
And their faces shone like snow.

And I saw two streams of fire,
And the light of that fire shone like a hyacinth,
And I fell on my face before the Lord of Spirits.

And the Archangel *Michael* seized me by my right hand,
And lifted me up and showed me forth into all the secrets,
And he showed me all the secrets of righteousness.

And he showed me all the secrets of the ends of the heaven,
And all the chambers of all the stars, and all the luminaries,
Whence they proceed before the face of the *Holy Ones*.

And he translated my spirit into the heaven of the heavens,
And I saw there as it were a structure built of crystals,
And between these crystals tongues of living fire.

And my spirit saw the girdle which girt that house of fire,
And on its four sides were streams of living fire,
And they girt that house.
And round about were *Seraphim, Cherubim, Ophanim*:
And these are they who sleep not,
And guard the throne of His glory.

---

12. From the Book of Enoch, XL.

And I saw Angels which could not be counted,
A thousand thousands, and ten thousand times ten thousand,
Encircling that house,

And *Michael,* and *Raphael,* and *Gabriel,* and *Phanuel,*
And the holy Angels who are above the heavens,
Go in and out of that house.

And they came forth from that house,
And *Michael* and *Gabriel, Raphael* and *Phanuel,*
And many angels without number.

And with them the Head of Days,
His head white and pure as wool,
And his raiment was indescribable....[13]

FROM THE *Book of Daniel:*

i

The prince of the kingdom of Persia withstood me one and twenty days: but, lo, *Michael,* one of the chief princes, came to help me....

ii

I will show thee that which is noted in the scripture of truth: and there is none that holdeth with me in these things but *Michael* your prince....

iii

And at that time shall *Michael* stand up, the great prince which standeth for the children of thy people: and there shall be a time of trouble, such as never was since there was a nation....[14]

---

13. Adapted from the Book of Enoch, as translated by R. H. Charles (London: SPCK, 1917) and also as translated by Richard Laurence (London 1883, republished Minneapolis: Wizards Bookshelf, 1976).
14. From the Book of Daniel, 10:13,21; 12:1. As Jahve, God of Israel, wages war against the gods of the heathens, so Michael, Jahve's prince, wages war against the princes of the angelic hosts of the Persians and Greeks.

FROM THE *Community at Qumran*:
My three names are: *Michael, Prince of Light*, and *Melchizedek*.[15]

* * *

CHRISTIAN

FROM THE *Epistle of St. Jude*:
When the Archangel *Michael* was arguing with the devil over the fallen body of Moses, he was too discrete to indict him in blasphemous terms, but simply said, "The Lord will punish you."[16]

FROM THE *Book of Revelation*:
And there was war in heaven: *Michael* and his angels fought against the dragon; and the dragon fought and his angels, and prevailed not; neither was their place found any more in heaven. And the great dragon was cast out, that old serpent, called the Devil, and Satan, which deceiveth the whole world: he was cast out into the earth, and his angels were cast out with him....[17]

FROM THE *Celestial Hierarchy of Dionysius the Psuedo-Areopagite*:
The revealing rank of *Principalities, Archangels*, and *Angels* presides over the human hierarchies, in order that the uplifting and return toward God, the communion and union, might occur according to the proper order and, indeed, so that the procession might be given by God benignly to all hierarchies and might arrive at each one in a shared way in a sacred harmony. So, then, it is the *Angels* who take care of our own hierarchy, or so the Word of God tells us. *Michael* is called the ruler of the Jewish people, and other angels are described as rulers of other nations, for "the Most High has

---

15. From Paul J. Kobelski, *Melchizedek and Melchiresa* (Washington, DC: Catholic Bible Association of America, 1981).
16. From the Epistle of Jude 9.
17. From The Revelation of John (The Apocalypse) 12:7–9.

established the boundaries of the nations by the numbers of his Angels (Deut. 32:8)...."

Here is another item for your understanding of the hierarchy. It was revealed to Pharaoh by the *Angel* presiding over the Egyptians and to the ruler of the Babylonians by their *Angel* that there is a concerned and authoritative Providence and Lordship over all things. Servants of the true God were established as leaders for those nations, and the manifestation of things represented by the angelic visions were revealed by God through the *Angels* to certain sacred persons near them, namely Joseph and Daniel. For there is only one ruling source and Providence in the world, and we must not imagine that the Deity took charge of the Jewish people alone.... But the theologians also say that *Michael* presides over the government of the Jewish people and that this is in order to make clear that Israel, like the other nations, was assigned to one of the *Angels*, to recognize through him the one universal ruling Source. For there is only one Providence over all the world, a Supra-Being transcending all power visible and invisible; and over every nation there are presiding *Angels* entrusted with the task of raising up toward that Providence, as their own source, everyone willing to follow, as far as possible.[18]

FROM A *Gothic Hymn*:

> *Michael!* Exalted, powerful Prince of Heaven,
> You bear upward the high golden radiance
> Of Christ, the King.
> Holy is your name, *O Michael*
> "who are like unto God."
> You are Companion of the *Thrones,*
> You are the foundation stone of the celestial canopy,
> You stand in the fortress of the *Dominions,*
> > You tower high among the *Virtues.*
> > You appear like the radiant light of heaven

---

18. Adapted from "The Celestial Hierarchy" in *Pseudo-Dionysius, The Complete Works,* translated by Colm Luibheid (New York: Paulist Press, 1987).

among the *Powers* and *Principalities*.
You bear the fire of expiation
Into the holy choir of the *Cherubim*,
And, supported by your holy spear,
Rule over the *Seraphim*.
As rightfully befits the eldest,
You lead the army of the heavenly host.
In the fourfold row of the eldest
You show yourself radiant in the course of ages.
You are the priest of the two times two rulers
Of the fourth globe.
You stay close to the Creator's throne—
For there is your rightful place.
You are the countenance
Of the ninefold hierarchy
Of the angelic orders.
And of the noble structure
Of the myriad heavenly hosts,
perpetually praising
the thrice Holy Trinity.
You cover the highest Godhead's
face and feet forever,
bowing in exchange
to its three aspects.
Companion of *Uriel*,
Of *Gabriel* and *Raphael*,
From the world's beginnings
You have covered the Godhead
with six rushing flames,
brightly blazing.
Truly, you will remain too
To the end of time
Always united to what is necessary....[19]

19. Adapted from Nora Stein von Baditz, *Aus Michael's Wirken* (Stuttgart: J. Ch. Mellinger Verlag, 1959).

FROM A *Liturgical Poem of Adam of St. Victor for St. Michael's Day*:

> Let all praise *Michael,*
> let none defraud themselves
> of today's great joy.
> This happy day, forever
> telling of the holy angels'
> solemn victory.
>
> The old Dragon is driven off!
> His legion, heaven's foe
> is put to flight!
> In confusion the confuser
> is expelled, the accuser
> hurled from heaven's height.
>
> Under *Michael's* tutelage
> there is peace on earth, peace in heaven—
> praise and jubilation.
> His courage, full of strength,
> defends the communal good,
> and triumphs on the battlefield....[20]

FROM *Joan of Arc*:

When I was thirteen, I had a voice from God to help me govern myself. The first time, I was terrified. The voice came to me about noon: it was summer, and I was in my father's garden. I had not fasted the day before. I heard the voice on my right and toward the church. There was a great light all about. I vowed then to keep my virginity for as long as it should please God.

I saw the light many times before I knew that it was *Saint Michael.* Afterward he taught me and showed me such things that I knew that it was he. He was not alone, but duly attended by heavenly

---

20. Adapted from the liturgical poem "St Michael and All Angels, September 28" in *The Liturgical Poetry of Adam St. Victor,* translated by Digby S. Wrangham (London: Kegan Paul, Trench, & Co.,.1881).

angels. I saw them with the eyes of my body as well as I see you.... Above all, *Saint Michael* told me that I must be a good child and that God would help me. He taught me to behave rightly and to go often to church....

He told me that Saint Catherine and Saint Margaret would come to me, and that I must follow their counsel; that they were appointed to guide and counsel me in what I had to do, and that I must believe what they would tell me, for it was at our Lord's command.

He told me the pitiful state of the Kingdom of France. And he told me that I must go to succour the King of France....

Twice and thrice a week the voice told me that I must depart and go into France.

And the voice said that I would raise the siege before Orléans. And it told me to go to Vaucouleurs, to Robert de Baudricourt, captain of the town, who would give me men to go with me.

And I answered the voice that I was a poor girl who knew nothing of riding and warfare.[21]

FROM *Pico Della Mirandola*:

If I may speak in dark and veiled words of the Mysteries—insofar as I am permitted to by our weakness; our heads sheathed in darkness by the Fall; our eyes darkened by passion and death—I will exhort you first to call upon Raphael, the heavenly physician who will bestow health upon you with his dialectics, which affect us like a health-giving herb. Next, the Archangel Gabriel will endow us with divine force, guiding us through the wonders of nature and demonstrating God's omnipotence at work within them. After this pilgrimage through the sphere of philosophy, Gabriel will hand us over to *Michael, the highest priest, whose grace will give us the Priesthood of Theology, like a crown made of precious stones.* [22]

---

21. From *Joan of Arc, A Self-Portrait*, compiled and translated from the original Latin and French sources by Willard Trask (New York: Stackpole Sons, 1936). Cf. Rudolf Steiner, *Occult History*.
22. Adapted from Nora Stein von Baditz, *Aus Michael's Wirken* (Stuttgart: J. Ch. Mellinger Verlag, 1959).

PUBLISHER'S NOTE

The lectures printed here were given by Rudolf Steiner to audiences familiar with the general background and terminology of his anthroposophical teaching. It should be remembered that in his autobiography, *The Course of My Life*, he emphasizes the distinction between his written works on the one hand, and on the other, reports of lectures that were given as oral communications and were not originally intended for print. For an intelligent appreciation of the lectures it should be borne in mind that certain premises were taken for granted when the words were spoken. "These premises," Rudolf Steiner writes, "include at the very least the anthroposophical knowledge of humanity and of the cosmos in its spiritual essence; also what may be called 'anthroposophical history,' told as an outcome of research into the spiritual world."

PART

1

A NOTE ON THE PRONUNCIATION
OF MI-CHA-EL

In a matter of language, I once knew Rudolf Steiner to be really angry; seeing me crestfallen, he quickly added: I do not mean you personally. In the accustomed English pronunciation of *Michael*—unlike the names of the other Archangels—we practically swallow the last two syllables. (It is a shock to admit it, but we pronounce the name in effect as though we should say "raffle" instead of Raphael.) Toward the end of his life, Steiner was often speaking of the present historic time—beginning with the year A.D. 1879—as the "Age of Michael." So, too, he did in his lectures at Torquay,[1] in interpreting which I naturally pronounced the name as we always do; it did not occur to me to do otherwise. When I visited him at his hotel that evening, he was indignant. The ending *-el,* he said, is the name of God; how can you slur it over in that way? Pronounce the vowels by all means in the accustomed English way, but do not slur them. In German, too, we have the Christian name "Michel" (which, in effect, is pronounced "Michl"), but when referring to the Divine Being you should articulate the full three syllables, *Mi-cha-el* Then, being evidently under the impression that I might think this impossible in English, he went on: You put a stop to spiritual progress if you will insist that your mother tongue can only be spoken according to present-day conventions. . . .[2]

---

1. Among others, this volume pp. 267–82.
2. From: George Adams, "Rudolf Steiner in England," in *A Man Before Others: Rudolf Steiner Remembered.*

ONE

RUDOLF STEINER'S EARLY ACCOUNTS
OF THE MICHAEL EVENT OF 1879

I
The Archangel Known as Michael and the Hosts of Mammon [1]
Berlin, November 3, 1905

All the European esoteric schools say that the bacterial illnesses of modern times—those caused by bacilli—have a similar origin which can be traced back to the spiritual world. This is an esoteric tradition among Rosicrucians and in other esoteric schools where such things are taught. A fundamental teaching exists in small circles of esoteric schools, which states that in the seventies [of the last century] quite definite battles took place in the astral world which caused things to take a better turn [Gap in text]. These events are called the battle between the hosts of the Archangel known to Christian esotericism as Michael and the hosts of the god Mammon. Mammon is the god of hindrances, who places destructive, hindering things in the path of progress. Furthermore, this god Mammon is seen as the creator of quite definite forms which work disturbingly in human life precisely in the sphere of infectious diseases. Certain infectious diseases, unknown in earlier times, are brought about by the god Mammon. [2]

---

1. From: Rudolf Steiner, *Foundations of Esotericism*, Lecture XXIX, pp. 234–5.
2. Cf. C. G. Harrison, *The Transcendental Universe*: "I have said that all great movements in the external world have their origin in the spiritual world, and that the conflict of ideas which marks the transition from one historical epoch to another is, as it were, a copy of a battle already fought and won in the spiritual region. On such a transition period we have just entered. . . . The year 1879 marked the close of an epoch in the intellectual life of Europe and America. In that year, the hosts of light, under S. Michael the Archangel, obtained a decisive victory over the hosts of darkness, led by Beelzebub and Mammon, in a series of battle extending over a period of thirty or forty years. . . ."

II
The Year 1879 [3]
Berlin, October 9, 1907

The year 1879 marks an epoch of the greatest significance in the evolution of humanity because of an event that took place on the astral plane. Since that event, our civilization has taken a different direction.

A certain spiritual stream began to flow in the year 1250 and reached its height in 1459, when Christian Rosenkreutz was raised to the rank of Knight of the Rose-Cross. In 1510, the age known in occultism as *the Age of Gabriel* began. *The Age of Michael* began in 1879. After that comes *the Age of Oriphiel*, when great conflicts will rage among human beings. Therefore a tiny handful of human beings is now being prepared to keep the torch of spiritual knowledge alight in that sombre epoch.

III
Michael, the Radiating Sun [4]
Münich December 5, 1907

All culture originates in the spiritual world. That is where the planets are formed, and they in turn determine the course of our lives on the physical plane. Here, on the earth, we merely witness the way in which one event follows the other according to physical laws, while the great spiritual causes remain hidden from us. But the events that occur on the higher planes of our being are the real cause of physical events. To make this clear, let us look at one example.

An especially important event took place on the astral plane in the year 1879, in November.

---

3. From: Rudolf Steiner, *Guidance in Esoteric Training*, p. 84.
4. From handwritten notes by Anna Weissmann in *Beiträge zur Rudolf Steiner Gesamtausgabe*, Nr. 67/68.

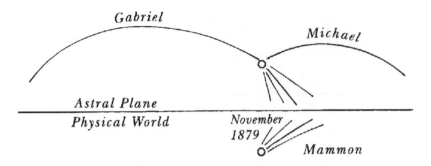

Beginning at that moment, esoteric life completely changed course and became quite different from what it had been previously. The esoteric stream that had been living in humanity since the fourteenth century was replaced by another stream. Between the fourteenth century and the year 1879, occult life took place in the greatest silence and secrecy. Under the guidance of a high spiritual being, the Archangel Gabriel, it was ripening towards the year 1879.

Gabriel means announcement, annunciation, foretelling. That is why the Archangel Gabriel plays the role of the messenger in the Gospels. Under Gabriel's guidance, spiritual life was ripening in complete stillness, well protected and surrounded like a child in its mother's womb. Then, in November 1879, on the astral plane, something quite similar to a birth occurred. What had been maturing since the fourteenth century could now be carried out into the world, even if only before a small minority of human beings, for the reign of Gabriel had been replaced by that of another Archangel, under whose guidance we now operate: the Archangel Michael. Michael is the radiating sun, through whom esoteric wisdom illuminates a small human band. Under Gabriel's guidance, esoteric wisdom remained hidden, while on the physical plane, materialism was developing. But let us not view materialism as something evil, for materialism too is part of the divine creative plan and has a goal and purpose in the cosmic whole. Now, however, the dark forces of materialism have taken the upper hand, and therefore the time has come for the esoteric sun to shine forth once more under Michael's radiant guidance.

Michael's radiant rule will be replaced in turn by a dark, terrifying age, which will begin around the year 2400. Even now, coincident with Michael, a dark god has proclaimed his power: Mammon.

For occultists, Mammon is not only the god of money. Mammon is the leader of all the lower, dark forces. His troops attack not just the human soul, but the physical bodies of humans as well, devouring and destroying them. People speak so much of bacilli nowadays not just because we know so much more about them than we used to, but also because the bacilli have actually taken a completely new form. And in the future, they will acquire even more frightening power.

When this dark age approaches, there will be raging quarrels between brothers, and wars between brothers. Poor human bodies will waste away, prey to dread illnesses and scourges. The seal of sin will be imprinted most visibly onto the human body. Then another Archangel will appear: Oriphiel. He is the one who must come to shake humankind, to jolt it through terrifying suffering, awakening it to its true vocation. For this to happen in the right way, however, there must be, starting now, a small handful of human beings capable of spreading esoteric life during the next four to six hundred years.

Anyone who feels an urge to participate in spiritual life under Michael's guidance is called to serve Michael and learn from him. This is the preparation for service under Oriphiel's terrifying rule. Sacrifice will be required of those who want to consecrate themselves to the spiritual life. The willingness to put oneself at the service of humanity is the necessary prerequisite from anyone who seeks to receive the spiritual life.

In four to six hundred years the handful of human beings who are now preparing themselves will be put in the service of Oriphiel, so that humanity can be saved. If the people who assume the leadership then have not prepared for it by holding their own against the troops of Mammon, they will not be able to play the role assigned them under Oriphiel. Then humanity will not be raised from its misery. Therefore, we must set to work now with the utmost seriousness.

But it is when the darkest forces are at their most violent that the brightest light also shines. Oriphiel has assumed the leadership in the past. The last time was when Christ appeared upon the earth, a period when the worst rottenness and decadence reigned all over the earth. It took terrible sufferings then for the human race to be jolted forward. Oriphiel has been called the Archangel of Anger, who purifies humanity with a strong hand.

The story of Christ's cracking his whip at the money-changers in the Temple has deep meaning in it. At this darkest of times in human history, Christ appeared to save humanity. Oriphiel's reign ended 104 years later and was replaced by Anael's. Then came Zachariel, then Raphael. Raphael reigned at the time of the Renaissance; Gabriel from the sixteenth century to 1879. Then Michael assumed the leadership. Around 2400, it will be Oriphiel's turn again. And, just as the last time, the spiritual light will shine radiantly in the darkness. Christ will appear again on earth, but in a different form. Our vocation is to receive Him, to serve Him.

TWO

THE INTEGRATION OF HUMANITY INTO
THE RANKS OF THE HIERARCHIES

I

Angels, Archangels, and Archai [5]
(Guardian Angels, Folk Spirits, and Time Spirits)
Düsseldorf, April 15, 1909

The Beings who, as we ascend, are closest to human beings are known in Christian esotericism as Angels, Archangels, and Prime Powers or Prime Beginners—*Angeloi*, *Archangeloi*, and *Archai*. In

---

5. From: Rudolf Steiner, *The Spiritual Hierarchies and Their Reflection in the Physical World*, pp. 67–69.

anthroposophical terminology, Archangels are also called Fire Spirits, and the Prime Beginners (or *Archai*) are also known as Spirits of Personality....

Let us first consider the Angels or *Angeloi*. These reached their human stage of development during the Old Moon period and are at present only as far evolved as humanity will be during its Jupiter phase of evolution.[6] Hence, Angels are one stage above humans. What is the task of these Beings? To deal with this question, we shall have to consider the evolution of humanity on the earth....

Every individual is endowed with a Being who, because it stands one stage above humanity, guides that individual from one incarnation to another. We should bear in mind that these are not the beings who order karma, whom we shall refer to later. They are simply Guardian Spirits, who preserve the memory of each incarnation until the next, because human beings cannot do so of their own accord. These are Angels or *Angeloi*. A human being is an individuality in each incarnation, and is watched over by a Being who carries from incarnation to incarnation the consciousness of what occurred in each life. This explains why, at certain lower stages of initiation, people may be able to ask their Angels about their former incarnations. This is within the bounds of possibility. The task of the Angels, therefore, is to stand watch over all the threads that human beings weave from one incarnation to the next.

Now let us consider the next group of Beings, known as Archangels, *Archangeloi*, or Fire Spirits. These are not concerned with single individuals. Their task is more encompassing. They bring about harmonizing influences among larger groups of humans, among peoples, races, etc. They have the task in earthly evolution of bringing individual souls into contact with the various Folk- and Race-Souls. For one who is able to penetrate cognitively and spiritually into the reality of things, Folk-Souls and Race-Souls are quite different from what one generally understands by these terms today, especially

---

6. For the evolutionary stages of (Old) Saturn, (Old) Sun, (Old) Moon, Earth, Jupiter, Venus, and Vulcan, see for instance Rudolf Steiner, *An Outline of Occult Science* and *The Apocalypse of St. John.*

modern, abstract scientists. A number of people live in a particular area—say, in Germany, France or Italy. And because our physical eyes can perceive a number of human beings only as so many outer physical forms, modern thinkers conceive of a Folk-Spirit or Folk-Soul as merely the abstract sum of so many people.

Only the individual human being is real for such modern think-ers, not the Folk-Soul or Folk-Spirit. But for one who is able to look into the true workings of the spiritual world, a Folk-Soul or a Folk-Spirit is a reality. A Fire Spirit or Archangel manifests itself in a Folk-Soul. It governs the relationship between individual human beings and the whole of a people or a race.

But if we rise a stage higher, we come to the Beings known as the Spirits of Personality, Primal Beginnings, Primal Powers, or *Archai*. These are still loftier Beings who have an even more exalted task in the total structure of human affairs. Essentially, they govern all the interrelationships of the whole of the human species on earth. They live in waves of time; they change their configuration from age to age, and are able to take on a different spiritual body at the appointed moment. You are all familiar with what is known abstractly today by the ugly expression "Zeitgeist" (Spirit of the Times, Time Spirit). These *Archai* beings, who are real to spiritual observation, are concerned with the significance and mission of a particular age of humanity. They encompass what goes beyond a sin-gle people or race—for example, the mission and significance of the first millennium following the Atlantean catastrophe. The Spirit of an Age does not restrict itself to a particular people; its influence goes beyond the frontiers of a country.

Such a true Time Spirit, or Spirit of an Age, is the Spirit-Body of an *Archai*, Primal Beginning, or Spirit of Personality. The Spirits of Personality, for example, are responsible for the fact that certain human individualities appear on the earthly scene at the ap-pointed time. You will readily understand that what must be done on earth must be done largely by earthly individualities. Certain epoch-making personalities have to appear at certain particular times. Utter confusion would reign in evolution if this were left to chance, if, for instance, a Luther or a Charlemagne were to appear

quite arbitrarily in one era or another. We must realize the significance of this in regard to the whole of human earthly evolution; the
right souls must appear at a particular moment in the overall pattern of earthly evolution, as it were. This is regulated by the Spirits
of Personality or *Archai.* . . .

II
Archangels and Archai: Folk Spirits and Time Spirits [7]
Oslo, June 7, 1910

In addition to the evolution of peoples and all that is associated
with their evolution, a progressive evolution of humanity as a whole
also takes place. Whether we consider a particular civilization to be
superior to another is unimportant. To express a preference for the
old Indian culture is a matter of personal opinion. A person who is
not swayed by personal opinions will be indifferent to such value
judgments. Human progress follows ineluctably upon the necessary
course of events, though some may later regard this course as a
decline. If we compare various periods—5000 B.C., 3000 B.C. and
1000 A.D., for instance—we are aware of the existence of something
that transcends the Folk Spirits, something in which several Folk
Spirits participate. You can observe this at the present time. How is
it that so many people can sit together in this hall, people who have
come here from many different countries and who understand each
other or try to understand each other when they touch upon vital
questions that have brought them together? They come from the
spheres of activity of very different Folk Spirits, and yet they have
some common ground of understanding. In the same way, different
people were able to understand one another in Atlantean times. In
every age there is something that is more or less universally understood, something that transcends the Folk Souls and can bring them
together. This is the *Zeitgeist* or Time Spirit, the Spirit of the Age, to
use an unfortunate term which is in common usage. Each epoch

---

7. From: Rudolf Steiner, *The Mission of the Individual Folk Souls*, pp. 31–36.

has its own particular *Zeitgeist*; the *Zeitgeist* of the Greek epoch is different from ours. Those who understand the Spirit today are drawn towards Spiritual Science. It is this Spirit which, reflecting the Spirit of the Age, transcends individual Folk Souls. When Christ Jesus appeared on earth, the forerunner, John the Baptist, characterized the Spirit which might be described as the *Zeitgeist* of that epoch in these words: "Repent, change your mental attitude, for the kingdom of heaven is at hand."

Thus, for every epoch, we can discover the Spirit of the Age. The Spirit of the Age is something that permeates the activity of the Folk Spirits, which we have already described as the activity of the Archangels. To today's materialists the Spirit of the Age is an abstraction, devoid of reality. Still less would they be prepared to accept the Spirit of the Age as an authentic entity. Nevertheless, the term "Spirit of the Age" conceals the existence of a real Being, who is three stages above humanity. It conceals the identity of the Beings, the *Archai*, who underwent their human stage on Old Saturn and who are now working on the transformation of the earth from its spiritual aura—in other words, they are undergoing the last stage in the transformation of their physical bodies into the Spirit Body or Atma. Here we are dealing with exalted Beings and the contemplation of their attributes might well overwhelm us. These are the Beings who might be described as the inspirers or—if we choose to use the technical expression of occultism—the "intuitors" of the Spirit or Spirits of the Age. They work in such a way that they take over from one another and mutually support each other. From epoch to epoch, they pass on their mission to their successor. The Spirit of the Age who was active in the Greek epoch handed on his mission to his successor, and so on. As we have already observed, there are a number of such Time Spirits or Spirits of Personality who work as Spirits of the Age. These Spirits of Personality, these inspirers of the Spirit of the Age, are of a higher order than the Folk Spirits. In every epoch one of these Spirits of Personality is predominant and sets his seal upon the whole epoch, assigning to the Folk Spirits their specific tasks, so that the whole spirit of the epoch is determined by the special or individual characteristics of the Folk

Spirit. Then, in the following epoch, another Spirit of Personality, another of the Archai, takes over.

After a certain number of epochs have elapsed, a Spirit of the Age has evolved further. We must picture this in the following way: when we die, having completed our present stage of evolution, our personality transmits the achievements of this earth-life to the next earth-life. The same holds good for the Spirits of the Age. In each Age we have one such Spirit of the Age, and at the end of an epoch this Spirit hands over to another, who, in turn, hands over to yet another, and so on. The earlier Spirits, meanwhile, continue their own development. Then, in a later epoch, while the other Spirits are proceeding with their own evolution, the original Spirit takes over again, infusing intuitively into humankind for the sake of a more evolved humanity what has been acquired for the higher mission. We look up to these Spirits of Personality, to these Beings who may be characterized by the somewhat colorless term "Spirit of the Age." We human beings pass from incarnation to incarnation; but we know for certain that, while we ourselves progress from epoch to epoch, when we look into the future, we see ever different Spirits of the Age determining events on earth. But our Spirit of the Age will return too and we shall meet once again. Because a characteristic feature of these Spirits of Personality is to perform cyclic revolutions and return to their starting-point, they are also called "Spirits of Cyclic Periods."[8]

These higher Spiritual Beings, then, who issue their commands to the Folk Spirits are also called Spirits of Cyclic Periods. We are here referring to those cyclic periods which humanity itself must go through when, from epoch to epoch, it returns to earlier conditions and repeats them in a higher form. This repetition of the characteristics of earlier forms may surprise you. But if you examine carefully the stages of human evolution on the earth in the light of Spiritual Science, you will find that these occurrences recur in many different forms. Thus the seven consecutive epochs following the Atlantean

---

8. See also Rudolf Steiner, *Spiritual Beings in the Heavenly Bodies and in the Kingdoms of Nature*, Lecture 2 ff.

catastrophe which we call the post-Atlantean culture-epochs, repeat themselves.[9] The Greco-Latin epoch, however, marks the turning point in our cycle and will not therefore be repeated. This stage is followed by a repetition of the Egypto-Chaldean epoch in our own age. This will be followed by a repetition of the Persian epoch, but in a somewhat different form. Then will follow the seventh epoch, which will be a repetition of the ancient Indian civilization, the epoch of the Holy Rishis, so that in this coming epoch certain aptitudes which were implanted in ancient India will reappear in a new form. The direction of these occurrences devolves upon the Spirits of the Age.

In order that, distributed among the various peoples of the earth, the progressive development of successive epochs may be realized, in order that the widely differing ethnic types may be moulded by a particular geographical area or community of language, in order that a particular form-language, architecture, art or science may flourish and their various metamorphoses receive all that the Spirit of the Age can pour into humankind—for this we need the Folk Spirits, who, in the hierarchy of higher Beings, belong to the Archangels.

But we require yet another intermediary agent between the higher missions of the Folk Spirits and those beings here on earth who are to be inspired by them. You will readily perceive, at least theoretically at first, that the mediator between the two different kinds of Spirits is the Hierarchy of the Angels. They are the intermediaries between the single human being and the Archangel of the folk. In order that the individual may receive into himself or herself that which the Folk Spirit has to pour into the whole people, this intermediary agent between the human being and the Archangel of his people is indispensable. . . .

Thus we see how humanity is integrated into the ranks of the Hierarchies, how, from age to age, from epoch to epoch, Beings whom we already know from another aspect, cooperate in its

9. See also Rudolf Steiner, *The Spiritual Guidance of the Individual and Humanity*, Lecture 3 and *An Outline of Occult Science*, Chapter 4, pp. 217 ff.

evolution. And we have seen how opportunities are provided for these beings to express themselves in a variety of ways peculiar to themselves and that what they have to offer can be imparted to humanity.

The guiding principles of the several epochs are determined by the Time Spirits (*Zeitgeister*). The single folk-individualities are responsible for disseminating the Spirit of the Age over the whole earth. While the Time Spirits inspire the Folk Spirits, the Angels act as mediators between the Folk Spirit and the single human beings, so that these individuals may fulfill the mission of the Folk Spirits....

III

Time Spirits: The Spirits of the Age [10]

Oslo, June 8, 1910

...I pointed out yesterday that [besides Angels and Archangels] other forces also are active—namely, the Primal Beginnings, the *Archai* or Spirits of Personality who, during earthly existence represent what is called the *Zeitgeist*, the Spirit of the Age. These work in such a way that from their own I, from their psychic organization, they work into the physical body and thus activate the forces of the physical body. If, at a certain moment, something arises as a result of the activity of the *Zeitgeist* and manifests itself in the Spirit of an Age to further human progress, we must assume that this corresponds to the utilization of physical forces in our earthly life. *A moment's reflection will show that definite prior conditions of a physical order are necessary to provide for certain contingencies in the Spirit of the Age.* Kepler, Copernicus and Pericles could not possibly have lived in any other age or under other circumstances. Personalities are the product of the specific conditions of their time, conditions which at a definite moment are created and determined by the higher Beings working on the physical plane. Now these physical conditions must not be regarded as isolated phenomena, but as particular configurations in

10. From: Rudolf Steiner, *The Mission of the Individual Folk Souls*, pp. 45–46.

the physical constitution of our earth. Sometimes these configurations stand out in bold relief; at other times, when the Spirit of the Age directs his influence in a certain direction, physical objects inevitably take on a quite definite pattern. You will recall that around the time when specially polished lenses were first used, some children playing in the glass polisher's workshop assembled them in a way that created the optical effect of a telescope, so that the inventor of the telescope, having thus discovered from observation the underlying principle, needed only to apply it to achieve practical results. This is an historical fact. Imagine the number of physical processes involved before this result could be achieved. The lenses had first of all to be invented, polished and then assembled in the appropriate manner. Chance would account for this, you might say, but only if you refuse to acknowledge the law that operates in such circumstances. This concatenation of outward circumstances is the work of the *Archai*, the Primal Forces. Their work is the consequence of focusing their activity at a particular place, an activity which otherwise, as the Spirit of the Age, is expressed in a variety of ways. Think of how many inventions would remain forever unknown if this work of the *Archai* had not taken place in their etheric bodies. It is really the work of the *Archai* which acts in this way and is directed to this end.

Now, if the activity of the *Archai* takes this form and is responsible for directing the Spirit of the Age, the question arises: how do these Spirits of the Age intuitively sense the progress of humanity? They create a situation in which a person appears to be stimulated fortuitously by external circumstances. It must not be accounted as pure fiction if this sometimes occurs. I need only remind you of the swinging lamp in the cathedral at Pisa where, by observing the regular oscillations of the lamp, Galileo discovered the law of the pendulum and how, later on, Kepler and Newton were stimulated to make their discoveries. I could quote innumerable cases of the coincidence of external events and human thought which would explain how the prevailing ideas of an age are intuitively sensed by the *Archai*, ideas which influence human development, determine human progress and subject it to law....

THREE

MICHAEL, THE MESSENGER OF CHRIST [11]   ✓
London, May 2, 1913

The Mystery of Golgotha is the most difficult of all Mysteries to understand, even for those who have already reached an advanced stage of occult knowledge. Of all the truths within the range of the human mind it is the one that can most easily be misunderstood. This is because the Mystery of Golgotha was a unique event in the whole evolution of the earth and of humanity on it, a mighty impulse that had never before been given in the same way and will never be repeated in a similar form. The human mind always looks for a standard of comparison by which things can be understood, but what is incomparable defies all comparison and because it is unique will be very difficult to comprehend. . . .

The Mystery of Golgotha should not be regarded as an event quite separate from the evolution of humanity, as if it came into consideration only during its duration of three or thirty-three years. We must remember that it occurred in the fourth post-Atlantean epoch, the epoch of the Greco-Latin civilization, and that it was prepared for during the whole period of the development of the ancient Hebrew people. What happened in humanity during the fourth post-Atlantean epoch was of the utmost importance for the Mystery of Golgotha; so too was the worship of Jahve which was practiced among the ancient Hebrews. It is therefore essential to consider the nature of the Being who revealed himself in those times under the name of Jahve or Jehovah. . . .

Above all, the factor of *evolution* must not be left out of account when thinking of the name of Jahve or Jehovah, especially in connection with the name of Christ. Even in the New Testament you will find—and in my books I have often referred to it—that in Jehovah the Christ revealed Himself, to the extent that it was possible to do so before the Mystery of Golgotha.

---

11. From: Rudolf Steiner, *Occult Science & Occult Development. Christ at the Time of the Mystery of Golgotha & Christ in the Twentieth Century*, pp. 21 ff.

If we want to make a comparison between Jehovah and Christ we would do well to take sunlight and moonlight as an illustration. What is sunlight, what is moonlight? They are one and the same, and yet very different. Sunlight streams out from the sun, but in moonlight it is reflected back by the moon. In the same way, Christ and Jehovah are one and the same. Christ is like the sunlight, Jehovah is like the reflected Christ-light, insofar as the Christ-light could reveal itself to the earth under the name of Jehovah, before the Mystery of Golgotha had come to pass. When contemplating a Being as sublime as Jehovah-Christ we must seek His true significance in the very heights of the supersensible world. In reality, it is presumption to approach such a Being with everyday concepts.

The ancient Hebrews sought to find a way out of this difficulty. Despite its inadequacy, human thinking made efforts to form an idea of this sublime Being. Attention was not turned directly to Jehovah (a name that in itself was held to be inexpressible), but to the Being whom our Western literature refers to by the name of *Michael.* Naturally, a great deal of misunderstanding can arise from this statement, but that is unavoidable. One person may say, "This will evoke the prejudices of Christians"; another will have nothing to do with such matters. Nevertheless, the Being whom we may call Michael, who belongs to the Hierarchy of the Archangels—whatever name we may give him—this Being does exist. There are many Beings of the same hierarchical rank, but this particular Being, who is known esoterically by the name of Michael, is as superior to his companions as the sun is to the planets Venus, Jupiter, Mercury, Saturn, and so on.

Michael is the most eminent, the most significant Being in the Hierarchy of the Archangels. The ancients called him the "Countenance of God." As human beings reveal themselves by their gestures and the expressions of their countenances, so in ancient mythology Jehovah was understood to reveal himself through Michael.

Jehovah made himself known to the Hebrew Initiates in such a way that they realized something they had never, with their ordinary powers of comprehension, previously been able to grasp, namely, that Michael was truly the countenance of Jehovah. Hence the ancient Hebrews spoke of Jehovah-Michael: Jehovah was unapproachable, unattainable by human beings, just as a person's thoughts, sorrows, and cares, lie hidden behind his or her outward physiognomy; Michael was the outer manifestation of Jahve or Jehovah, just as the manifestation of the I in a human being may be recognized in the brow and countenance.

We can therefore say that Jehovah revealed himself through Michael, one of the Archangels. Knowledge of the Being described above as Jahve was not confined to the ancient Hebrews, but was far more widespread. Indeed, if we investigate the last five hundred years before the Christian era, we find that throughout this whole period revelation was given through Michael. This revelation can be discovered in another form in Plato, Socrates, Aristotle, in Greek philosophy, even in the ancient Greek tragedies, during the five centuries before the event of Golgotha.[12]

When with the help of occult knowledge we try to shed light upon what actually took place, we can say that Christ-Jehovah is the Being who has accompanied humankind throughout the whole course of evolution. And during the successive epochs Christ-Jehovah always reveals Himself through different Beings of the same rank as Michael. But at different times he chooses a different countenance, as it were, to turn toward humankind. And according to which Being from the Hierarchy of the Archangels is chosen to be the mediator between Christ-Jehovah and humanity, widely different ideas and conceptions, impulses of feeling, impulses of will, are revealed to human beings. In a sense, the whole period surrounding the Mystery of Golgotha may be described as the Age of Michael, and Michael may be regarded as the messenger of Jehovah.

During the period which preceded the Mystery of Golgotha by almost five hundred years and continued for several decades afterwards, the leading form of culture bore the stamp of Michael. Through his power he poured into humanity what was destined to be imparted at that time. Then came other Beings who were equally Inspirers of humankind from the spiritual worlds—other Beings

---

12. See this volume pp. 145–47.

from the rank of the Archangels. Yet, as has been said, Michael was the greatest, the mightiest, among these. Therefore an Age of Michael is always the most significant, or one of the most significant, that can occur in human evolution. For the Ages of the different Archangels are repeated; and it is a fact of supreme importance that every such Archangel gives to the Age its fundamental character. These Archangels are leaders of different nations and peoples, but because they become leaders of particular epochs, and because they were also such leaders in bygone times, they become in a certain sense also leaders of humanity as a whole.[13]

As regards Michael, a change has now taken place. Michael himself has attained a further stage of development. This is of enormous importance for, according to occult knowledge, in the last few decades we have entered a new epoch inspired by the same Being who inspired the Age during which the Mystery of Golgotha took place. Since the end of the nineteenth century, then, Michael may again be regarded as the leader of the epoch.

To understand this we must consider the Mystery of Golgotha from another point of view and ask ourselves: What, in this Mystery, is of chief importance? The fact of supreme importance is that the Being who bears the name of Christ *passed through the Mystery of Golgotha and through the gate of death* at that time. Never, throughout the evolution of the earth, will one be able to speak of the Mystery of Golgotha without considering the fact that the Christ passed through death—that is the very core of the Mystery....

There is no death for any Being belonging to the higher Hierarchies, with the exception of Christ. But for a supersensible Being such as Christ to be able to pass through death, that Being must first have descended to the earth. And the fact of immeasurable significance in the Mystery of Golgotha is that a Being who, in the realm of his own will, could never have experienced death, should have descended to the earth in order to undergo an experience connected inherently with humankind. Thereby an inner bond was

---

13. See Rudolf Steiner, *Karmic Relationships: Esoteric Studies*, vol. III, lecture VII, "The New Age of Michael."

created between earthly humanity and Christ, in that this Christ-Being passed through death in order to share this destiny with humankind. As I have already emphasized, that death was of the greatest possible importance, above all for the present evolutionary period of the earth. A Being of unique nature, who until then was only cosmic, was united through the Mystery of Golgotha, through Christ's death, with the earth's evolution. At the time of the Mystery of Golgotha, He entered into the very process of earthly evolution. This had not been the case before that event for He then belonged to the cosmos alone; but through the Mystery of Golgotha He descended out of the cosmos and was incorporated on earth. Since then He lives on earth, is united with the earth in such a way that He lives in human souls and experiences earthly life with human beings.

Thus the whole period before the Mystery of Golgotha was only a preparatory period in earthly evolution. *The Mystery of Golgotha imparted to the earth its meaning and purpose.*

When the Mystery of Golgotha took place the earthly body of Jesus of Nazareth was given over to the elements of the earth, and from that time onward Christ has been united with the spiritual sphere of the earth and lives within it.

As already said, it is extremely difficult to characterize the Mystery of Golgotha because there is no standard with which it can be compared. Nevertheless, we will try to approach it from still another point of view.

For three years, after the Baptism in the Jordan, Christ lived in the body of Jesus of Nazareth as a human being among earthly human beings. This may be called the earthly manifestation of Christ in a physical, human body. How, then, does Christ manifest Himself since the time when, in the Mystery of Golgotha, He laid aside his physical body?

We must naturally think of the Christ Being as a stupendously lofty Being, but although He is so sublime, He was nevertheless able, during the three years after the Baptism, to express Himself in a human body. But in what form does He reveal Himself since that time? No longer in the physical body, for that was given over to the physical earth and is now part of it. To those who have developed the power to see into these things through the study of occult science, it is revealed that the Christ-Being can now be recognized in a being belonging to the Hierarchy of the Angels. Just as the Savior of the world manifested Himself during the three years after the Baptism in a *human* body—in spite of His sublimity—so, since that time, He manifests Himself directly as an Angel, as a spiritual Being belonging to the hierarchical rank immediately above that of humanity. As such, He could always be found by those who were clairvoyant, as such He has always been united with evolution. Just as truly as Christ, when incarnated in the body of Jesus of Nazareth, was more than human, so is the Christ Being more than an Angel— that is His outer form only.

But the fact that a mighty, sublime Being descended from the spiritual worlds and dwelt for three years in a human body also includes the fact that during that time this Being Himself progressed a stage further in His development.

When such a Being takes on a human or an angelic form, He Himself progresses. And it is this that we have indicated in speaking of the evolution of Christ-Jehovah. Christ has reached the stage where He reveals Himself henceforth not as a human being, not through His reflection only, not through the name of Jehovah, but *directly.* And the great difference in all the teachings and all the wisdom that have streamed into the evolution of the earth since the Mystery of Golgotha, is that through the coming of Michael—the Spirit Michael—to the earth, through his inspiration, human beings could gradually begin to understand all that the Christ-Impulse, all that the Mystery of Golgotha, signifies. But in that earlier time Michael was the messenger of Jehovah, the reflection of the light of Christ; Michael was not yet the messenger of Christ Himself.

Michael inspired humanity for several centuries, for almost five hundred years before the Mystery of Golgotha, as was indicated in the old Mysteries, by Plato and so forth. But soon after the Mystery of Golgotha had occurred and Christ had united Himself with the evolution of the earth, the direct impulse of Michael ceased. At the time when the old documents we possess in the form of the Gospels

were written—as I have said in my book *Christianity as Mystical Fact*—
Michael himself could no longer inspire humankind. Nevertheless,
human beings continued to be inspired by Michael's companions
among the Archangels in such a way that much soul-force was
received unconsciously through inspiration.

The writers of the Gospel themselves had no clear occult knowledge, for the inspiration of Michael came to an end shortly after the
Mystery of Golgotha and the other Archangels, the companions of
Michael, could not inspire humanity in such a way as to make the
Mystery of Golgotha comprehensible. This accounts for the diver-
gent inspirations of the various Christian teachings. Much in these
teachings was inspired by the companions of Michael. That is, the
teachings were not inspired by Michael himself but bear the same
relation to his inspirations as the planets do to the mighty sun.

Only now, in our own age, is there again a Michael influence, a
direct inspiration from Michael. Preparation for this direct inspiration from Michael has been going on since the sixteenth century. At
that time, it was the Archangel who is closest to Michael who gave
humanity the inspiration that led to the great achievements of modern natural science. This natural science is not attributable to the
inspiration of Michael, but to that of one of his companions, Gabriel. The tendency of this scientific inspiration is to create a science,
a world-picture, connected with the physical brain, that promotes
understanding of the material world alone.

Within the last few decades Michael has taken the place of the
Inspirer of science. And in the next few centuries Michael will give
to the world something that, in a spiritual sense, will be equally
important—indeed more important, because more spiritual—
immeasurably more important than the physical science which has
advanced from stage to stage since the sixteenth century. Just as his
companion Archangel Gabriel endowed the world with science, so
Michael will endow humankind with spiritual knowledge, of which
we are now only at the very beginning. Just as five hundred years
before the Mystery of Golgotha Michael was sent as the messenger
of Jehovah, as the reflection of Christ, to sound the keynote of that
era, just as he was then still the messenger of Jehovah, so now, in our

own epoch, Michael has become the messenger of Christ Himself. Just as in ancient Hebrew times, which were a direct preparation for the Mystery of Golgotha, the Initiates among the Hebrews could turn to Michael as the outer revelation of Jahve or Jehovah, so we now are able to turn to Michael—who from being the messenger of Jehovah has become the messenger of Christ—to receive from him during the next few centuries increasing spiritual revelations that will shed more and more light upon the Mystery of Golgotha. What happened two thousand years ago could be made known to the world only through the various Christian sects and its profundities can be unveiled only in the twentieth century when, instead of science, spiritual knowledge—our gift from Michael—will come into its own. This should fill our hearts with deep feelings for spiritual reality in our present time. We shall be able to realize that within the last few decades a door has opened through which understanding can enter.

Michael can give us new spiritual light which may be regarded as a transformation of the light that was given through him at the time of the Mystery of Golgotha; and people today can receive that light. If we can realize this, we can grasp the significance of the new age that is now issuing from our own; we can be aware of the dawn of a spiritual revelation that is to enter into the life of humanity on the earth within the next few centuries. Indeed, because human beings have become freer than in former times, we shall be able through our own wills, to progress to the stage where this revelation may be received.

Reference shall now be made to the event in the higher worlds that has led to this altered state of affairs—to this time of a renewal of the Mystery of Golgotha. . . .

Let us remember what has been said—that in the invisible worlds there is no death. Christ Himself, because he descended to our world, passed through a death similar to that of human beings. When He again became a spiritual Being, He retained the memory of His death; but as a being of the rank of the Angels, in which He continued to manifest Himself outwardly, He could experience only a diminution of consciousness.

Through what, since the sixteenth century, was a necessity for earthly evolution—namely, the triumph of natural science at ever higher levels—something entered human evolution that was also significant for the invisible worlds. With the triumph of science, materialistic and agnostic sentiments of greater intensity than ever before arose in human nature. There had been materialistic tendencies in earlier times, but not the intense materialism that has prevailed since the sixteenth century. Increasingly, human souls who passed through the gates of death into the spiritual worlds bore with them the outcome of the materialistic ideas they had on earth. After the sixteenth century, more and more such seeds of earthly materialism were carried over—and these seeds developed in a particular way.

Christ came into the old Hebrew race and was led to His death within it. The angelic Being who, since then, has been the outer form assumed by Christ, suffered an extinction of consciousness in the course of the intervening nineteen centuries as a result of the opposing materialistic forces that had been brought into the spiritual worlds by materialistic human souls who had passed through the gate of death. This onset of unconsciousness in the spiritual worlds will lead to the resurrection of the Christ-consciousness in the souls of human beings living on earth in the twentieth century. In a certain sense, it may be said that, beginning in the twentieth century, the consciousness lost by humanity will arise again for clairvoyant vision. At first only a few, and then an ever-increasing number of human beings in the twentieth century will be capable of perceiving the manifestation of the Etheric Christ—that is to say, Christ in the form of an Angel.[14] It was for the sake of humanity that what may be called an extinction of consciousness occurred in the worlds immediately above our earthly world, where Christ has been visible in the period between the Mystery of Golgotha and the present day.

At the time of the Mystery of Golgotha something took place in a little-known corner of Palestine, something that was the greatest event in the whole of human evolution, but of which little notice

---

14. See Rudolf Steiner, *The Reappearance of Christ in the Etheric.*

was taken by the people of the time. If such a thing could happen, need we be astonished when we hear what conditions were like during the nineteenth century, when those who since the sixteenth century had passed through death and confronted Christ?

Thus Christ-consciousness may be united with the earthly consciousness of humanity from now on into the future; for the dying of the Christ-consciousness in the sphere of the Angels in the nineteenth century signifies the resurrection of the direct consciousness of Christ—that is to say, Christ's life will be felt in human souls more and more as a direct personal experience from the twentieth century onward.

Once the few who could read the signs of the times were able to realize, contemplating the Mystery of Golgotha, that Christ had descended from the spiritual worlds to live on the earth and undergo death so that through His death the substances incorporated into Him might pass into the earth; in the same way, today, we are able to perceive that in certain worlds lying immediately behind our own a sort of spiritual death, a suspension of consciousness, took place. This was a renewal of the Mystery of Golgotha, in order to bring about an awakening of the previously hidden Christ-consciousness within human souls on earth.

Since the Mystery of Golgotha many human beings have been able to proclaim the Name of Christ, and from the twentieth century onwards an ever-increasing number will be able to make known the knowledge of the Christ that is given in Anthroposophy. Out of their own experience they will be able to proclaim Him.

Twice already Christ has been crucified: once physically, in the physical world at the beginning of our era, and a second time spiritually, in the nineteenth century, in the way described above. It could be said that humanity experienced the resurrection of His *body* in that former time and will experience the resurrection of His *consciousness* from the twentieth century onward.

The brief indications I have been able to give you will gradually make their way into human souls, and the mediator, the messenger, will be Michael, who is now the ambassador of Christ. Just as he once led human souls towards an understanding of Christ's life descending from heaven to the earth, so he is now preparing humankind to experience the emergence of Christ-consciousness from the realm of the unknown into the realm of the known. And just as at the time of Christ's earthly life the greater number of Christ's contemporaries were incapable of believing what a stupendous event had taken place in earthly evolution, so, in our own day, the outer world is striving to increase the power of materialism, and will continue for a long time to regard what has been spoken of today as so much fantasy, dreaming, and perhaps even outright folly. This, too, will be the verdict on the truth concerning Michael, who at the present time is beginning to reveal Christ anew. Nevertheless many human beings will recognize the new dawn rising which during the coming centuries will pour its forces into human souls like a sun—for Michael can always be likened to a sun. And even if many people fail to recognize this new Michael-Revelation, it will spread through humanity nevertheless.

FOUR

THE ARCHANGEL MICHAEL: THE TIME SPIRIT [15]
Stuttgart, May 18, 1913

We have to distinguish quite sharply from other epochs the period which began about the fifteenth and sixteenth centuries and received its character from the rise of the new natural sciences. This epoch brought natural science to the height it attained in the nineteenth century, a greatness which cannot be admired enough. When one surveys the work done by humanity as a whole in natural science in these centuries, one sees that it has been accomplished by certain peoples who were guided from the supersensible world by a Being appointed from among the Hierarchy of the Archangels, and

---

15. From: Rudolf Steiner, *The Festivals and their Meaning*, pp. 359–66.

that this Being is quite distinct from the one who from the supersensible world directs the spiritual culture of the epoch which is just beginning. If one uses the names which in the West have become customary for these leaders among the Hierarchy of the Archangels, then from the Christian era onward one can point to different Beings who have guided the progress of civilization. Without wishing to lay stress on the names as such, I will list the names of Beings in the Hierarchy of the Archangels, just as one lists the names of those who have taken part in something on the physical plane. The Beings in the Hierarchy of the Archangels who have in turn controlled the progress of civilization are: Oriphiel, Anael, Zachariel, Raphael, Samael, Gabriel, and Michael.

Gabriel was the guiding Spirit in the cultural epoch which came to an end for the spiritual world with the last third of the nineteenth century. For with the last third of the nineteenth century—and this is a fact that will become more and more evident—an epoch opens into which quite different influences and impulses flow from the supersensible into the sense world. Whereas during the previous period human souls were bound to what the senses can observe and what the mind can grasp, in the coming period the human being who is not sleeping through the march of evolution will above all have to observe how supersensible wisdom and knowledge flow increasingly from the supersensible world into earthly sense-evolution.

Speaking in an external way, one might describe it as follows. In the period of evolution now passed, supersensible Beings guided the forces from the supersensible worlds, so that, as far as possible, these flowed into our earthly physical bodies. The Hierarchies had to prevent these forces from flowing into human souls. From now on, however, supersensible forces will be directed and guided from the supersensible world so that as much as possible may flow into human souls—so that a knowledge of Imagination, Inspiration, Intuition may lay hold of the human soul.[16] The truly living

---

16. See Rudolf Steiner, *The Stages of Higher Knowledge*; *The Effects of Spiritual Development*; and *Boundaries of Natural Science*.

impulses in the civilization of the coming epoch will be as charged with Inspiration and Intuition as the preceding epoch has been lacking in all Inspiration and in all knowledge of the spiritual.

Fifty years ago, it would have been impossible to speak to people of things that through the necessary course of world evolution may be said to them to-day; because at that time it would have been impossible for people to receive these things directly out of the spiritual world. The door has only now been opened, and as the times that are past were the most favorable for the development of the intellect, so will the immediate future be the most favorable for the development of Inspiration and Intuition.

Two epochs of time meet sharply at this point: one to which all Inspiration was denied, and one in which, though mighty forces will undoubtedly use every available means to fight against it, it will nevertheless be possible to receive Inspiration and make it the determining element in the mood and character of the soul.

And if we look further into the question, we discover that the supersensible forces which did not flow directly into the soul in the past epoch were by no means inactive. What an external physiology cannot prove is nevertheless true: in the Gabriel period the supersensible world was at work in the world of the senses, influencing the human physical body. During that period delicate structures arose in the front parts of the brain, and were gradually implanted into the reproductive system. Thus the majority of human beings were born with a brain possessing other and more delicate structures than was the case, for example, in the twelfth and thirteenth centuries. That was the special task of the age in which human beings turned their minds to the physical plane of the senses and were shut off from Inspiration. The consequence was that the impulses of the supersensible world poured themselves into the body and developed this fine structure in the brain.

This structure will be increasingly present in those who now feel themselves capable of progressing to active thinking and to an understanding of Spiritual Science. In our epoch, in the epoch at the beginning of which we stand, supersensible forces will not be used to form structures in the brain but to work in the soul through

Imagination and Inspiration, to flow directly into the human soul. This is what the Michael Rulership means.

Hence two archangelic Beings must be distinguished: one, Gabriel, who guided human beings immediately before our time, working upon the structure of the brain; and another, Michael, who works upon humanity now and must let receptiveness for spiritual wisdom stream into the human soul. Thus we distinguish from one another Beings belonging to the Hierarchy of the Archangels.

In these two examples I have tried to present concrete attributes and characteristics of these Beings. We cannot remain satisfied with names alone; for even as we know nothing about someone if we merely know he or she is called "Miller", so we know very little about Gabriel if we only know the name. But we do know something about a person if we can say that they are compassionate, or have done this or that. The same is true in the case of a supersensible Being of whom we can say that this Being causes forces to flow into the human physical body, forces which can instill certain structures into the power of propagation, or of another Being of whom we can say that this Being helps stimulate the perception of intuitive truth. Michael does not work so much for the spiritual investigator, the initiate, but for those who wish to understand spiritual investigation, for those who are striving to achieve active thinking. It is for these that Michael will work, as these forces accumulate in humankind during the coming centuries.

This transition from Gabriel to Michael is an important one in another respect. Through what happened then, a race of people is being formed who, owing to the whole way in which they are organized will in future incarnations be in a position to look back on their earlier earthly lives.

Humanity, however, must first give itself this possibility. One cannot remember something one has not thought about. If at night you take off your shirt without thinking, and without thinking put away your cuff links, then you cannot find them next morning, because you did not think about them when you took them off. If you had taken care to impress upon yourself a picture of the whole surroundings where you put your cuff links down, then next morning you would go straight to the place.

If this is true as regards memory in ordinary life, we must look in the same way on the wider horizon of our different earth-lives. It is the innermost nature of the soul that we must remember what we really wish to pass over into the being of the soul; but in order to remember, we must first understand the life of the soul. And that can only be done through occult training. If one has not taken care to have thoughts about the nature of the soul in one's earlier incarnation then of course one cannot recollect it. People will be constituted so as to remember, but they will at first experience this new constitution as illness, as a dreadful nervous condition. For they will be constituted to remember the past, yet they will have nothing that they can remember. When people have impressions which they cannot turn to account, organs that they cannot use, then they fall ill.

This is the state of things we are approaching. Human beings will be organized to remember, but only those who have something to remember will be able to do so—that is, those who through occult training have recognized the special nature of the human soul as a member of the spiritual world. In every life that follows one in which a person has recognized the soul as a spirit-being there will be remembrance of former earth-lives.

We are standing at an important turning-point. To understand Spiritual Science means fundamentally nothing else than to have a true feeling for the turning-point to which we have come in our age.

Now, all the Beings who belong to the Hierarchy of the Archangels are not of the same nature, nor of the same rank. When we speak of the Hierarchy of the Archangels we can say that they "relieve" one another in the way I have described to you in the case of Gabriel and Michael, but the highest in rank, the chief as it were, is the one who takes over the leadership in our age—that is, Michael. Michael is one of the order of Archangels, but he is from a certain aspect the most advanced. Now there is, as you know, evolution; and evolution embraces all Beings. Beings are in an ascending evolution, and we live in the era when Michael, the chief of those of archangelic nature, passes over into the nature of the *Archai*. Michael will gradually become a Guiding Being, he will become the Spirit of the Time, the Being who leads and guides the whole of humanity. It is of the utmost importance that we should understand this. It means that something which, in all previous epochs, was not available to all humanity, now can and must become a possession of all humankind. What formerly appeared among certain peoples, here and there—spiritual deepening—can now be something for the whole of humanity.

If we can point in this way to something taking place behind the world of the senses, then we can also point to something taking place in the sense-world as an imprint or reflection of that event — for instance, the promotion, as it were, of an Archangel. Hitherto human beings have been able to possess personality. In the future they will still possess personality, but in a different way. Humanity has always participated to some extent in the supersensible worlds—at least, human beings were always able do so with their soul lives; but the *personal* note, the personal coloring which a person then showed in the sense world in his or her life did not come down from above, it rose up from below, from Lucifer. It was Lucifer who gave us personality. One could therefore say: Human beings cannot enter the supersensible world with their personalities, they cannot bring them into the spiritual world, they must blot out their personalities—otherwise they will pollute the spiritual world.

In future human beings will be required to allow their personalities to be *inspired from above,* so that they can receive what flows out of the spiritual world. A personality will receive its stamp from what it has been able to absorb of spiritual knowledge; personality will become something quite different. In a sense, formerly people were personalities through what separated them from the spiritual through what was impressed into them through the body. In future, we must become personalities through what we are able to receive from the spiritual world and work upon in ourselves.

In the past, blood and temperament determined personality, and into this personality impersonal elements streamed from the supersensible world. Less and less will we be personalities on account of our blood and temperament. In future we will be able to become a personality through the character that we acquire by our participation in the supersensible world. The Michael-Impulse—which brings an understanding for the spiritual life into the human soul—will achieve this. Those with a pronounced character and personality will, in the future, have this character and personality because of what they bring to expression out of their understanding of the spiritual worlds. The Alexanders, the Caesars, the Napoleons belong to the past. Certainly, the supersensible element flowed into them too, but they received their highly personal coloring from what came to them from below. Those who are personalities on account of the way in which they carry the spiritual world into the sensible, who carry personality into humanity *from the soul,* will take the place of the Alexanders, the Caesars, and the Napoleons. In the future, the strength of human deeds will come from the strength of the spiritual influence working into these human deeds.

All this belongs to what is important in the transition from one epoch into another. And the transition in our time from the Gabriel epoch to the Michael epoch has all the characteristics of a transition of the utmost significance.

One can, even with ordinary sound human reason, come to an understanding of what has been said today, if one is unprejudiced enough to observe our times and see how two possibilities came up against one another in the last third of the nineteenth century. The first possibility is the formation of a world conception based on natural science. Today, that is out-of-date. It has become antiquated—it is no longer in the character of the age. People still form their world conception on the basis of natural science because they simply carry forward what comes from the past. It lies in the character of our age, however, to construct a world conception from Inspirations received from the spiritual world and an understanding of them. We must receive this into our souls as a feeling, as an experience; then we shall learn what the anthroposophical world conception means for individual souls, we shall learn to perceive what evolution is for humanity. It is given to us to participate in things of great significance.

And now let me remind you of something that I mentioned in the last lectures I held here in which I spoke of the change in the function of the Buddha.[17] This is where the tomorrow's lecture will join on to today's.

Today's lecture may therefore close with a question. This question can arise in every soul and will lead us from the important matters that have occupied us today to considerations of still greater importance. Once a promotion of Michael has been accomplished, once he has become the guiding Spirit of Western civilization, who will take his place? His place must be filled. Thus we find ourselves saying: "Then some Angel must also have been promoted, and must enter the ranks of the Archangels." Who is it?"

FIVE

MICHAEL AND THE BUDDHA[18]
Stuttgart, May 20, 1913 ·

While in the past human beings could look up to Jahve or Jehovah and know that Jahve was the Being who sent out Michael to prepare the way for the transition from the "Jahve Age" to the "Christ Age," it is now the Christ who sends us Michael.

This is the new and important fact which we must transform into a feeling. As formerly one could speak of the Jahve-Michael, the leader of the age, so now we can speak of the Christ-Michael. Michael has been exalted to a higher stage—from Folk Spirit to Time Spirit. From being the messenger of Jahve he has become the Messenger of Christ. And so when we speak of a right understanding of the Michael-Impulse in our age, we are speaking of a right understanding of the Christ-Impulse.

Abstract understanding always deals simply in names, and believes it will get somewhere if it asks: "What kind of Being is Michael?" It wants to be told that Michael comes from this or that Hierarchy,

17. Rudolf Steiner, *Occult Research into Life Between Death and a New birth.*
18. From: Rudolf Steiner, *The Festivals and their Meaning,* pp. 376–79.

that he is an Archangel, that Archangels have such and such qualities. Then all is defined and people think now they know what such
a Being is. But they do not know anything if they speak of Michael
in this way. If one wants to understand human evolution—the evolution of humanity—then one must understand that Michael too
has evolved: one must understand that the same Being paved the
way for the preparation of the Mystery of Golgotha who now in our
own day paves the way for the understanding of the Mystery of
Golgotha. At that time, however, he was a Folk Spirit, now he is a
Time Spirit; then he was the messenger of Jahve, now he is the messenger of Christ. We speak of the Christ rightly when we speak of
Michael and his mission, knowing that Michael, who was formerly
the bearer of the mission of Jehovah, is now the bearer of the mission of the Christ.

My dear friends, we have been able to follow the path of Michael,
a Spirit from the rank of the Archangels who has, as it were,
ascended—or rather is ascending—to the rank of the *Archai* in
order to communicate a new impulse to human beings. His place
will therefore be filled by another Being who succeeds him.

I have spoken here on different occasions of the evolution which
Buddha passed through. The puerile objections which are now
being made against us are brought also against our understanding
of the Christ-Impulse in the world[19]—as though we had ever been
one-sided in our representation of the Christ Impulse. We turn
our gaze to evolution as a whole and describe what different
impulses underlie it, giving to each its due value. Again and again
we have spoken of the Bodhisattva who was born as Gautama Buddha and have shown that for us it is truth that he became "Buddha." We have followed his evolution until the time when he
received his mission on Mars. And of that mission we have also spoken here.[20]

---

19. A reference to the attempts made by some members of the Theosophical Society to put forward Krishnamurti as the new Bearer of the Christ for the West.
20. See also Rudolf Steiner, *The Spiritual Foundations of Morality; Man in the Light of
Occultism, Theosophy, and Philosophy*; and *Esoteric Christianity and the Mission of Christian Rosenkreutz.*

ANGEL

As long as humanity dwells on earth, human beings, however high, always have an individuality guiding them from incarnation to incarnation. The individual guidance of human beings is subject to the *Angeloi*, the Angel-Beings. When a human being who is a Bodhisattva becomes a Buddha, then the Angel of this Bodhisattva is, as it were, set free. And such Angels, after the fulfillment of their mission, ascend into the realm of the Archangels.

If we really understand how to penetrate more deeply into the supersensible evolution which lies behind our sense evolution, we are actually able to perceive at some point how an Archangel ascends to the nature of the *Archai*, and an Angel Being to an Archangel Being.

My dear friends, I have not told you all this about the spiritual background of the world in which we live and in which we wish to take our stand as Anthroposophists in order that you may merely theorize over these things, but rather that you may transform into feeling and experience what has been expressed in words and ideas. Yes, to be an Anthroposophist in our age means to know the nature of the supersensible world underlying the sense world of human evolution. It is to feel oneself in the spiritual world, just as one feels himself physically as a physical being in the atmosphere. But merely repeating, Spirit, Spirit, Spirit is in us! will not bring us to feel ourselves in the spiritual world. Just as one has to gauge in a practical, concrete way—from the formation of the clouds, from the humidity and other phenomena—the state of the earth's atmosphere, so also we must "feel" quite concretely the spiritual world into which we are submerged every night when we fall asleep. We must feel and know that what is now happening in the spiritual world is a result of the mission entrusted by Christ to Michael. That is what is happening behind our physical-sensory evolution. And if we feel ourselves to be in such happenings in the spiritual world, in the same way as we feel ourselves physically to be within the atmosphere we breathe in and out, then we have the consciousness we ought to have today in relation to the spiritual world.

Try to receive into your whole heart and soul these results of occultism which I have sought to lay before you; try to have a sensitive understanding of them, and to consider what it means now in this age to live consciously in the spiritual events that are taking place around us, to live consciously in that world whither our soul goes every night when we fall asleep and whence we come every morning when we awake. Try to lead the soul into the direct and concrete experience of what is so often abstractly called Divine Providence. It lies in the true character of our age to do this. Try now, in this present time, to know and experience as individual beings what humans in past ages could feel only in an undefined way as Providence moving through the world.

Place as a picture before your souls that the task of the previous epoch was to find natural science. At that time the laws of nature were good if they were rightly used to build up external world conceptions. But there is nothing absolutely good or bad in the external world of Maya. The laws of Nature would be bad and evil if they were still used in our day to construct a world view at a time when spiritual life is flowing into the sense world. These words are not to be taken as directed against what past ages have done; they are directed against what wants to remain as it was in earlier ages and will not put itself at the service of the new revelation.

Michael did not fight the present dragon in ages past, for then the dragon now meant was not yet a dragon. It will become a dragon only if those concepts and ideas which belong to natural science are used to construct the world conception of the coming age. For the monster who will then rear its head among human beings will be rightly seen to be the image of the Dragon that Michael, whose age begins in our own time, must vanquish.

Michael overcoming the Dragon is an important imagination. *To receive the inflow of spiritual life into the sense world: this is the service of Michael from now on.* We serve Michael by overcoming the Dragon that is trying to grow to its full height and strength in ideas, which during the past epoch produced materialism and which now threaten to live on into the future. To defeat this dragon means to stand in the service of Michael. That is the victory of Michael over the Dragon. It is the old picture, which for earlier times had another meaning, and which must now acquire the right meaning for our age....

SIX

BEHIND THE SCENES OF EXTERNAL HAPPENINGS:
THE FALL OF THE SPIRITS OF DARKNESS [21]

I

Zürich, November 6, 1917

I have often indicated to circles of friends here and there that the year 1841 was a critical time, a year of decision and crisis. This, of course, is not discovered by looking merely at the events which happened in the physical world, but only by studying these events in connection with what was going on in the spiritual world. The year 1841 was, in truth, the critical year for the onset of the age of materialism, for at that time a very definite battle began in the spiritual worlds—a battle waged by certain Spirits, Spirits of Darkness we may call them, belonging to the hierarchical rank of the *Angeloi*. In the spiritual worlds they fought out this battle until the autumn of 1879. They were striving for many, distinct aims, only one of which will be mentioned today. Between 1841 and 1879, a decision was to be made as to whether a certain store of spiritual wisdom could be matured sufficiently to trickle gradually down to the earth from the last third of the nineteenth century onward, that is to say, to enter into human souls as a stimulus to the spiritual knowledge described today as Spiritual Science, which has been possible only since that time.

The aim of these *Angeloi*-Spirits between 1841 and 1879 was to prevent what was to flow down to the earth from coming to maturity in the spiritual world. But these Spirits of Darkness were defeated in the war they waged against the Spirits of Light during this period. In 1879, an event occurred that, on a smaller scale, was of a kind that has occurred several times in the course of evolution, and has always been pictured symbolically as the victory of Michael, or St. George, over the Dragon. This time, too, in 1879, the Dragon was overcome in a certain realm. This time the "Dragon" was the

---

21. From: Rudolf Steiner, *Behind the Scenes of External Happenings*, pp. 25–27, 38–54.

Angeloi—Spirits who were striving for, but could not achieve, the aim I have indicated. In 1879, therefore, they were cast out of the spiritual world into the earthly-human world—and here, in this world, they wander among humanity. They are present here, sending their forces into human thoughts, feelings and impulses of will, egging them on to one undertaking or another. These Spirits were not able to prevent the onset of the age when the spiritual knowledge flows down—their defeat in the battle lies precisely in this. Indeed, the spiritual knowledge is here and will unfold increasingly; and human beings will be able to acquire the faculty of seeing into the spiritual world.

But having been cast down to the earth, these *Angeloi*-Spirits are intent upon doing harm with the downflowing knowledge; they seek to guide it into the wrong channels, to rob it of its power for good and lead it into paths of evil. In short, having been cast down since 1879, their aim is to achieve here on earth, with the help of human beings, what they were unable to achieve with the help of the Spirits in the other world. Their aim is to bring ruin to that part of the benevolent plan of cosmic evolution that consists in allowing knowledge of the control of masses—as well as knowledge of birth, illness, and death, among other things—to spread among humanity when the time is ripe. The Spirits of Darkness want to spread such knowledge too soon by means of premature spiritual births. . . .

The only way to combat the influence of these Ahrimanic Beings is to realize that nothing avails against some of Ahriman's aims, except to see through him, to know that he is there. I have indicated this repeatedly in the *Mystery Plays*. Think only of the end of the last play.[22] Human beings in the fifth post-Atlantean epoch must evolve to the stage where they can address the Ahrimanic Beings and Powers as Faust addresses Mephistopheles: "In thy Nothingness I hope to find the all."[23] We must resolve to look into that realm where materialism sees "Nothingness" and see the spiritual world. . . .

---

22. Rudolf Steiner, "The Soul's Awakening" (see bibliography, *The Four Mystery Plays*).
23. See Goethe's *Faust*.

II
Zürich, November 13, 1917

The most beautiful and meaningful fruits of such concrete relationships with the spiritual world are prophetic utterances such as those of Daniel and the Apocalypse. Here people are not just told to trust in a God, to believe in a God. Instead, they are told in all concrete reality of the connection of the spiritual world with the physical, material world—of the first, the second, and the third heavenly kingdom. Humanity has lost all aptitude for speaking concretely of the relation of the spiritual to the physical. People would prefer everything to be painted the same color, as it were. Best of all, people like to devise theories by which all human beings throughout the world can find equal material happiness. The socialists today insist that certain ideas are right and proper for the human life— right for England, America, Russia, and Asia; they believe that if everyone arranged national affairs according to socialist principles, the happiness which is the dream of modern humanity would come to the earth by itself. But all these ideas are abstract, unreal. Ignorance of the fact that something quite specific arises in one region of the earth from a particular people, while something quite different arises in another region from another people—this inability to understand the great difference between West and East—this causes endless confusion and chaos. For only when people are able to build a bridge from the soul to objective realities can they cooperate fruitfully in shaping earthly existence.

But people are unwilling to build such a bridge. Inner reasons have lately caused me to speak to friends in many different places of a momentous event—momentous in its effect upon evolution— that took place in the last third of the nineteenth century. This is an event known to all occult schools although these are not always able to give accurate details of its actual course. I will speak of it briefly. Starting in 1841, in regions of the spiritual world, a battle was waged between certain Beings of the higher Hierarchies and other superior Beings. The Beings who rebelled and waged war between 1841 and 1879 had been used, before that time, in the service of the wise guidance of worlds. Even those Beings who rebel and hence become evil Beings of Darkness may, at other times, serve good and useful purposes. I am speaking, therefore, of Beings who up to the year 1841 had been used by higher Spirits in the service of the wise guidance of worlds, but whose aims, from then on, ran counter to the aims of the Beings superior to them. These Beings of lower rank thus fought a great battle in the spiritual world—one of those battles which often take place, but at different levels, is portrayed in legend and symbolism as the battle of Michael with the Dragon. In the autumn of 1879, this battle ended with certain Spirits of Darkness being cast down from the spiritual world to the earth. Since that time, they have been working among human beings, creeping into their impulses of will, into their motives, into their ideas, indeed into all human affairs. And so, since the autumn of 1879, certain Spirits of Darkness have been among humanity and if human beings wish to understand earthly happenings, they must be alive to the presence of these Beings.

It is absolutely correct to say that in the year 1879 these Beings were cast down to the earth. This made the heavens free of these Beings, but made the earth full of them. From then on, their habitation is no longer to be found in the heavens, but on earth.

To describe the aim pursued by these Beings in their war of rebellion from 1841 to 1879, I must say the following. They wanted to be able to prevent the spiritual wisdom, which will be revealed from the twentieth century onward, from flowing into human souls. Only by removing these hindering Spirits of Darkness from the spiritual realm could human minds and hearts be opened to receive, from the twentieth century onwards, the spiritual knowledge destined for them—only thus was the flow of this spiritual knowledge possible. Wandering among us as they now do, these Spirits of Darkness make it their business to spread confusion. From their arena here on earth, they seek to prevent the establishment of the right attitude toward spiritual truths. They want to withhold from us the blessings which the spiritual truths are intended to bring.

Intimate and penetrating knowledge of these things is the only means whereby the aims of the Spirits of Darkness may be counteracted. Certain occult brotherhoods, however, make it their business to work in exactly the opposite sense. They want to retain the wisdom of the spiritual truths exclusively within their own narrow circles—in order to exploit it in connection with their lusts for power. We are living in the midst of this struggle. On the one side is the necessity for humanity to be led along the right paths by the assimilation of the spiritual truths. On the other side are closed occult brotherhoods of an evil kind, who desire to prevent these truths from finding their way to human beings, so that these remain dull and stupid as regards the spiritual world, and thus making it possible for those within the narrowly enclosed brotherhoods to carry on their intrigues.

Contemporary events bristle with such intrigues and machinations, and calamity looms if we fail to realize that these machinations are in full swing. You will immediately feel that light has been shed upon the real background of these things when I tell you of certain truths that have matured in our time—truths that must fall like ripened fruit as it were from the spiritual world into the human kingdom, but are prevented from spreading—truths against which, moreover, humans are instinctively prejudiced because they are afraid of them.

In this connection I must speak as concretely as possible. The fact that, in 1879, a number of Spirits of Darkness were cast into the human kingdom has profound and significant consequences. One of these is that since that time clear thinking has assumed a far, far greater importance than it ever had before. At no other period could it have been said, with regard to the inner necessities of evolution, that clarity of thinking is as essential as eating and drinking are to the maintenance of physical life. For if human thinking lacks clarity in the present age, in times to come we will be unable to see in the right light the ripened truths which are to fall from the spiritual world. Above all, we will fail to realize the vast and profound significance of the Mystery of Golgotha, of the Coming of Christ, for the whole of human evolution. Many people speak of Christ Jesus. Modern theology, however, would actually like to prevent anyone from speaking of the deep purpose imparted to earthly human evolution by the Mystery of Golgotha. Naturally, the fulfillment of what was to come to pass through the Mystery of Golgotha has been, and is, both slow and gradual. But in our present century, for the first time, this process becomes intensely evident.

Previous epochs still enjoyed a heritage from the days when spirituality pervaded the more atavistic inner life of human beings. Now, for the first time, we must actively *strive* for spirituality—if we desire it. And so, in our day—actually only from 1879 onward—very definite phenomena appear. Because external observation has become so crude, they are clearly to be perceived only when the eyes of the soul are directed to that realm which human beings enter when they pass through the Gate of Death. For souls born before the year 1879 and those born after it pass into the spiritual world in different ways. Truly, it is a momentous event of which we are speaking here.

One consequence of this event is that human beings in their souls more and more come to resemble their thought—to resemble what they regard as knowledge. This will seem a strange truth to the modern mind, but is so, nevertheless. To see certain things in their proper light, with clarity of thought, with thoughts saturated with reality is vitally important. It is good to see Darwinism in the proper light, as I tried to present it in yesterday's public lecture,[24] to regard Darwinism as the only valid conception of the world, to believe the only possible truth to be that human beings descend from animals—and repeating the thought: "I descended from the animals; I descend entirely from forces which also produce the animals." Such thoughts, in our age, tend to make the soul resemble its own conception of itself. This is an important matter! When the body is left behind, the soul is confronted with the sorry fate of having to perceive its resemblance to its own thought! People who live in the physical body, believing that animal forces alone were at work in their evolution, fashion a kind of consciousness for themselves in which they perceive their own likeness to animal nature.

---

24. November 12, 1917, "Anthroposophy and Natural Science" (GA 73), not translated.

For since the event of 1879, the character of the fifth post-Atlantean epoch has been such that human souls are transformed into the ideas human beings form of themselves. That is why I said that it is not necessary to be particularly biased in favor of anthroposophical Spiritual Science to be willing to advocate it. All that is necessary is compassion for our fellow human beings who need these thoughts and ideas because these thoughts are creative powers in the life of soul, because it is ordained that in the future what human beings consider themselves to be, that they will become. This development is part of the wise guidance of worlds, so that human beings may attain full and free consciousness of the Self. The Gods were bound to make it possible for human beings to become what they make of themselves. And Christ Jesus fulfilled the Mystery of Golgotha in order that we might imbue this self-created being with supersensible meaning, that we might be able to find in this self-created being something that gives us an eternal aim. When we understand Christ Jesus in the light of Spiritual Science, in the light of true thought, we find the way to Him: the way that leads from the animal to the Divine.

One truth stands out strongly when the eyes of the soul are able to look into the world entered by the human being after death. Those who were born before 1879 always carry with them a certain heritage that protects them from becoming purely what they have pictured themselves to be here on earth. And for a long time to come—these things are only gradually approaching—this protection will still be possible, but only through pain, only when humans can suffer, when, paradoxically, they can take on themselves the inner pain of knowing and feeling the shortcomings of their conception of the human being. Harmony with the Self, together with a knowledge which lets a human being after death be truly *human*—this will arise in the future only if we become aware, here, in the physical body, of our true connection with the spiritual world. Those who, because of their materialistic ideas, are afraid of concrete facts of spiritual knowledge will, of course, for a long time to come still be unwilling to acknowledge that any such change took place in the year 1879. Nevertheless, it will have to be acknowledged sooner or later. It is clear from all this that one thing above all is essential, and will become increasingly so in the future, namely, that all available spiritual knowledge be spread over the earth. Therefore, in order to further their aims, the Spirits of Darkness will attach particular value to breeding of confusion among human beings so that they will fail to form in the right way the thoughts and ideas into which, after death, they will be transformed. What we think ourselves to be, that we are obliged to become.

This is a truth that was destined, after the great changes in the nineteenth century, to find its way to humanity. Human beings must be *voluntarily* anything that they can be really—they must be able to think about their own being if they are to be truly themselves in their soul lives. For even now the dead could announce as a ripened truth that *the soul is what it thinks itself to be.* But, at the time when it was evolutionarily necessary to spread the truth that the soul is what it thinks itself to be, exactly then the Spirits of Darkness inspired human beings to proclaim that "We are what we eat." And although this is not, in theory, widely acknowledged, the practical conduct of life amounts very nearly to being an acknowledgment of the principle that humanity is what it eats and nothing else. Indeed, this principle is increasingly applied and developed in external life. To a far greater extent than people believe, the grievous and tragic events of the present time are an outcome of the tenet "We are what we eat." In a much deeper sense than is supposed by the superficial modern mind, a terrible amount of the blood that is shed today is shed over unseemly issues.

That is why the spread of thoughts and ideas corresponding to the realities of the times is so necessary. Thought will gradually have to be known as a concretely real power of the soul, not merely as the miserable abstraction produced so proudly by the modern age. People living in earlier times were still linked, by an ancient heritage, with the spiritual world. Although for many centuries now, atavistic clairvoyance has almost entirely ebbed away, this heritage still lives in the feeling and in the will. But the time has come when everything that is *conscious* must become a real power. Hence the Spirits of Darkness strive to counter really effective thoughts by abstract thoughts in the form of all kinds of programs for the world. This connection must be realized and understood. Thoughts must be imbued with greater and greater reality.

There are still many people who say: "Oh, well, in good time we shall find out what happens after death; why bother about it now? Let us attend to the demands of life and when we reach the other world we shall soon discover what it is...." Well and good, but if it is true that in the other world a person becomes what he or she has pictured himself or herself to be, then something else is also true. Take an idea that is not at all uncommon nowadays. Somebody dies, leaving relatives behind. Although thought may not be entirely lacking in these relatives, they may be materialistically-minded, and then, quite inevitably, they will think either that the one who died is decaying in the grave or that what still exists of him is preserved in the urn. Only if thought is entirely absent can people be materialists and *not* hold this view. If materialism were to triumph, the conviction would still further increase that all that remains of the dead is disintegrating in the urn or in the grave. This though is, however, a real power. It is an untruth. When those left behind think that the dead no longer live, are no longer there, this is a false thought—but it is real and actual in the souls of those who form it. The dead themselves are aware of this thought-reality—they are aware of its significance. And it is by no means a matter of no consequence but, on the contrary, of fundamental importance, whether those left behind cherish in their souls the thought of those who have died living on in the spiritual world, or whether they succumb to the woeful idea that the dead, well, they are dead, there they lie, decaying in the grave. Far from being a matter of no importance, there is a very great and essential difference in these points of view.

Coming to Zürich nowadays one can hardly fail to be attentive to what is known here—and also elsewhere, but here it is pursued very actively—as Analytical Psychology or Psychoanalysis. Naturally, it is the case that the psychoanalysts have become alive to many things that have to do with the realm of soul-and-spirit. Indeed, they are beginning to think of the soul-and-spirit simply because it confronts

them so insistently. Let me here say a word or two about one characteristic feature in this Psychoanalysis.[25]

A patient suffers from symptoms of hysteria. The forms taken by
these manifestations of hysteria are very typical at the present time,
and for this reason attract attention. Illnesses particularly common
at any given period are always a matter of concern, and efforts are
made to discover where the causes lie. Psychoanalysis has actually
reached the point of stating that the causes of these frequent manifestations of hysteria lie in the life of soul. As it is quite impossible to
look for them in the material domain, or in the field of physiological
or biological processes as such, they must lie in the Psyche—in the
life of soul. The present tendency is to seek in the subconscious life
of soul for causes of the various forms of hysteria. The psychoanalysts say: "Such and such a person shows signs of hysteria; the cause is
that something is working in him or her below the threshold of consciousness, and is constantly surging upward like waves from subter-
ranean, subpsychic depths—and that is what we must look for."

This is where the dangerous game begins. The psychoanalysts try
to find all kinds of happenings which constitute an isolated, subterra-
nean, hidden province of the Psyche, as they put it. For example, in a
hysterical subject of age thirty, they look for "perversions" at the age,
perhaps, of seven, which were not fully lived through or satisfied
then, and which must be made conscious again, because this will
cure the subject and so forth. It is a game with extremely dangerous
weapons, my dear friends! Yonder on the physical battlefields, war is
being waged with very dangerous weapons. Here, in many domains,
with weapons of knowledge no less dangerous, a game is being
played because people are unwilling to deepen their thought in the
direction of Spiritual Science so as to acquire a true understanding
of these phenomena. The problem is approached with inadequate
means of knowledge and it is a very dangerous game. It is, of course,
perfectly true that the subconscious works in many people today,
without ever rising into consciousness. But what the psychoanalysts

---

25. See also, for instance, Rudolf Steiner, *Psychoanalysis and Spiritual Psychology* and
Community Life, Inner Development, Sexuality, and the Spiritual Teacher.

believe they have unearthed is usually of the least significance of all and, for this reason, successes so far as cures are concerned are in most cases highly dubious. When hysteria in a woman of thirty is put down to some sexual perversion which occurred, say, at the age of fourteen and has gone on simmering in the subconscious—this is probably the most unimportant factor of all. In a few cases it may actually be correct and then, if its importance has been wrongly estimated, it will be all the more misleading. Nevertheless, it is absolutely true that countless factors lurk within human beings today, trouble them and give rise to the diseases of modern civilization.

Think of what I said before. The thought of the absent dead dwells in some way in the soul, although little attention is paid to it. This thought dwells in the soul because the soul is still heedless— and is rather susceptible to these heedless thoughts. According to an eternal law, those who have died are then forced to dwell with these thoughts; the dead haunt the souls of those who are still living. True contact with those who have died can be established only by knowing: "the Dead live!" Human beings on the physical plane will be more and more prone to psychological illnesses as a consequence of the prevailing disbelief in the existence of those who have died. The causes of these hysterical manifestations are not, as a rule, early sexual troubles but *unbelieving thoughts.* For thoughts in our age are destined to become powers in more senses than one. They work as powers of thought as such, in that after death the soul takes on a stronger and stronger likeness to what, in the body, it pictures itself to be. And, in a higher sense still, thoughts become real powers in that they fetter beings—in this case, the Dead—in a wrongful way to the living. Only by sustaining the thought that the dead lives on, can one guard oneself, as well as others, against the link with the dead becoming a source of danger to those who have been left behind. Indeed, in a certain sense the same applies to the dead themselves, who under an eternal, wisdom-filled law are compelled to lurk in the survivors in such a way that this influence remains subconscious and manifests, ultimately, as illness.

Ask yourselves now, What is the real remedy for many phenomena confronting psychoanalysts today? The universal remedy, the universal therapy, is the spread of knowledge of the spiritual world—not these individual treatments.

Life demands that we abstain from the thought that here on earth we must devote ourselves exclusively to physical existence because the world of after-death existence will reveal itself to us in its own good time. We must abstain from this thought because it is also true that, just as our life here is important for the existence into which we pass between death and a new birth, so too the life of souls living between death and a new birth is important for the soul living here on earth.

What I have now said refers to *one* thought—namely, disbelief in the existence of the dead. But the dead are and should be connected by *many* links with the living. The link of which I have just spoken is improper, but there are many true links which must be made and which constitute the right connection with the spiritual world. Anthroposophical Spiritual Science strives to establish the true connection with the spiritual world, for earthly human life will only take its rightful course, if this true relationship is established with the spiritual world. Failing this, it will become increasingly possible for certain individuals to embark upon intrigues and machinations in order to gain power over others.

Let us be quite clear about one thing. We can understand the deeply symptomatic events now proceeding in Eastern Europe only when we have a clear, inner conception of the nature of these lands and people. Think of what we have been saying for many years about the qualities of the peoples there as a basis for the sixth post-Atlantean epoch.[26] Only then can light be shed on all the difficult events and confusing influences, stemming quite inevitably from these Eastern lands. Something altogether different, in fact, must evolve in the course of time from what is happening there. What is destined to evolve there is, however, not so easy for people of our time with their comfortable ways of thought, to understand. No wonder, therefore, they are taken aback by what happens there from day to day. But the important point is to find the right way into

---

26. See also Rudolf Steiner, *Preparing for the Sixth Epoch.*

all the streams and currents which are now arising and will arise in the future. And if Spiritual Science is our guide to knowing and understanding the spiritual world then we shall find the right way little by little. Thereby, too, we shall establish the right relationship with the spiritual world.

In my last lecture here I told you of an improper relationship to the spiritual world which certain quarters want to establish. I said that certain individuals are deprived of life here and sent into the spiritual world as the outcome of deliberate machinations; these individuals have not wholly lived out their life here and therefore are still able to turn certain forces to account in the world where they live between death and a new birth. Then certain brotherhoods working with dishonorable motives, desiring only to satisfy their own lust for power, can use mediums for the purposes of receiving from the dead the knowledge which the dead have thus been able to acquire.

Occult brotherhoods of this kind are also, as a rule, those who lead people astray with regard to the events of greatest importance in the spiritual world. If I tell you that, in 1879, in November, a momentous event took place, a battle of the Powers of Darkness against the Powers of Light, ending in the image of Michael overcoming the Dragon . . . then the point is not simply to tell you that such and such an event took place. For you can read in many books—it is not an esoteric truth at all—that such an event is appointed for world evolution. What I really want to bring home is the significance of the event and the attitude which you should adopt towards it. Eliphas Lévi, Franz von Baader, Saint-Martin,[27] all knew and spoke of such an event—there is nothing really esoteric in the fact itself. But in our time, attempts are afoot to spread confusion about such events—confusion that makes people regard them as mere superstition, although they have long been proclaimed by

---

27. Louis Claude de St. Martin, 1743–1803, the "Unknown Philosopher," French Christian esotericist and theosopher, often mentioned by Rudolf Steiner. Franz von Baader 1765–1841, profound Catholic theosopher, philosopher, and metaphysician, "*naturphilosoph*" etc. Eliphas Lévi, 1810–1875, is the *nom de plume* of the French occultist, Alphonse Louis Constant. Lévi was a major figure in the nineteenth century occult revival. His sphere of influence—which included Madame Blavatsky—was enormous, both in his native France and in Britain (where his contacts were extensive).

ancient learning. Here, again, is a reason why correct and true ideas about these things are so important.

Today a right and proper path of approach exists to the spiritual truths which, since 1879, have been filtering down from the spiritual to the physical world. It is the path indicated by Spiritual Science. And if in the stream of Spiritual Science there is no deviation from sincerity and purity of intention, Spiritual Science will lead to the establishment of the right relationship between the physical and the spiritual worlds. But what is attained thereby and must arise among human beings involves and demands strenuous effort. Laziness in all its many forms must be put away. Strenuous effort is essential....

SEVEN

SIGNS OF THE TIMES: MICHAEL'S WAR IN HEAVEN AND ITS REFLECTION ON THE EARTH [28]
Münich, February 17, 1918

Today, it will be my task, on the basis of the spiritual way of seeing we have been developing here, to move on to a discussion of the spiritual processes that in a certain way lie immediately behind contemporary events now speaking so earnestly to our souls.

Certainly, as you know, we can observe in all vividness precisely what spiritually underlies so difficult a time if we consider what we call in Spiritual Science our coexistence, our community, with forces that stream from the so-called dead into the realm where we ourselves are incarnated. But of course people nowadays seek very little to know the spiritual background of existence. In fact, this lack of seeking the spiritual background of existence is much more closely connected than one might think with the great catastrophe that has befallen humanity in the present age.

---

28. From: Rudolf Steiner, *The Mission of the Archangel Michael,* pp. 133–54.

I have drawn your attention before to the fact that, when compared to earlier periods of history, extraordinary and sweeping
changes affecting the whole of human evolution occurred in the
period we may call the last third of the nineteenth century. In this
connection, I have pointed repeatedly to the end of the 1870's. I
pointed out that the end of the 1870s signified a decisive turning-
point in human evolution. Yet very few people today seem to be
aware of how fundamentally different spiritual life since the end of
the 1870s is from what preceded it. Perhaps people have had too
little distance from this moment and so cannot see the change.
Indeed, as a rule, such an event becomes apparent only when one
is no longer directly involved and has acquired a certain distance,
and so can observe the differences. Today, then, if humanity is not
to be confronted with still greater misery, we must gain the distance we need to experience these changes as soon as possible.

Viewed spiritually, our present age is governed by a very strange
and truly startling contradiction. If I describe this contradiction to
you, you will actually find it grotesque. The contradiction is that there
has never been a time in human historical evolution that is as spiritual
as the time we now live in—the time since the end of the 1870's. From
a historical point of view, we live in the most spiritual of times. Still, it
is undeniable that the way we live today is such that most people who
consider themselves spiritually developed believe that our time is
completely materialistic! As far as reality is concerned, however, our
time is *not* materialistic; it is materialistic only as far as people's
beliefs—and what results from their beliefs—are concerned. But what
do I really mean when I say, "Ours is a spiritual time"?

Well, first of all we have our contemporary natural-scientific world
view. Compared to our present natural-scientific world view, all that
came before it in the way of natural science was materialistic! Today,
we have a natural science that rises to the most subtle, the most spiritualized concepts. We will see this best if we consider the realm of
existence that lies just beyond the realm of what is immediately
physically present.

Most concepts that, with the best intentions, we use today with a
spiritual meaning offer little to the so-called dead. Contemporary

natural-scientific ideas, however, reflected upon without prejudice, have extraordinarily much to offer them. Indeed, it is interesting that so-called materialistic Darwinism is understood and used in a completely spiritual fashion in the realm of the dead. Things appear quite differently in reality than they do in the beliefs—the often very erroneous beliefs—produced by what people experience in the body.

But what do I really mean by pointing to the scientifically spiritual? Well, you see, in order to be able to form these scientific concepts, to rise up to such thoughts as are thought today with regard to evolution and so forth, we need a spirituality that did not exist in previous times. It is much easier to see ghosts and to take them for something spiritual than it is to form finely chiseled concepts for what seems to be only material. Consequently, we develop the most spiritualized concepts in our soul lives and then deny them, mistakenly believing that they relate only to material things. This materialistic interpretation of contemporary scientific ideas is nothing but a defamation of the true character of the world view of natural science. It springs from a general tendency to cowardice! We cannot bring ourselves to live with lively feelings in these spiritualized concepts. We are unable and unwilling to grasp this spirituality in the dilution needed to form clear-cut concepts about nature. We do not dare acknowledge that when we develop these rarified, spiritualized concepts we are living in a spiritual realm—in the spirit— and so we deceive ourselves by saying that these concepts relate merely to material things. But this is simply not true, it is mere self-deception.

The same is true of other spheres of life. I pointed out two days ago that many contemporary works of art demonstrate values that did not exist in the art of earlier epochs, also because of such a spiritualized, refined feeling.[29] It is undeniable that many artistic developments appear in contemporary works of art that one would seek in vain in the works of Raphael or Michaelangelo.

---

29. Rudolf Steiner, *Das Sinnlich-Übersinnliche in seiner Verwirklichung durch die Kunst.* (not translated).

These changes in human spiritual-cultural life were brought about by a quite definite spiritual event. Today, I would like to characterize this spiritual event from certain points of view.

When the middle of the nineteenth century had not yet quite been reached, in fact more or less at the beginning of the 1840's, a certain spiritual Being—names here are irrelevant, but in order to have a name, we can choose one taken from Christian theology, the Archangel Michael—prepared himself to evolve gradually from an Archangel to a Time Spirit, to undergo an evolution that would enable him to work into human life, not merely from the super-earthly point of view, but directly from the earthly standpoint. This Being had to prepare himself to descend to the earth itself, to emulate, as it were, the great process of the Christ Jesus, so as to take his starting point here on earth and to be active thereafter from the point of view of the earth. From the 1840s to the end of the 1870s this spiritual Being prepared himself for this task.

In other words, it may be observed that the period approximately between the 1840s and 1879 represents a significant battle in the supra-earthly sphere, specifically in the supra-earthly sphere that borders immediately on the earthly sphere.[30] This spiritual Being, whom we call the Archangel Michael, had to fight a hard, difficult battle against certain opposing spirits. If, then, we wish to understand what actually occurred at this moment, we must look more closely at these opposing Spirits.

The spiritual Beings, who had to be fought by the Archangel Michael, who in turn became a Time Spirit, have always affected human life and evolution. During the millennia preceding the middle of the nineteenth century, their task in the spiritual world was to create differentiation among human beings. The spiritual Beings who are the direct followers of the Archangels strive in a certain sense to lead human beings back to the group soul: in a certain sense they seek to pour unity or homogeneity over the whole of humanity. This would not have worked in the right way, however, if they had been alone in affecting humanity. If they had been working alone,

---

30. See also pp. 63–66; and Steiner, *The Fall of the Spirits of Darkness.*

humanity would have become more or less blended into indistin-guishableness—it would have represented merely a species, similar to an animal species, but on a somewhat higher level.

The spiritual Beings, whose task it was to fight against the Michaelic principle, were the same ones whose task it was to bring differentiation into humanity, to split unified humanity into races and peoples, to bring about all those differences connected with the blood, with nerves, with temperament. This had to happen. We may call these spiritual beings who had to bring such differentiation into humanity "Ahrimanic" Beings. We may call them such, but we must realize that the Ahrimanic principle was a necessity in the whole course of human evolution.

Then the moment came, which was important for the evolution of humanity—the time arrived—when, beginning with the 1840's, the old differentiations had to vanish, and the divided human race had to be formed into a unity of humankind.

The cosmopolitan views (which admittedly sometimes turned into cosmopolitan slogans in the eighteenth and the first half of the nineteenth centuries) are simply a reflection of what occurred in the spiritual world. The tendency already existed among human beings to wipe out the various differences fostered by blood, and the nervous temperament. The spiritual worlds have no tendency to differentiate humanity any further. On the contrary, their tendency is now to pour out a cosmopolitan element over humanity. Under the influence of our catastrophic times, people have little under-standing of this. But we must own up to this truth. Indeed, this fact, mirrored in earthly events, when observed in its spiritual back-ground, leads to a clairvoyant vision which shows how the Spirits of race, those Folk Spirits that produced the differences between peo-ples, were fought against from the 1840s onward by the spirit who was to become the Time Spirit of the modern age.

An event that has always been represented by a significant symbol took place during this time, although at a new, different stage. The symbol refers to other stages of evolution besides this one, for things repeat themselves again and again at various stages. Thus what I am telling you now is only a repetition at a certain stage of a

spiritual event that took place at other stages also. This spiritual
event is represented by the symbol of the Archangel Michael conquering the Dragon. This conquering of the Dragon by the Archangel Michael—which means that the counterstriving powers were
cast out of the realm where the Archangel Michael rules—occurred
in a certain sphere, beginning in the 1840s. Certain spiritual Beings
whose task in the spiritual world was to differentiate humanity into
races and peoples, were, if I may use the expression, cast out of
heaven down to earth. These spiritual Beings, who up to the 1840s
had created these differentiations among humankind, now no
longer have any power in the region bordering the earthly world.
They have been cast down among humanity on the earth with all
that they could bring with them. It is this event, the pushing down
upon the earth of certain Spirits resisting him, which took place at
the end of the 1870s, that Spiritual Science designates as the victory
of the Archangel Michael over the counterstriving Spirits.

Thus, since the end of the 1870s we have two things. On the one
hand, since 1879, we have had on earth—for those who may be said
to be of good will, if we understand this expression in a qualified
sense—the dominion of the Time Spirit Michael, who enables us to
acquire spiritualized concepts, a spiritualized intellectual life. We
also now have on earth the counterstriving Spirits, who deceive us
into denying the spirituality of the present time. If we fight against
the materialism of our time, we should be constantly aware that we
must not fight against what is good in our age but only against the
lies of our age. For the Spirits that have been pushed from heaven
down upon the earth are chiefly Spirits of falsehood, who, as Spirits
of hindrance, prevent us from looking for what is spiritual in our
understanding of natural existence.

If we come to know those human beings who descended from the
spiritual world into earthly incarnations after the year 1841 and who
since died, we can indeed see how these things are considered from
the other side, as it were. One can then correct much of what is very
difficult to comprehend here in the physical world.

When, at the beginning of the twentieth century, it gradually
became clear how necessary it was to point once more to the most

varied areas of spirit in life, those who drew attention to this fact were precisely those human beings who, following the year 1848—actually, beginning already in 1840—had themselves participated in the hard battle waged by the Archangel Michael in the spiritual world, of the counterstriving Spirits into the life of the earth, where they now are among human beings. Indeed, if one rises against these Spirits and tries to drive them from the field one is essentially fighting alongside the Archangel Michael.[31]

Now, a certain law exists, my dear friends, which states that evolution may be traced backward as well as forward from every point. We may focus our attention on any given point in human historical development and say, here is a point in time, at this moment this or that happened. Then time goes on, and we observe events as they unfold. But the flow of time may also be observed backward. We may go back from 1879 to 1878, 1877, 1860, 1850, and so on. We may then observe how one can follow something backward in the spiritual world. We will see the following. We will see a repetition of what went before in the deeper structure of events as they unfold. Often, if one expresses something great in a simple way, it sounds trivial. Nevertheless, I shall speak simply.

If we consider the point in time that is 1879, we can either proceed forward to 1880, or we can go back to 1878. If we proceed forward to 1880, we will notice in the deeper spiritual structure that what occurred in 1878 is still in a certain way active in the events of 1880. The event of 1878 still stands as an active force behind the event of 1880. And behind the event of 1881, as an active force, stands the event of 1877. It is as if the line of time reverses itself the farther back we go, so that events belonging to a past time lie behind events that lie ahead of that time. If we grasp these things, we can understand much.

Now, please remember that I have been speaking about the year 1879 for many years, and not only since 1914, when it became reasonable to do so. This is important, dear friends. I ask you now to

31. See Rudolf Steiner, *Goethestudien und goetheanistische Denkmethoden* (not translated).

make a simple calculation with me. Count back with me from the year 1879 to the year which I have often designated as the other extreme. I have always stated that the battle of which I am now speaking started at the beginning of the eighteen forties, around 1840 or 1841. Count back then: 1879, 1869, 1859, 1849, and 8 or 9 years more, i.e., 38 or 39 years. Now count forward: 1879, 1889, 1899, 1909, 1914, and right up to today. You also have 38 or 39 years. Thus if you observed the year 1917, you would find a surprising result. You would realize the deep significance of the occultist's statement that, starting from an incisive historical event, you find the preceding spiritual event repeated in the subsequent one. Behind the present events of our time here on the earthly plane lie the spiritual events beginning in the 1840s that we designate as the Archangel Michael's battle against the counterstriving Spirits. These events are behind today's events. We have a repetition today of what took place in the early 1840's. You can imagine how differently one looks at the events of our time when one pays attention to this law. If one pays attention to this law, one develops a deeper understanding of events that now pass silently by human ears, that do not penetrate our souls. We may say that today the battle of the Archangel Michael against the counterstriving powers has to a certain degree returned to its starting point.[32]

In general, it is always difficult nowadays to speak to human beings concerning such deeper relationships, because people today energetically reject anything that would help them understand the present time correctly and enable them to act in the proper manner. The times we live in require that we rid ourselves of old prejudices. The times are such that we must understand and bring into consciousness the events that are now taking place. For things are now happening here on the physical plane that are much more spiritual in nature than events generally are. This has to do with the descent of the Archangel Michael into our earthly region. Many people are talking of this descent of the Archangel Michael into the region of the earth. But when it is a question of

---

32. See also Steiner, *The Fall of the Spirits of Darkness*, especially lectures 9–14.

taking this as seriously as it really ought to be taken, in its true background, then people do not want to go along. Yet exactly this taking of the Michael event in all seriousness is what is required. A spiritual understanding of the most important impulses of our time must take hold in ever wider and wider circles. For this reason it was absolutely important during all the years of our branch meetings to draw attention to this Michael event—to ensure that we did not sleep away the stream of events, which in our time is so strongly influenced by the spirit.

To sleep away events is plainly a characteristic of our time. We pass by events as if we were asleep. Indeed, the more incisive and significant an event entering the physical plane, the more human beings sleep through it.

To give you a concrete example: March 1917 was so powerful in character—and will produce results of such great importance as humanity cannot even dream of—that it is quite grotesque how little understanding exists today of the need for a complete revision of almost all judgments, a complete revision of everything people believed prior to 1914.[33]

Perhaps I may be permitted to point to the fact that in 1910 I delivered a number of lectures in Christiania [Oslo] on the European Folk Souls. In the first of these lectures you can read that human beings will soon be called upon to understand something about the relations of the European folk souls.[34] In my lectures I have repeatedly mentioned that we must turn our gaze toward the immediate East—that what happens there is important for human evolution. How often have I said this! Anyone who has listened to me knows this is so. Likewise, in the spring of 1914, in my Vienna lecture cycle about the life between death and a new birth,[35] I dared to make the emphatic statement that the social life of our time may be compared in a very real sense with a special form of disease, namely, with a carcinoma. I dared say that a creeping

---

33. Outbreak of the Russian Revolution and abdication of the Czar (ed).
34. Rudolf Steiner, *The Mission of Folk Souls*, see this volume pp. 36–40.
35. Rudolf Steiner, *The Inner Being of the Man and Life Between Death and a New Birth.*

cancerous disease is running through our social life. Naturally, under our present conditions these things cannot be stated in any other way; but they must be understood.

We must not think of world events as following one another in a neat continuous progression. It is a fable told by historians that a later event always develops out of a preceding one and that this event, in turn, developed out of the one preceding it, and so forth. We may leave this prejudice to those who do not have the sense for reality that anthroposophically schooled thinkers ought to develop. We may leave this prejudice to the politicians of the old school, as well as to a great many of today. Reality deals with something quite different. We must think of the course of events as of a pair of scales in full motion: the scale-beam sinks first to the right, then to the left. From this point of view, the time since the beginning of the 1840s may be characterized as follows. Much would have been possible if an attempt had been made during the period 1840–1914 (the period divided in two by the year 1879) to prepare adequately for the spiritualization of humanity that is striven for through the Archangel Michael—that is, if the attempt had been made, on a large scale, to imbue human beings with spiritual concepts, spiritual ideas. If by free human volition—since modern humanity depends on freedom—this attempt is not made, then the scale-beam sinks to the other side. What could have been achieved in spiritual ways now occurs through the blood. The spiritualization occurs in an as it were super-physical manner. What we experience in our catastrophic times is such a balancing of the scales. Humanity, which has rejected spiritualization, must be forced into spiritualization. This can happen through a physical catastrophe.

This idea can be verified if we firmly place ourselves upon the following foundation. We live here in the physical world; but, as I recently described, we are awake there only through our perceptions and our ideas—with our feelings we are dreaming and as far as our will impulses are concerned we are asleep. This is the way things are for human beings. But if, through imagination, inspiration, and intuition, we acquaint ourselves with the spiritual world, which is always around us like the air, and where the so-called dead exist together with us and where their impulses are active, then we perceive how life here in the physical world is connected with the life of the so-called dead. And these so-called "dead" are able to receive from the hearts of living human beings only spiritual thoughts.

Recall what I told you three days ago. If someone dies when young, in a spiritual sense he or she has not actually left the family. He or she remains there, in reality is still there. But for the one who is dead something else is connected with this other than just being here. I beg you to take this very seriously. For the dead, it is a question of being able to bear this existence, to comprehend it. If the person who has died comes from a materialistically inclined family which does not cultivate spiritual thoughts, he or she is, to be sure, still present in this family, but present in a way that is constantly oppressive and distressing. The family becomes something like a nightmare, like the air which we too deeply inhale, through which we experience the nightmare. Only spiritual thoughts from the rest of the family can rid the departed one of this nightmare and make life bearable and possible for them.

I told you too that, when older people are torn from their families, they take their family's souls with them. They take them along, draw them to them. But again, if they are not permeated by spiritual thoughts, they constitute a nightmare.

Now let us consider the following. We can learn a great deal if we observe the sudden death of a human being by outer circumstances or abnormal inner conditions. Let us say that someone is slain or shot. In such an instance, death is brought about in a way which is very different from gradual, natural death by illness. Now imagine someone who is shot in the thirty-fifth year of life; his or her life is suddenly destroyed through outer circumstances. If the bullet had not struck (certainly, there are karmic connections, but what I am going to say nevertheless holds true), this person's constitution might have allowed another thirty-five years of life. Inwardly, this person still has as it were the constitution for another thirty-five years. This causes something quite special.

Those who die violently when their life forces are still very active experience something quite tremendous. Condensed into a single moment, they experience things that would have been spread over a long period of time. What they could have experienced during the next thirty-five years, what would have been spread over the next thirty-five years, is condensed in a single moment. For in the hour of death, the most important experience is that a human being comes to see his or her true physicalness from outside. A person sees the transition the physical body passes through as it moves from being under the control of the forces it possessed when the soul dwelt in the body to becoming a nature-being, given over to natural, external physical forces. The tremendously significant experience at the moment of death is that the human being then beholds the relinquishing of his or her organism to physical nature forces. Human beings who suffer a violent death are not only delivered over suddenly to the forces of nature, which are the normal ones, but in addition the organism is treated by the bullet as if it were an inorganic, lifeless body: it is completely relegated to the inorganic world. There is a great difference if a person dies a slow death through illness or suffers a sudden death by the intrusion of the universe from outside, be it in the form of a bullet or in another form. A sudden flaring up occurs, a sudden flashing forth of an infinite amount of spirituality. The flaming over of a spiritual aura takes place, and the one who has passed through the portal of death looks back upon this flaming up. This flaming up is very similar to what takes place when human beings devote themselves to spiritual concepts. These are values which are interchangeable. It is extremely interesting to see, when viewed from the other side, from the side of the dead, how similar the thought, the feeling thought that one has when one enjoys or creates an image, a painting, born of spiritual life, is to the sensation a person has—though he or she is of course unconscious of this—when he or she suffers an external injury, let us say, to his arm and pain arises from it. There is a profound relationship between the two events so that one may take the place of the other.

Now you will grasp the karmic connection that exists between the events of 1841 and 1917. Naturally, quite a few people knew the, let us say, "position of the stars" when the 1840s approached. This is only a technical expression used by occultists when they wish to designate such an event as the battle of the Archangel Michael with the Dragon. They say: "This is the position of the stars." Of course, quite a number of people at that time knew that such a significant event was taking place. There were some who wanted to take certain precautions, but, we may say, the other side of the balance was too heavily weighted: people's materialistic sense was too strong. Thus the falsest measures possible were resorted to. People understood that spiritual life must enter humanity. This was quite obvious. Many people in the 1840s understood the signs of the time and were convinced that spiritual life must enter humankind.[36] Had a new spiritual life entered humanity beginning with the 1840s, humanity would have been spared many catastrophes. Certainly, what took place would have taken place anyway, but it would have taken place in a different form. What is karmically necessary happens, but it may occur in different forms. This must always be kept in mind.

I shall express myself more explicitly. When as human beings today we consider what should happen in the social sphere or in any other field, there are two ways of doing this.

We can construct a program, form programmatic concepts, and think out how the world should develop in a certain area. We can present this in beautiful sounding words. We can swear by these words and take them as dogmas—but nothing will result from them, nothing at all! We can have the most beautiful ideas about what ought to happen, but nothing will come of them. For ideas, however beautiful, need not result in anything. In fact, contrived programs are the most worthless things in life.

But there is another way of proceeding. We can do something in contrast to this programmatic approach, and many people achieve it without any special clairvoyance. Out of a naive intuitive knowledge of the condition of the times, can we simply ask ourselves what is bound to happen in the next twenty or thirty years? What in our time wishes to become reality? Then, once we have discovered what will inevitably happen, we can say to ourselves: "Now we must

---

36. Rudolf Steiner, *The Occult Movement in the Nineteenth Century*.

choose. We can either come to our senses and guide the course of events in the direction they must inevitably take—in which case matters will turn out well; or we can fail to do this and allow matters to run their course—in which case we are asleep, simply not awake. And then the course of events will be brought about by "catastrophes." In that case, revolutions, cataclysms, and so forth will follow. No statistics, no programs, however well thought out, are of any value. The only thing of value is observation of what the times engender. What the times engender must be taken up, must be penetrated: the intentions of the present must be governed by this.

Last century, in the 1840s, many different kinds of people, program-people, were victorious over the few who understood what I have just stated. Thereby all kinds of attempts to spiritualize humanity sprang up: for instance, spiritualism, which is only an attempt to spiritualize humanity with inadequate means. Spiritualism seeks to reform humanity in a materialistic way, to represent and reveal the spiritual worlds to human beings materialistically. It is easy to be quite materialistic in one's thinking. A person is being materialistic when he or she says: "Yes, this or that particular group of human beings is right, why don't the spiritual powers intervene and help them assert their cause?" How often do we hear people asking today, "Why don't the spiritual powers intervene?" Recently I answered this in a more abstract form: Humanity today must rely on its own freedom. Those who ask, "Why don't the spiritual powers intervene?" proceed on the assumption that ghosts should make politics instead of human beings. We could certainly progress if ghosts instead of human beings introduced the necessary reforms! They do not do this, of course, because human beings must rely on their freedom. Waiting for ghosts is what makes human beings most confused. It draws their attention away from what ought to happen. Thus, at precisely the same time as humanity, in its own life, was familiarizing itself with refined spiritual concepts—which clearly live in some people—it was also exposed to the starkest materialistic temptations. Human beings are quite unable to distinguish between refined spiritualized concepts and sensations on the one hand, and what approaches them as temptation on the other, working against the comprehension of what they have spiritualized in themselves—which really is something spiritual. Therefore, because people did not understand at the right moment how evolution ought to proceed, the present catastrophic age—our present, difficult times—became necessary. Without these present difficult times humanity would have sunk still deeper into doubt about itself. To be sure, it would have been even more capable of developing spirituality, but it would also have rejected it to a still greater degree.

This is part of the background of historical development. Naturally, on this basis, I should like to throw light on much that lies in the foreground, but this cannot be done today for reasons you will readily understand. It must be left for each individual to illuminate for himself or herself out of this background what lives in our immediate present.

The sleeping away of events, as I have characterized it, makes us overlook the sharp angles and contours of life. But when we overlook the sharp angles and contours of life, compromises arise. Now, there are times that are very suitable for compromises. The time that preceded the 1840's, for instance, was such a time; but this is not true of our time. Our time demands that we see things as they are, with all their angles and contours. But precisely because these sharp angles and contours are there the urge also arises in our souls to close our eyes sleepily to these things. What I have just stated may indeed be observed even in regard to the greatest, the most significant events in human evolution.

Human evolution has even brought about just such angles and contours in relation to the greatest event in world history, namely, the Mystery of Golgotha. We know all that the development of theology in the nineteenth century has to say about the Mystery of Golgotha—from the time of Lessing[37] right up to the time of the theologian Drews,[38] all kinds of things have been said. Indeed, it

---

37. Gotthold Ephraim Lessing, 1729–1781. German dramatist, literary critic, translator, and editor.
38. Arthur Drews, 1865–1935. German philosopher, professor at Karlsruhe, author of works on: German philosophy since Kant, Nietzsche, Plotinus, the Christian Myth, and the psychology of the unconscious.

may well be said that the whole development of theology in the nineteenth century provides complete proof that people have entirely forgotten how to understand anything at all of the Mystery of Golgotha. And yet there are some very interesting publications concerning Christ Jesus. For instance, there is a Danish publication written entirely from the standpoint of a modern natural-scientific thinker.[39] The author states his point of view as follows: "I am a psychologist, a physiologist, a psychiatrist; I observe the Gospels from my point of view." What conclusion does this author reach? Absolutely factually, judging as a modern psychiatrist, he concludes that the picture which the Gospels sketch of Christ Jesus is pathological. From the point of view of psychiatry, one can only conceive of the Christ Jesus as suffering from insanity, epilepsy, morbid visions and similar conditions. All the symptoms of a serious mental illness are there.

If one reads aloud the most important passage of this book, as I have recently done, people are shocked.[40] This is understandable, for people are horrified when what they consider sacred is described in terms of pathological symptoms. But what is really happening here? What is happening is that among a great number of dishonest compromisers, one arose who is dedicated completely to the natural-scientific viewpoint and makes no compromises whatsoever, but states without equivocation: "I am totally a scientist; and therefore must speak as I do, for these are the facts. If others would place themselves honestly on the standpoint where natural science has placed itself, they would have to hold the same views." There are these sharp angles and contours, and one cannot do otherwise. They cannot do otherwise than either forsake the natural-scientific point of view and cross over to the spiritual-scientific point of view— in which case they remain honest—or they may choose to remain honest upon the natural-scientific point of view, in which case they must observe matters, without making compromises, in the manner

---

39. Emil Rasmussen, *Jesus, A Comparative Psychopathological Study.*
40. See Rudolf Steiner, *Geistige Wesen und ihre Wirkungen* [Spiritual beings and their effects], vol. 4, lecture 1 (not translated).

of such a narrow-minded scientist, who, although honest in his field, is thoroughly limited in his views and does not try to conceal his narrow-mindedness. Such a scientist is narrow-minded, but consistent. This has to be understood. If people would see today what makes certain nuances necessary, when clearly examined, then they would begin to see life without compromise.

Someone recently handed me an interesting slip of paper. I already knew of the book mentioned on the paper, but since I do not have the book with me here, I can only read you what is written on this slip of paper. It was handed to me in order to show me what kinds of things are possible today.

Anyone who has ever attended high school will remember the unforgettable hours when in the study of Plato he or she could "enjoy" Socrates' conversations with his friends. Unforgettable, because of the fabulous boredom that flowed from these conversations. One will perhaps remember that these conversations of Socrates struck one as extremely stupid; but, of course, one did not dare utter this opinion, for after all, the human being in question was Socrates, "the greatest philosopher." Alexander Moszkowski's book *Socrates, the Idiot* completely does away with this unjustified overestimation of the good Athenian. In this small, entertainingly written book, the polymath Moszkowski undertakes nothing less than to divest Socrates thoroughly of his philosophical honors. The title *Socrates the Idiot* is to be taken literally. One is not wrong in assuming that this book is based on scientific investigations.

Now, you may think it dreadful that such things are written. But I do not find it dreadful at all. I think it is self-evident and quite honest of Moszkowski. For, according to his concepts and sentiments, Moszkowski cannot do otherwise than to call Socrates an idiot, if he wishes to remain consistent. This is obvious. And by doing so he is more honest than many others who, in keeping with their views, would also have to call Socrates an idiot, but who prefer to make compromises instead. I need not tell you that no one should now spread the news through the porous walls of the Münich Branch that I have proclaimed myself in agreement with Moszkowski when he declares Socrates to have been an idiot.

However, I must also acknowledge that people arrive at certain judgments today because they make dishonest compromises. One cannot think about mental illness as modern psychiatry does and not write a book such as the one written by the Danish author about Christ Jesus. That cannot be done. One is being dishonest if one does not either reject such concepts and replace them with spiritual ones, or take the point of view that Jesus was mentally ill. And if one is acquainted with Moszkowski's peculiar views on radiation theory, quantum theory, boundary concepts, and the whole structure of the world, then, if one is honest and consistent, one cannot help but consider Socrates and Plato idiots.

Hence, the impulse to reject compromises—to make no compromises, above all in one's soul life—belongs among the impulses that are especially essential to humanity. It is extraordinarily important that we consider this as a demand of our age. For precisely this rejection of compromise is one of the most significant of the impulses of Michael, the Spirit of the Age—namely, to pour clarity, absolute clarity, into human souls. If we wish to follow the Archangel Michael, then we must infuse human souls with clarity and overcome sleepiness. Such sleepiness, of course, arises in other spheres too, but above all it is absolutely necessary today to overcome sleepiness if we are to gain insight into the consequences of things. In previous ages this was different. During the centuries prior to the Michaelic age, when European humanity was governed essentially by the Archangel Gabriel, the compromises which human beings thought of were diminished by the influence of the spiritual world. Michael is the spirit who works in the most eminent sense with the freedom of humankind. Therefore Michael will always do the right thing. You must not believe that Michael fails to do the right thing—he does indeed do the right thing.

In the unconscious regions of the soul every contour and angle of spiritual life is today sharply outlined in every human being. It is there. Those who possess even the slightest ability—be it ever so small—of bringing to the surface what exists as latent visions in the depths of soul life know what lives as discrepancies and incongruities in the soul today. They know that in souls today modern materialistic psychiatry, which does not shrink from seeing an epileptic in Christ Jesus, even lives side by side with the actual acknowledgment of Christ Jesus. We know that this is so. If these things were only called just a little into consciousness, if we had only the minimal ability needed to call these things into consciousness, we would become aware of these facts. It would be interesting if a good painter who had a real understanding of our present time would paint "Christ, seen from the point of view of a modern psychiatrist," and would depict it expressionistically. It would be very interesting to see what the result would be if the painter had a real understanding of what takes place at the present time in the depths of human soul life.

You see, today we must plumb the depths if we wish to grasp what takes place on the surface of existence. But one can understand, on the other hand, that people are seized by a certain cowardice and discouragement if they are to approach what we have been talking about.

You see, it is especially necessary today to dig deeply if we wish to understand what is taking place on the surface of existence. On the other hand, we can also understand that human beings are overcome with a certain cowardice and timidity when they get too close to the things we are speaking of here. This, indeed, is the other quality necessary today: courage, and even a certain audacity in perceiving, in thinking; an audacity that does not dull our concepts but rather perhaps makes them highly acute. I have said these things so that they may be observed by everyone, to the extent that they are spiritually accessible to everyone. You can observe them yourselves, if you really wish to observe spiritual life in the present.

Everything that has been said today can be found in external events. The spiritual researcher simply describes it more precisely because he sees it against its proper background. And if the researcher then describes this background, outer events will all the more corroborate what has, for example, been indicated today.

Many people ask what they should do. It is so obvious what one should do! One should open one's eyes, one's spiritual eyes, to be sure! Once we open our eyes, our will follows. Our will depends upon our life situation. It is not always possible in our particular circumstances to do the right thing according to our karma; but we must try to open our eyes spiritually. Nowadays, however, it often happens that if one tries to impart verbally what is necessary for the present age, people quickly close their eyes and swiftly turn their minds away from it. This is the falling of the scales on the other side. When one speaks as I am doing here, it could very well be considered a criticism of our age. I have never intended such criticism. My purpose is to draw attention to the impulses that must enter human souls, human minds, from the spiritual world. As I have stated, it is not possible to enter into concrete details. Each of you can do that for yourselves.

PART

2

The Mission of
the Archangel Michael

*Revelation of Essential Secrets of
the Human Being*

SIX LECTURES GIVEN IN DORNACH

NOVEMBER 21–NOVEMBER 30, 1919

LECTURE ONE

INTRODUCTION

The contrast between the evolution of the head and the rest of the organism—Triad and duality in the world and human understanding—The abolition of the tripartite human being at the Eighth Ecumenical Council of Constantinople of 869—The Christ-Impulse as the balance between Lucifer and Ahriman

Dornach, November 21, 1919

During the next few days I would like to discuss how human beings today can relate to the spiritual force wielded by Michael both in the spiritual world and in all earthly events.[1] Today's lecture will prepare us for this task. A variety of viewpoints will be necessary if we are to read the true influence of this Michaelic force in the symptomatic events constantly occurring around us.

Whoever would speak seriously of the spiritual world must remember always to include what the spiritual powers reveal of themselves in the physical realm. We must try to pierce through the veil of the physical world, as it were, to see what is taking place in the spiritual. We can all observe what is present in the physical realm. And what is active in the spiritual world serves to throw light on and solve, from a spiritual point of view, the riddles presented by the physical world. We must only experience these riddles of physical existence in the right way. In important matters of this nature it is essential to grasp the full meaning of what I spoke of here recently,[2] namely, that subjective and personal views of the world bear no relation to the true understanding of what is so

1. These lectures were translated from *Die Sendung Michaels* (GA194) by Marjorie Spock.
2. Cf. Steiner, GA 191, [Social Understanding out of Spiritual Science] (not translated).

vitally important—not only to humanity as a whole but also, and preeminently, to the earth and the cosmos. We must free ourselves of what is merely personal and subjective. Indeed, only by doing so, by freeing ourselves from the narrower aspects of this personal element, can we gain insight into the true role and value of personality in the world.

Now, you know that the earthly phase of our evolution was preceded by other evolutionary phases, that we are involved in a whole process of cosmic evolution.[3] And you know, likewise, that this evolution continues, and in fact has reached a point when it will progress to further, more developed stages. And you are also aware that, from a cosmic standpoint, we human beings are linked not only to beings we encounter in the earthly realm—those of the mineral, plant and animal kingdoms—but also to beings of a higher order, of the higher hierarchies. When we speak of evolution as a whole, therefore, these higher beings too must always be included.

These beings of the higher hierarchies are involved, like us, in an evolutionary process, one that we can understand by analogy both with our own human development and with the evolution of the other earthly kingdoms.

Consider first, for example, the following. As human beings, we have passed through the evolutionary phases of Saturn, Sun, and Moon and have now arrived on the earth. Therefore, surveying the cosmic evolution we have undergone, we may say that as human beings who perceive themselves in earthly surroundings, we have reached the fourth (earthly) stage of our evolution.

Consider next the beings called *Angeloi* (Angels), who are at the stage immediately above our human level. Continuing the analogy with our own evolution, we can say that, although these beings are constituted quite differently than we are and remain invisible to our physical senses, they have already arrived at what will be for us, when we reach it, the fifth or Jupiter stage of evolution.

Going on, the next hierarchy, the *Archangeloi* or Archangels are those beings at what will be for human beings the evolutionary stage

---

3. See Steiner, *An Outline of Occult Science.*

of Venus; while the *Archai*, the Spirits of Time, who are especially involved with our present, earthly phase of evolution, are already at the Vulcan stage.[4]

Here an important question arises. The next class of spiritual beings belongs to the hierarchy of the so-called Spirits of Form (the Powers or *Exusiai*). But these beings have reached an evolutionary level *beyond* the level that we human beings envision as our future Vulcan stage, and have attained what, if we count as *seven* the stages required for our current human evolution, must be called an *eighth* stage. In other words, we may say that as human beings we are now at the fourth stage of evolution, while the Spirits of Form are at the eighth stage.

Of course, we must not think of this sequence of evolutionary stages as existing successively, one after another. Rather we must picture them as interpenetrating each other. Just as a mantle of air—the atmosphere—surrounds and permeates the earth, the eighth evolutionary sphere or stage, to which the Spirits of Form belong, permeates the fourth or earthly stage within which humanity exists.

Let us consider these two spheres or stages of evolution more closely. First, recall that as human beings we exist in a sphere that has reached the fourth evolutionary level. But at the same time, leaving all other considerations aside, we also exist in the (eighth) realm of the Spirits of Form, who surround and permeate us.

Let us picture human evolution concretely. We have often traced the evolution of the various parts of the human organism. We have distinguished the development of the head from that of the rest of the body, dividing the latter into two parts—the chest and the limbs. For the moment, we will disregard this last division and simply picture the development of the head, together with all that belongs to it, on the one hand, and the rest of the human being on the other.

Imagine now the following. Picture the surface of an ocean and a person wading there, moving forward through the water, with only the head protruding. This is an image—but only an image—of our present human situation. From this point of view, all that has made

---

4. See Steiner, *The Apocalypse of St. John.*

the head what it is today must be reckoned as belonging to the *fourth* evolutionary level, while everything through which the human being is wading or (we might say) swimming, we would have to call the *eighth* evolutionary stage. Strange as it is, human beings have outgrown, as far as their heads are concerned, the element in which the Spirits of Form unfold their particular nature. With regard to the development of our heads, we have, as it were, become emancipated from that element which is completely impregnated by the essence of the Spirits of Form.

Any true understanding of human nature must be based on a thorough grasp of this fact for only then is a proper perspective of humanity's special place in the universe possible. Only then do we realize that when we sense the creative influence exerted upon us by the Spirits of Form, we do not sense it directly through the capacities in our heads but indirectly through the effects of the rest of the organism upon our heads.

You all know that we breathe and that, physiologically speaking, breathing is bound up with the circulation of the blood. But the blood is also driven into the head, connecting the head in an organic, living relation with the rest of the organism. In this way the head is nourished and enlivened by the rest of the body.

Here two things must be carefully distinguished. On the one hand, the head is directly connected with the outer world. That is, when we look at something, we perceive it with our eyes, setting up an immediate connection between the surrounding world and the head. On the other hand, if we study the life of the head—the way its life is maintained by the processes of breathing and blood circulation—we notice that blood shoots up into the head from the rest of the organism. In this case, we would have to call the connection between the head and the surrounding environment indirect, rather than direct.

Naturally, we must not be pedantic, pointing out that the air we breathe is inhaled through the mouth, and hence also belongs to the realm of the head. As I said, we are dealing here only with an image. Organically, what we take in through the mouth does not really belong to the head, but rather to the rest of the organism.

Now, we should focus on these basic concepts and hold fast to the idea that we belong to two spheres, the fourth or earthly sphere— the evolutionary stage to which we belong as a result of having passed through Saturn, Sun, and Moon stages of evolution—and the eighth sphere —the life which belongs to the Spirits of Form in the sense that the earth belongs to us, and which penetrates our earth, excluding only our heads, so that we live within this sphere with every part of our organism not involved in sense perception. If we can hold these things in our minds, then we will have prepared a foundation for what is to come.

But, before going any further, I want to lay another foundation for what is to follow by including some further ideas. Certainly, if we are to study influences of a spiritual order we cannot leave out the Luciferic and Ahrimanic beings who are also involved in the cosmic process.[5] Let us for the moment focus on the outermost aspects of these Luciferic and Ahrimanic beings, who also dwell in the spheres that human beings occupy. We may say that we conceive of the outermost characteristics of *Luciferic* beings properly when we imagine that they possess such forces as we human beings manifest when we become visionaries, when we abandon ourselves one-sidedly to fantasy, let ourselves be carried away, and, speaking pictorially, lose our heads. In other words, whenever we tend to go out beyond our heads, we are dealing with forces that, while they play a certain role in our organism, actually belong cosmically to the beings we term Luciferic. If we picture beings who are wholly formed of that within us that strives to go out beyond our heads, we are picturing the Luciferic beings who are related to our human world in certain ways.

Now, in contrast, think of everything that presses us down upon the earth, that makes us dull and philistine, leading us to develop materialistic attitudes, penetrating us with a dry intellect, and so on: there you have a picture of the Ahrimanic powers.

All these aspects I have just described from a psychological perspective may also be expressed more physiologically. We may say that human beings always occupy a median position between what

---

5. See Steiner, *The Influences of Lucifer and Ahriman.*

their blood wants and what their bones want. Our bones are constantly trying to solidify, densify, and ossify us—to stiffen and harden and make us Ahrimanic in a bodily sense. Our blood, on the other hand, seeks to drive us out beyond ourselves. In pathological cases, it becomes feverish, driving us organically into producing fantasies (hallucinations). The bones can likewise extend their essential tendency to the whole organism—in this case we become sclerotic, as almost everyone does to some extent in old age. In old age, indeed, the Ahrimanic tendency, the death element, spreads throughout the organs. It can be said therefore that everything that has to do with the blood tends toward the Luciferic, whereas all that has to do with the bones tends toward the Ahrimanic. As human beings we are the point of balance between the blood and the bones, just as we must strive for the psychological balance between visionary excesses and dry philistinism.

We may characterize these two kinds of beings still further. For instance, we may contemplate Luciferic beings from the standpoint of the kind of interest they take in cosmic existence. We find that their chief interest lies in making the world, particularly the human world, unfaithful to the spiritual beings whom we must regard as the true creators of humanity. Their one desire is to make the world disloyal to these divine beings. They are not interested in claiming the world for themselves. You will have gathered from previous remarks about the Luciferic beings that such is not their chief aim. Their aim is rather to make human beings forsake their divine creator-beings—they wish to free the world from the beings felt by humankind to be the real divinities.

The Ahrimanic beings have a different interest. Their firm intention is to get the human kingdom and thereby the earth along with it into their sphere of power, to make human beings dependent on them, to control humanity. Whereas the Luciferic beings strive, and have always striven, to alienate us from the beings whom we feel to be our Gods, the Ahrimanic beings seek to draw humanity and everything connected with it into their power.

In other words, Luciferic beings, striving for universal freedom and Ahrimanic beings, striving for lasting dominion are constantly waging war in this cosmos we are part of. This battle involves us and affects everything, and I ask you to keep it in mind as the second important theme in our further deliberations. The world we live in is permeated by Luciferic and Ahrimanic beings, and as we have described it there is a tremendous contrast between the freeing tendency of the Luciferic beings and the power-seeking tendency of the Ahrimanic beings.

Contemplating all this, you will notice that the world can really be understood only in terms of a triad. On one side we have everything Luciferic, on the other everything Ahrimanic, and, in the third, central, place, the point of balance between the two, humanity, with a sense of its relationship to the Divine, of its divine essence. We can understand the world in the right way only when we see it based on this triad and are perfectly clear that human life is the beam of the scales. Here is the fulcrum: on one side is the Luciferic element, actually pulling the pan upward; opposite is the Ahrimanic element, pushing the pan downward. Our human task—our human essence—is to keep the beam balanced.

Initiates into such secrets have always emphasized, when speaking of human spiritual evolution, that the cosmic existence in which we find ourselves can be understood only in terms of the triad. They knew that it cannot be understood on the basis of any number other than the number three. Expressed in our own terminology, we may say that in cosmic existence we have always a Luciferic element (one side of the scales), an Ahrimanic element (the other side of the scales), and the state of balance, represented by the Christ-Impulse.

Now, as you may well imagine, it lies in the deepest interests of the Luciferic and Ahrimanic powers to conceal this secret of the number three—after all, only the proper penetration of this secret would allow humanity to bring about the state of balance between the Luciferic and Ahrimanic powers. This means that we must make beneficial use of the Luciferic tendency toward freedom, on the one hand, and of the Ahrimanic tendency on the other. For human beings, the healthiest spiritual condition is to enter into a proper relationship with this cosmic trinity, this cosmic structure based on the principle of three.

There is now and has been for some time a powerful tendency in cultural and spiritual life to confuse people about the significance of this holy triad. During the next two days we shall examine the sources of this confusion more closely. For the moment, however, let me repeat: a strong tendency exists to confuse people on the subject of the number Three, which we may well call a sacred number. Certainly, we can see clearly that this triadic structure has been almost totally eclipsed in modern culture by a dualistic one. Just think for a moment that to understand Goethe's *Faust* correctly, as I have often mentioned, we need to realize that this confusion around the number three has crept into even this tremendous cosmic work.[6] If Goethe in his day had thoroughly understood how things stand in this regard, he would never have represented the Mephistophelean power as Faust's only enemy and seducer; rather, he would have shown Lucifer as complementing and opposing this Mephistophelean power whom we recognize as identical with Ahriman; and so Lucifer and Ahriman would have appeared in *Faust* as *two* elements. I have often discussed this here. Anyone who studies the figure of Mephistopheles can see plainly how Goethe's characterization of Mephisto everywhere confuses Luciferic and Ahrimanic elements. Goethe has in some way made the figure of Mephisto a mixture of two elements rather than a consistent single one, and the two are fantastically intermingled. My monograph, *Goethe's Standard of the Soul* [*Goethe's Geistesart*], explores these questions more completely.

This confusion which thus plays even into Goethe's *Faust* is based on the delusive modern concept—it was different in earlier times and has arisen in the course of evolution—that puts dualism or the principle of two in place of the triad or principle of three when considering the structure of the world. That is, a good principle on one side and a bad principle on the other: good as opposed to evil, God opposed to the Devil. People in earlier times did not make this mistake.

So you see, we have to be clear that a realistic view of the structure of the cosmos requires that we recognize the role that three plays in

6. See lecture of November 3, 1917, "Faust and the Problem of Evil" [typescript].

it. We must acknowledge the opposing roles of the Luciferic and Ahrimanic powers, while recognizing that the divine role consists in holding a balance between the two. This needs to be contrasted with the delusion of the duality of God and the Devil that has entered human spiritual evolution—the notion of divine spiritual powers above and diabolical powers below. It is as if human beings have been deprived of the possibility of balance because a healthy human understanding of the world consists in a proper grasp of the triad and this has been, as it were, concealed from them, causing them to believe that the world structure is somehow determined by duality. Some of the loftiest human striving has fallen victim to this delusion.

To weigh this matter adequately we must completely overcome all prejudice. We must enter an unbiased sphere of thinking. We must carefully distinguish between a thing and its name. We must be determined not to be deceived into believing that because we have given a certain name to a being we have therefore experienced that being in the right way.

If we wish to form conceptions of those beings whom we experience as true divinities, we must realize that we can rightly experience them as such only when we think of them as bringing about a balance between Luciferic and Ahrimanic principles. Our own divine being cannot be experienced correctly unless we admit such a threefold structuring. Consider, from this point of view, poems like Milton's *Paradise Lost,* or Klopstock's *Messiah*, which it inspired.[7] In these works, no trace is to be found of any real understanding of the threefold structuring of the universe. Instead we find just a battle between supposed good and supposed evil, heaven and hell. In other words, the deluded notion of duality has been introduced into human spiritual evolution—the illusory opposition between heaven and hell that had taken widespread root in popular consciousness was introduced into these two works of world literature.

---

7. Cf. John Milton, 1608–1674, *Paradise Lost* [1671]. Friedrich Gottlieb Klopstock, 1724–1803, *Messiah* [1748–1773].

It makes no difference that Milton and Klopstock describe their heavenly beings as "Divine." They would be truly divine beings, as human beings ought to experience them, only if they were presented as members of a threefold structuring of cosmic existence. Only then would it be possible to say that a battle was raging between the principles of good and evil. But, as it is, a duality is assumed. All good attributes are ascribed to one pole, and names are found and attached to the beings of this pole who are presented as divine, while the diabolical element antagonistic to the Divine occupies the other pole. And what really happens then? Why, the Divine is erased from people's consciousness and is replaced by a Luciferic element, which is given the label of divinity. The actual result is that we have a battle going on between Lucifer and Ahriman, but Luciferic characteristics are attributed to Ahriman, and Lucifer's kingdom is conceived of as divine.

You see how far-reaching the implications of such considerations are. People think that they are dealing with the Divine and the diabolical in such works as Milton's *Paradise Lost* and Klopstock's *Messiah*, whereas in fact they are dealing with Luciferic and Ahrimanic principles. No real consciousness exists of the truly divine element. Instead, the Luciferic element is endowed with the label of divinity.

Now, Milton's *Paradise Lost* and Klopstock's *Messiah* are just spiritual creations that stand out in modern consciousness. What is expressed in them corresponds to the overall state of awareness of the human race: the delusion of duality has taken over modern consciousness, and the reality of the triadic principle has been consigned to oblivion. Some of the most profound creative works of recent times, justly revered as such, are cultural maya, illusion, founded on the great modern human delusion. Everything born of this delusion or maya is basically the creation of the Ahrimanic influences that will one day be concentrated in the incarnation of Ahriman himself, of which I have already told you.[8] For this delusion, to which we have all succumbed, is simply the outcome of a

8. See Steiner, *The Influences of Lucifer and Ahriman,* lectures 1 and 2; and *The Ahrimanic Deception.*

false way of looking at the world. It is common to everyone in the current state of culture and civilization who opposes heaven and hell. Heaven is viewed as the divine pole, and hell as the devilish pole. In fact, of course, we are actually dealing only with a Luciferic element, which we term heavenly, on the one hand and an Ahrimanic element, which we term hellish, on the other.

We must realize what interests rule recent spiritual history. I have often emphasized that the threefold membering of the human organism, or of human nature as a whole, was done away with for posterity by the Eighth Ecumenical Council of Constantinople in 869. The dogma was then established that Christians must not believe in a threefold human membering, but only in a twofold one. Acknowledgment of the existence of the third element, spirit, was forbidden. Theologians and philosophers of the Middle Ages, who were well aware of the true facts, had a hard time working with them, for the threefold membering of body, soul, and spirit— known as the trichotomy—was declared heretical. Scholars were compelled to teach duality—that the human being consists of body and soul only and not of body, soul, and spirit. But, as certain beings, certain human beings, were well aware, replacing a threefold membering by a twofold one was of tremendous consequence for human spiritual life.

Profound questions of this kind must be borne in mind if we are to understand why in the November issue of *Stimmen der Zeit* [*"Voices of the Time"*] the Jesuit Father Zimmermann draws attention to the fact that one of the recent decrees of the Holy Office in Rome prohibits Catholics, under pain of denial of absolution at confession, from reading or possessing Theosophical literature or participating in anything Theosophical. In this article in *Die Stimmen* (which was earlier called *Stimmen aus Maria-Laach* [*Voices from Maria Laach*]) Father Zimmerman interprets this decree as applying primarily to Anthroposophy and states that all those who wish Rome to recognize them as good Catholics should not read Anthroposophical literature. As one of the main reasons for this, he cites the fact that Anthroposophy differentiates human beings into body, soul, and spirit, a heretical teaching counter to the orthodox belief that regards human beings as composed only of body and soul.

I have mentioned before that modern philosophers have unconsciously adopted this differentiation of body and soul. They believe they are pursuing science without prejudice or prior assumptions, and that accurate observation alone has led them to see human beings as consisting only of body and soul. But the truth is that they too are merely succumbing to the dogma that has infiltrated the evolution of consciousness in recent times. What passes as science nowadays is actually completely subject to the influence of such unconscious trends that have made their way into the world in the course of recent human evolution. Don't let yourselves believe that any favorable words you might often feel impelled to speak to people who talk harshly of Anthroposophy could convert them, or that you could change their attitude to one of some degree of benevolence toward it. Anthroposophy has to make its way in the world on its own merits, not as the result of any protection given it—even by powers thought to be highly Christian. Inner strength alone can enable Anthroposophy to achieve the goals it must achieve.

Keep in mind that the impulse of the Christ may be understood only when it is recognized as the impulse that maintains the balance between the Ahrimanic and the Luciferic elements and so is assigned its proper place in the Trinity. It might be asked what is required to lead people astray on the subject of the true Christ-Impulse. They would have to be kept from recognizing the true threefold ordering of the world, and led to accept the delusion of duality, or two, which applies only in instances where manifestation is involved, not where the question is one of penetrating beyond the manifested world to the sphere of reality from which manifestation issues.

We need to be clear that it is essential to get beyond mere labels in such matters. Calling a being the Christ does not make it so. It does not mean that we have encountered the Christ. In fact, putting duality in the place of the triad can prevent the Christ from being encountered in His true Christ-name. Anyone who wanted to be sure of keeping people from forming a true concept of the Christ would only have to replace the triad with duality. To refer truly to the impulse of the Christ requires only replacing duality with three-ness. But there is no need to join the ranks of the Inquisitors. There is no need, starting today, to condemn *Paradise Lost* or Klopstock's *Messiah* as works of the devil. We can certainly continue to enjoy their beauty and grandeur. But we should be aware that works of this sort—which in their way are high points of recent culture—have no connection whatsoever with the Christ. Instead, they are products of the delusion that anything that falls outside the bounds of human evolution must be accounted either devilish or divine. On the contrary, in such works we meet only what is Luciferic. And Mil-ton, in writing *Paradise Lost* is actually describing the expulsion of humanity from the realm of Lucifer into the realm of Ahriman. What is portrayed there is not the human longing for the Divine, but the longing for a lost paradise that is actually Lucifer's kingdom. You will find beautiful descriptions of the longing for Lucifer's king-dom in Milton's *Paradise Lost* and Klopstock's *Messiah*, but they should be seen for what they are. And that is what they actually are.

Certain concepts that have made their way into modern humanity stand in direst need of revision. If we commit ourselves seriously to anthroposophical thinking and feeling, we face great, not small, decisions. We confront the need to take seriously a phrase often used by Nietzsche—"the transvaluation of all values."[9] This phrase needs to be taken very, very seriously. The achievements of modern times stand in dire need of transvaluation.

This does not mean that we ourselves must become denouncers of heretics. We continually present scenes from Goethe's *Faust* here,[10] and I devoted decades to a study of Goethe.[11] But you can gather from my monograph *Goethe's Standard of the Soul* that appreciation of Goethe in no way blinded me to the mistaken characterization of his

---

9. Cf. Nietzsche's *Antichrist*, section 62.
10. Performed on the stage of the Goetheanum, Switzerland.
11. From the 1880s to the turn of the century Rudolf Steiner worked with Goet-he's ideas, including time spent at the Goethe Archives in Weimar. See Rudolf Steiner: *An Autobiography*, *Goethean Science*, *Goethe's World View*, and *The Science of Knowing Implicit in the Goethean World View*.

figure of Mephistopheles.[12] It would be philistine and narrow-minded to say, "Goethe's Mephisto is wrong, so away with it." That would be adopting the witch-hunting methods of the heretic-hunters. As modern human beings we should not behave like that. On the other hand, we must not be lazy and content to adopt ideas ready made from the spiritual life of recent times just because they have been absorbed into the very blood and bone of the great masses of people today. Humanity has an incredible amount to learn, and will have to undertake a revision of a great many of its values.

All this has to do with the mission of Michael in relation to those beings of the higher hierarchies with whom he is once more connected. The next two days will therefore be devoted to the theme of how we can come to an understanding of the impulses radiating from the Michael-Being into our human existence here on earth.

LECTURE TWO

The head as retrogressive, the rest of the organism as progressive
—Pre-Christian Revelations: Day Revelations through the head
(Lucifer), Night Revelations through the rest of the organism
(Jahve)—Michael, the Countenance of Jahve—The transformation of Michael from Night Spirit to Day Spirit— Michael's Task
in the past and the future: The Word becomes flesh and the
flesh becomes Spirit

Dornach, November 22, 1919

Yesterday I spoke of an error that has crept into modern spiritual life, one that only few people today notice or understand in the right way. You probably sensed from my comments that reference to this error marks a very important point in our spiritual scientific

12. See *Goethe's Standard of the Soul (as Illustrated in Faust and in the Fairy Story of the Green Snake and the Beautiful Lily)*.

studies. In fact, it is absolutely necessary to have a clear grasp of this matter if the spiritual life of humanity is to develop properly.

I drew your attention to such cultural witnesses as Milton's *Paradise Lost* and Klopstock's *Messiah*. These works arose from the kind of popular thinking that has become widely accepted in recent centuries. I also pointed out that it is precisely in the arts—in highly acclaimed cultural accomplishments such as those of Milton and Klopstock—that we see what dangers threaten human soul life when people fail to recognize that it is impossible to reach a true and adequate concept of God, and thereby of Christ, as long as they believe that the structure of the universe, including the spiritual world, is understandable in terms of duality. Because people differentiated only duality—with good occupying one pole and evil the other—they fell into the error of lumping together as "evil" all that we have learned over the course of time to attribute to the Luciferic and Ahrimanic principles. They did not realize that they had lumped together two universal elements. In this way the Luciferic element was shifted to the other side, the "good" pole. In other words, people believed they were perceiving and revering the Divine, speaking of the Divine by name, whereas in fact they were infusing what they called "Divine" with a Luciferic element. This is why it is so difficult for people today to arrive at a pure concept of God and of the Christ-Impulse in human and cosmic evolution.

Furthermore, the acceptance of this duality by the culture of recent times has given us the habit of speaking either, on the one hand, of a soul element or, on the other, of a physical-bodily element. We have lost the connection between thoughts that convey knowledge of the soul-spiritual element and those that convey the bodily element. When we speak nowadays of thinking, willing, and feeling, what we say amounts to scarcely more than empty words. Nowhere is this truer than in conventional psychology. Nowhere do we find a genuine, inner, meaningful understanding of the soul. At the same time, we speak of a de-spiritualized material element, devoid of soul and spirit, and hammer away, as it were, at this externally hard, stonelike, soulless material element, unable to build a bridge from it to the soul.

The spiritual that is everywhere present and the bodily that is actually also spiritual have split into two. Mere theories cannot provide a bridge to link them, and since they cannot the whole realm of scientific thinking has taken on, above all, this character of a split between the bodily and the soul-spiritual elements. We might express it thus. On one hand, we have the different religious confessions which have degenerated into pointing toward the spiritual without being in a position to show how it creatively takes hold of and directly affects the body. On the other hand, we have a soulless science, a soulless observation of nature that today, because of the way it regards the body, can nowhere see through bodily processes to the soul-spiritual element that rules them. Against this background, anyone surveying the scientific world view as it developed through the nineteenth century and into our own time must realize that what appears there is a result of what I have just described.

Before we can gain complete insight into the delusion that presently obscures the truth, however, we must begin by finding the right approach. And we shall do this if we consider the different principles that have emerged from many of our previous studies. People today speak of the human being as a single, unified being, regardless of whether they are referring to the soul or the body. They speak of both the soul and the body as one and uniform in their essence. But you have learned from our discussions here that in the human constitution a great contrast exists between what belongs to the head structure and what belongs to the rest of the organism. In addition, as you know, the rest of the organism can also be seen as made up of various further parts, but for our present purposes we will consider these as constituting a single whole.

Our subject is human evolution. But any inquiry into the evolution of the human head must be conducted quite differently from an inquiry into the evolution of the rest of the human body.

If we wish to consider, from a merely physical point of view, the formation of the human head—as a structure housing the organism that serves sensory perception and thinking and mental picturing— then we must seek its origins far back in human-cosmic evolution.

We must realize that what is expressed today in the form of the head has gradually evolved and been transformed. That is, the head has evolved through the developmental stages of the ancient Saturn, Sun, and Moon periods and has continued to evolve further in the Earth period. This is not so, however, with the rest of the body. It would be quite wrong, in fact, to think that the whole human organism has undergone a single, unified evolutionary process.

Therefore we may say the following. The head structure goes back to earlier Saturn, Sun, and Moon stages of the earth. In other words, what culminates in the human head is the result of a long evolutionary process. On the other hand, if we wish to seek the origins of the rest of the human organism, we cannot look back to the Saturn stage. Rather, we are forced to conclude that, as far as the rest of the human organism is concerned, we can trace the chest structure only as far back as the ancient Moon stage, while the limbs were added only during subsequent, earthly, stages of evolution.

We view the human being correctly only when we do so somewhat as follows—however, please take this statement only as a comparison. Hypothetically, then, we can easily imagine that some organic situation or other in the cosmos—some conceivable adaptive capacity linked with inner growth conditions—might enable human beings to develop new limbs. In that case, we would not trace the whole human form back to earlier developmental stages. Rather, we would say instead that, though we do indeed have to trace human evolution in general back into the past, this or that limb was added only at a certain moment. We are not tempted to think this way about the head's relation to the rest of the body simply because the head takes up so much less physical space than the rest of the human form does. But the truth is that the formation of the head reaches furthest back in evolution, while the remainder of the human form results from later additions to it. If, then, we wish to speak of an evolutionary connection between the human being and the animal world we can only say that everything pertaining to the human head goes back to an earlier animal form. The human head is a metamorphosed, indeed very extensively metamorphosed, animal form.

At one time, before there were any animals and when entirely different physical conditions prevailed, human beings had outwardly an animal form. The animals developed in addition to human beings only later on in evolution, while the original animal form of the human being developed into what is today the human head. The rest of the human organism was added to the human head at the same time as the animals entered evolution. Therefore the head has nothing to do with an actual descent from the animals. The truth of the matter is that the human head, seemingly the noblest part of the human being, has in fact an animal origin. That is, at an earlier stage, the human head did indeed have an animal-like form. But the rest of the human organism only developed as an organic addition to the head at the same time in cosmic evolution as the animals developed.

In a certain sense, the head has become the organ of thinking. Our organ of thinking is thus precisely the part of us which is traceable to an animal origin. But it is an animal descent of a remarkable, peculiar kind. If you examined a human head, you would probably not immediately note the anatomical traits traceable to an animal form. But if you looked more closely and were able to make a correct analysis of the structure of the head organs you would recognize that they were metamorphoses of animal organs.

In this connection, I must emphasize that the transformation of the human head from an animal form came about because a retrogressive development had already entered into the head. What once teemed with life and vitality during earlier evolutionary stages is now involved in a dying, regressing process in the human head. I once said that if we human beings were nothing but heads we could not possibly continue to live. We would be continuously dying. For, from an organic point of view, the forces active in the head are death processes rather than life processes. The head is constantly being revivified—enlivened—by the rest of the organism. Only thanks to the rest of the body is the head able to participate in the overall life of the human organism. If the head had to depend solely upon the forces for which it is organized—namely, the forces of sense perception and conceptualization—it would be continuously dying. The head has a continuous tendency to die: it must be constantly revived. When we are thinking or engaged in sensory perception, the processes going on in our heads and nervous systems or in connection with the senses are not up-building, life-oriented, growth-serving processes. If such processes took place in our heads we would only fall asleep. We would fall into deep slumber, and become quite incapable of wide-awake thinking. Thinking and sensory perception, in fact, find an organ for their activity only because death moves continuously through our heads—because a continuous retrogressive evolution is occurring there, and organic processes are constantly being held back.

People who try to explain thinking and sensory perception materialistically as based on brain processes, while remaining totally unaware of the processes actually taking place in the head, believe these processes to be comparable to those of organic growth. But this is not the case. The processes that run parallel to sense perception and imagination are death processes: processes of dissolution and destruction. Organic and material elements must first be broken down and destroyed before the processes of thinking can rise above and supplant the organic process of destruction.

People today try to deduce these things from the outside. As human beings, we think and perceive with our senses, but we have no idea of what organic processes accompany these functions. They remain quite unconscious. Only the exercises I describe in my book *How To Know Higher Worlds*[13] make it possible for a person to ascend gradually to a kind of insight that goes beyond what is usually called, in an empty way, the "soul element" in thinking and sense perception. If one undertakes the kind of soul development described in my book, one can learn to surrender to thinking and sensory perception while, simultaneously, seeing what is taking place in the brain. Then one sees that the processes going on in the brain are not growth processes, but breaking-down processes that require constant restoration of life by the rest of the organism.

That is the tragic concomitant of real insight into the nature of our head's activity. Clairvoyant individuals—seers—take no pleasure

---

13. Previously titled *Knowledge of the Higher Worlds and Its Attainment*.

in the unfolding of organic processes in the head during thinking or perceiving with the senses. Instead, they become familiar with a process of destruction. They become aware that materialists assume processes to be taking place in the head that cannot actually occur in acts of thinking and perceiving. Materialism assumes the exact opposite of the truth.

In the human head, then, we are dealing with an evolutionary structure that goes back to an animal origin, but is now caught up in a retrogressive evolution, a process of dissolution. But the rest of the organism is involved in a progressive, ascending evolution. However we should not for that reason think that the rest of our organism plays no part in our human soul-spiritual element and our experience of it. Not only is blood continuously sent up into the head from the rest of the organism, but the soul-spiritual thought-forms out of which the world and the human organism are both woven also rise continuously into the head. Constituted as we are today, we do not normally perceive these soul-spiritual thought-forms. But the time has come when we must begin to perceive what rise as thought-forms out of our own being.

As you know, we sleep not only between when we fall asleep and when we wake up again. Actually, we are asleep with part of our being during the whole day. In fact, during the day, only our thinking, conceiving, and sense perceiving are actually awake. With regard to our feeling life, we are in a state of dreaming, while with respect to the life of our will, we are sound asleep. All we know of our will-life are the thoughts and ideas that prompt it to action. We remain as unconscious of the actual process of willing itself as we are in the period between sleeping and waking. We cannot follow its workings. And yet if we were to ask, "By what paths can knowledge of the genuinely Divine reach a human being?", we would not point to the path through the head nor to the path through sense perceptions or thinking, but only to the path that leads through the rest of our organism.

Here we face the tremendous mystery that humanity has evolved the head through a long series of evolutionary phases, while the rest of the organism was gradually and later added to it; that the head has already entered upon a retrogressive phase of evolution; and that what we can sense of the Divine has to reach us through the rest of our organism, not through the head. It is very important to be clear that only Luciferic beings have addressed us through the head. In fact, it may be said that the rest of the organism, apart from the head, was created to allow the Gods to speak to us. We do not read in Genesis that in the beginning God rayed a beam of light into the human being and the human became a living soul, but rather that God breathed the breath of life into the human and the human became a living soul. In other words, the Bible recognizes correctly that human beings received a divine impulse through a means other than the head.

You will have gathered from this that the divine impulse could reach human beings initially only in the form of unconscious clairvoyance, or at least through understanding what was received in that form. If you examine the Old Testament you can only regard it as a product of unconscious clairvoyance—you know this from previous studies. And those who helped to bring the Old Testament into being were also conscious of this fact. I cannot describe today how the Old Testament came into existence; I simply want to point out that I have already dealt with this question before.[14] How consistently we find that the teachers of the ancient Hebrew people were aware that their God did not speak to them through immediate sensory impressions or ordinary thinking—where the head serves as the mediator—but through dreams. These were not ordinary dreams, of course, but dreams saturated with reality. God spoke to them in clairvoyant moments, as when He spoke to Moses from the burning bush. When the Hebrew initiates of ancient times were asked how they conceived of these divine communications, they replied that the Lord, whose name it was forbidden to pronounce, spoke to them, but that He spoke to them through His "countenance." And they called this countenance of their Lord "Michael," the spiritual power we reckon among the hierarchy of the Archangels. They conceived of their God as one who remains invisible,

---

14. See Rudolf Steiner, *The Bible and Wisdom.*

even to clairvoyant experience. When they achieved a clairvoyant state of soul that lifted them to their God, it was Michael who addressed them. But Michael spoke only when human beings were able to enter into a certain state of non-ordinary, clairvoyant consciousness in which they became aware either of what lives in and works upon human beings while they are asleep, or else of what lives and works upon will, which remains unconscious and asleep even during waking conscious.

In ancient Hebrew secret doctrine this revelation of Jahve was called "the night revelation." This revelation of Jahve—experienced through the revelation of Michael—was experienced as a "night revelation." When people of that time looked upon the world and saw there what sensory perception and rational thinking could reveal to them, they realized: "The insights that we gain on the path of perception and thinking do not contain the Divine. But when we develop beyond this state of ordinary consciousness to a higher one, then Michael, God's countenance, speaks to us and reveals the true secrets of human nature. This Michael revelation then builds a bridge between human beings and those powers that are imperceptible in the world of the senses, powers neither reachable nor thinkable by brain-bound minds."

This is to say that in pre-Christian times people had access, on the one hand, to sense-derived insights that provided guidance in earthly affairs, while at the same time they were also aware of the possibility of another kind of insight that human beings would possess in ordinary consciousness only if their consciousness could stay awake—and it could not—during periods of sleep. In Old Testament times, people knew that during their waking hours they were in the company of spiritual beings, and that these beings were Luciferic, not creator beings. They knew that the beings they recognized as their creators worked in them from the time they fell asleep until they awoke, and they knew, too, that these beings were active in those parts of human nature that slept through waking day-consciousness. At the time when the Old Testament originated, the God Jahve was called "the Ruler of the Night," and his servant Michael, "Jahve's countenance," was called "the Servant of the Ruler of the

Night." Indeed, Michael was the being people had in mind when they spoke of prophetic insights that enabled them to understand more than they could by means of knowledge gained from mere sensory experience.

What sort of consciousness lay behind all this? Behind this lay a consciousness that grew out of the sphere of existence where the powers linked with Jahve lived and had their being. The human head, on the other hand, is surrounded by Luciferic beings.

There was a secret, preserved in all ancient temples, that actually came very close to the truth. This secret was that, with the extension of the head beyond the rest of their organism, human beings had given their head-allegiance to Lucifer—were turned by their heads toward Luciferic beings. In a certain way, people were aware that Lucifer protruded beyond the organism just as the head did. The power that brought the head out of its animal beginning into its present shape is Luciferic. And the force that is to be recognized as Divine streams up into the head out of the night-condition of the rest of the organism. This was what human beings could know in pre-Christian times.

Then the Mystery of Golgotha entered earthly evolution. As we know, the Mystery of Golgotha means that a celestial being united with the earth's evolution through the body of Jesus of Nazareth and that through the death on Golgotha this Being, whom we call the Christ-Being, united Himself with earthly humanity. And what effect did this have on earthly evolution? Why, through this event it first received its meaning—the source of its whole significance. This earth would have been without meaning if we human beings had developed on it equipped only with our senses and head-bound intellects, which are of Luciferic origin. The earth would have no meaning if we could perceive it around us and the light-world of the Sun and stars that streams down upon it, but had to remain in a state of sleep in order to perceive the Divine. Under these conditions, the earth would never have attained its true significance, for the earth needs a humanity that is awake. Waking humanity and the earth belong together. Sleeping human beings, on the other hand, are unconscious of their connection with the earth.

Because the Christ-Being lived in a human body and passed through death, earthly evolution received something of a jolt: a new impetus. Everything in it took on new meaning. Gradually, human beings acquired the possibility of cognizing the divine creative powers not only during sleep but in ordinary, waking day-consciousness as well. People do not realize this only because not enough time has yet elapsed since the Mystery of Golgotha to bring to human consciousness a waking perception of the world that the Old Testament prophets experienced as pervaded by revelations of Jahve, the "Ruler of the Night," and his countenance, Michael. A time of transition was necessary. But with the end of the nineteenth century—a turning point, whose significance is noted in all Oriental wisdom, though from an entirely different point of view[15]—the time has come when humanity must realize that something has been brought to fulfillment that could not previously be fulfilled. Namely that there is now latent in human beings a ripened capacity to awaken, to perceive by means of waking- or day-revelation what was formerly conveyed by Michael only at night.

However, this revelation had to be preceded by a great error, by what might be termed a "dark night of knowledge." I have often said that I disagree completely with those who call our time a time of transition. I am perfectly aware that every age is actually a time of transition. But I cannot rest satisfied with such formal, abstract definitions. The point is to indicate clearly what any given transition in a particular time consists of. In our day, the transition consists in coming to the realization that what used to be revealed by night must now become waking day-knowledge. In other words, Michael was once the revealer by night, but now he must become the revealer by day. Michael, having been a spirit of the night, must become a day spirit. For Michael, the Mystery of Golgotha signifies this change from night-spirit to day-spirit.

But this insight, which humanity was meant to attain much faster than we suppose today, had to be preceded by a great error, by what is perhaps the greatest possible imaginable error in human

---

15. Rudolf Steiner is referring here to the end of the Kali Yuga.

evolution—despite the fact that it is widely regarded by many people today as a particularly important and essential truth. The origin of the human head and its connection with Luciferic spirituality have been completely concealed from modern humanity. As I have said, a human being has come to be regarded as a single whole, as a unified being, physically as well as in other respects. And the answer to the question of human origins is that humanity has descended from animals, whereas in actual fact, of course, only what is Luciferic in human beings has this animal origin.

As I have said, only the part of human beings through which the divine creators once addressed humanity in the sleep state—i.e., the rest of the body—came into being concurrently with the coming into being of the animal kingdom *as an addition to the head.* But now everything is lumped together as it were and given an animal origin. This is something like a "cognitive punishment"—though I am using the word "punishment" here in a somewhat unusual sense.

If the truth regarding the origin of the head and the rest of the organism is as I have described, what could account for this tendency to invent the fiction of humanity's animal origins? What could inspire people to invent the fiction that the entire human being descends from the animal?

You see, what happened was that the Ahrimanic element gradually stole its way into human evolution in the period between the Mystery of Golgotha and our own time. In a certain sense, this was a period of preparation for the understanding of the Mystery of Golgotha, a period when the ancient pagan wisdom, which had helped humanity's first attempts to understand Christianity, was receding and the new knowledge of the spirit had not yet matured enough to understand it. And since people were unable to recognize the Luciferic element in the formation of the head, they were naturally also unable to recognize in the rest of the organism the Ahrimanic element that was engaged in a battle with the Divine. In this way, the purely Ahrimanic fiction arose that humanity descended from the ranks of the animals.

The theory that human beings are descended from animals is inspired by Ahriman. Evolutionary science of this kind is purely

Ahrimanic. The darkening of the wisdom that the head is of Luciferic formation made possible the delusion that human beings descended from animals. The loss of a right understanding of the origin of the human head opened the way to a loss of right understanding with regard to the rest of the human being. As a result, the idea that human nature, as a whole, was related to the animal kingdom entered insidiously into human thinking. And at the same time another view entered, impregnating all our recent cultural history: the view that the head was the noblest part of the human being. The head was contrasted with the rest of the organism, as good was contrasted with evil, heaven with hell. In other words, dualism instead of the triad, twoness instead of threeness. What ought to have prevailed was the insight that what human beings achieve in the world with their heads is indeed the product of cosmic wisdom—but Luciferic wisdom—and that this must be gradually permeated by other elements.

The spiritual power we call Michael organized the inclusion of the Luciferic essence in the structuring of the human head. This happened once earthly evolution had begun, following the completion of the Saturn, Sun, and Moon evolutionary phases. "And he cast his enemies down upon the earth"[16] means that by Michael's casting down of his opponents—the Luciferic spirits—humanity was permeated with human reason, with what springs from the human head.

Thus Michael loosed his opponents upon humanity in order to endow humanity with this opposing Luciferic element, reason. And this deed was followed in human evolution by the Mystery of Golgotha. The Christ-Being, in the person of Jesus of Nazareth, underwent death, uniting Himself with human evolution.

But now the time of preparation has passed. Michael himself participated in the results of the Mystery of Golgotha in the supersensible world. Indeed, since the last third of the nineteenth century Michael has had a very special position in human evolution and in relation to humanity. And the first thing that must happen as a consequence of a genuine understanding of this position is insight into

---

16. Cf. Book of Revelation, 12:7–9.

secrets such as those I have tried to present today concerning the human head and the rest of the organism.

The essential thing to see is that since we did not recognize the true origin of the human head, we could not avoid falling into delusion about the origin of the organism as a whole. Because people were unwilling to conceive of Lucifer's role in forming the human head, they could succumb to the mistaken notion that everything that has to do with the head is attributable to the same origin as that of the rest of the human being. Humanity must now get to the bottom of these secrets. We must become able to face fearlessly and courageously the insight that we can improve the inner life of all we receive through mere head insight, through mere earthly human wisdom and cleverness, if we take hold of these new divine Mysteries. And first of all we must correct the great error that had to precede this change in thinking, namely, the materialistic interpretation of evolutionary theory which sees the whole human being as descended from the animal.

Only in this way will we be able to see once more in a human being standing before us not just a pure soul-spiritual element living in an unensouled body, but a *concrete* spiritual element working in the head, albeit Luciferically, and a concrete *divine-spiritual* element working in the whole human being, except for the head, albeit subject to a hostile Ahrimanic element.

Speaking in images,[17] we may point back to how the Luciferic principle was embodied in human beings with the help of the Michael-Impulse. Now, likewise, the Ahrimanic element must be removed with the help of what Michael has become. Outer science presents modern consciousness with a picture of the human being based on anatomy and physiology—and on direct sensory observation—and says that it is the truth about human nature. But we must become able to look at a human being in such a way that we perceive the spiritual—the concrete-spiritual—being, along with bodily aspects, in every fiber. We must be aware that the blood coursing in living human beings is not the same as that which can be drawn out,

---

17. Literally, "in Imaginations."

a blood outside the living being. The blood that flows within us is an element suffused with spirit in a special manner. We must learn to know the spirit that pulses in the blood, that pulses in the nervous system, just when the latter is in a declining phase, and so on. We must be able to see the spiritual element in every single manifestation of the life within us.

Michael is the spirit of strength. With his entrance into human evolution, Michael must make it possible for us to get beyond the point of having, on the one hand, an abstract spirituality, and on the other, a material world that can be hammered on and dissected without our having any conception that it, too, is simply an outer manifestation of the spirit. Michael must penetrate us as the strength, the force, who can see through matter to the spirit everywhere present in it. St. John the Evangelist, pointing to an earlier stage of human consciousness, said that in ancient times the Word lived in a spiritual form, but that It had become flesh and dwelt among us. The Word united Itself with a fleshly body, preceded by the Michael revelation. The processes indicated here are all processes in human consciousness. And now the reverse process, a process of inversion, must begin. We must add another passage to the words of the Evangelist. We must develop in our consciousness the strength to see how we can absorb what united itself with the earth out of the spiritual world through the impulse of the Christ—which must unite with humanity to keep it from perishing along with the earth. We must see to it that human beings take up the spiritual, not just into their heads, but into their whole being. We must permeate ourselves wholly with the spiritual. Only the impulse of the Christ can help us to do that. But the impulse of Michael must help by interpreting the Christ-Impulse to us. Then we can add to the words of the Evangelist the following: *"And the time must come when the flesh will again become the Word and learn to dwell in the kingdom of the Word."*

The statement at the end of the Gospel, that much has been left unsaid, is no invention of a later commentator. It is a reference to what can only gradually be revealed to humanity. The Gospels are little understood by those who think they must remain exactly as

they are and may not be tampered with.[18] They must be interpreted, as I have often told you, in the light of Christ's words: "*Lo, I
am with you even unto the end of the earth.*"[19] That means, "I have
revealed myself to you not only in the days when the Gospels were
written, for through my day-spirit, Michael, I will always speak to
those who seek the way to me."

By this continuous, ongoing Christ-Revelation we are permitted
to add to the Gospels things that could not be known and recorded
in the Gospels of the first millennium, things that will be known in
the second millennium; and to these things new insights shall be
added in the millennia to come.

For true as it is, as the Prologue to the Gospel of St. John says, that
"*In the beginning was the Word, and the Word became flesh and dwelt
among us,*" it is also true that we have to add, "*And human flesh must
again be permeated by the spirit in order that it may dwell in the realm of the
Word and behold there the secrets of divinity.*" That the Word became
flesh—the Incarnation—is the first Michael-Revelation. The spiritualization of the flesh must be the second.

LECTURE THREE

Luciferic and Ahrimanic influences—Michaelic thinking—The
true concept of evolution—Progressive and regressive evolution—Beauty in art and the battle between beauty and ugliness

Dornach, November 23, 1919

The day before yesterday, in our first lecture, I spoke of how, as
members of the human race, we live in a sphere that we may designate as our fourth phase of evolution. We know that the evolution of

---

18. See John, 21:25: "And there are also many other things that Jesus did, which,
if they should be written every one, I suppose that even the world itself could not
contain the books that should be written."
19. Matthew 28:20.

the earth is such that what is now earthly evolution formed only gradually, by stages, beginning with Saturn evolution, which became Sun evolution, and then Moon evolution, out of which our present earthly stage of evolution emerged.

Turning our attention to these four successive forms of the earth to which humanity as such naturally belongs, we must remember that by "human beings" we mean here only "head-beings." We must also be clear that we are using the term "head" symbolically to cover all that belongs to human sense perception and intelligence, as well as to what spills over into social life from both of these sources. In addition, we must include within the general designation "head-being" all that a human being experiences *developmentally*, as a being endowed with sense perception and intelligence. In other words, when I speak of "a human being as a head-being," I am using the term metaphorically to cover all that I have just mentioned.

Now, we speak casually of the fact that, as physical human beings, we live in the atmosphere—an air sphere. We should realize that this atmosphere is likewise part of us. After all, the air that is within us now was outside us a moment ago. In fact, as human beings we could not exist—we are inconceivable—without this atmospheric envelope of air.

As human beings today, we have grown used to believing that this has always been the case—that people of earlier times spoke of things like the air in the same way that we do. But in fact it is not so, and we talk of them in the modern manner. Today we would find it strange enough if someone were to say that just as we move about in the air, so we move too in a sphere containing the conditions enabling us to develop as beings of sense and intelligence, that is, to possess all the faculties that justify our being referred to symbolically as "head-beings." And yet, as I have said, this is just *one* of the spheres that we inhabit. We actually inhabit several different spheres.

Let us now go on to a sphere of practical importance for human beings. Let us consider all that affects our lives as a result of having passed through the three evolutionary stages preceding the fourth, Earth, stage that we are currently involved in.[Rudolf Steiner draws a red circle.] At the same time, however, besides living in this fourth sphere, we also live in another evolutionary sphere which belongs to the spiritual beings who created us, just as the fourth, earthly, sphere belongs to us.

Now, if we disregard humanity for a moment and turn our attention to those creator beings in the ranks of the hierarchies above us whom we have always called the Spirits of Form, the spirits responsible for all form-creation, for all creative form-being, [20] we find that the sphere to which these beings belong must be thought of as a sphere that humanity will attain only *after* the earth has passed through the next three post-earthly evolutionary stages (described in *An Outline of Occult Science* as the Jupiter, Venus, and Vulcan stages) and has arrived at the *eighth* stage. In other words, these creative Spirits of Form presently inhabit the sphere that we will reach only after we have passed through the seventh, Vulcan, phase of evolution. That is their sphere. It belongs to them in the same way that the fourth sphere belongs to us. Now, these two spheres must be thought of as permeating and interpenetrating one another. [Rudolf Steiner here draws a larger circle, colored orange, encompassing the smaller red one.] In other words, if I describe the outer circle as the eighth sphere, we human beings live not only in the fourth sphere—our Earth sphere—but also in the eighth sphere,[21] in the company of our divine creators.

This eighth sphere, however, is inhabited not only by these divine creative beings, but also by Ahrimanic beings. In other words we, too, live in a sphere inhabited both by the spirits we regard as our divinities and by Ahrimanic beings as well. Luciferic beings, on the other hand, strictly speaking, are those who inhabit the fourth sphere with us. This is how, as it were, these spiritual beings are apportioned. We can understand these beings once we have grasped how we are related to the environments that correspond to their respective spheres.

---

20. See Rudolf Steiner, *The Spiritual Hierarchies* and *Spiritual Beings in the Heavenly Bodies and in the Kingdoms of Nature.*
21. See Steiner, *The Occult Movement in the Nineteenth Century.*

The power of perception available to initiation science reveals, first of all, that it is *because* we now live in the fourth sphere of evolution that we are capable of intelligence and sensory perception. We must never forget, however, that the power of Lucifer plays into human intelligence, which must always be understood to include sensory perception. Luciferic power is thus intimately related to the special brand of intelligence that human beings regard as innate, and like to claim as their own.

In fact, however, we possess our intelligence only because the higher Being, whom I referred to as Michael, cast down the Luciferic spirits into this fourth, earthly-human, sphere. This accounts for the presence of intelligence in human beings.

You can feel what this impulse of intelligence means in humanity if you consider the impersonal element at work in intelligence today. You know how many personal interests we human beings have. They enter into our encounters with each other. They individualize us; it is our personal interests that individualize us. But this individualization does not extend to our intelligence. Where intelligence and logic are concerned, we all have the same—we count upon them as a common possession, we expect to agree. But this commonness of intelligence would not be the case had not Michael made it possible for Lucifer's influence to be loosed upon humanity.

We are able to understand each other as easily as we do only because the Luciferic powers gave us this common intelligence. Intelligence—this Luciferic spirituality—came into being because Michael imbued humanity with Luciferic influences, and these have continued to develop throughout our evolutionary history. Of course, much else also developed in us alongside these influences. Nevertheless, Luciferic spirituality, which we think of as our intelligence, is widely considered today as the most distinctive human characteristic.

To make the matter clearer, we must direct our soul's gaze upon something else which, were it to spread throughout the world, could unite all human beings living on the earth. This is the Christ-Impulse. But the Christ-Impulse is very different from the impulse of intelligence. The latter has something coercive about it. You cannot make human intelligence your personal affair. You cannot, without being rejected by society as insane, suddenly decide in a personal manner something that has to be decided by intelligence. On the other hand, you can only have a personal relationship to the Christ-Impulse. You cannot interfere with another person's relationship to Christ. Each person's relationship to Christ is an entirely personal affair. Yet because Christ passed through the Mystery of Golgotha and united with the earth's evolution, the relationship of all human beings to the Christ-Impulse will be, quite of its own nature, the same no matter how many people form this relationship personally and independently of one another. In other words, people will be brought together by a deed that every individual makes a personal affair, rather than by the inducement of intelligence. The Christ-Impulse itself will bring about a right relationship to the Christ in a way that makes all such relationships the same. This is the distinction between the Christ- Impulse and the impulses governed by intelligence. The Christ-Impulse is one and the same for all humanity while still remaining a personal question for each individual human being. Intelligence, on the other hand, is not personal.

Where and how, then, does the Christ-Impulse fit in? We can find the answer in indications I have already given. We know that the head's evolution is regressive, that with respect to our heads we may be said to be involved in a process of continuous dying. We can point to a cosmic fact: Michael cast down the Luciferic hosts into the human realm. And, as their dwelling place, the Luciferic hosts were given the human head—but the human head in a state of dying.

These Luciferic hosts then began a continuing battle with the death process in the human head. Here we touch upon what was once a widely known fact of human nature, one that is now almost totally hidden from humanity. Namely, that, from the standpoint of divine evolution, human beings bear in their heads a continuous process of dying. But paralleling this dying tendency is a kindling of life by Lucifer. Lucifer is constantly trying to make the head as alive as the rest of the organism. From an organic perspective, were Lucifer actually to succeed in enlivening the head to the same degree as the rest of our organism, human evolution would turn counter to its divine direction.

This enlivening of the head is precisely what the divine direction of human evolution must oppose, for the human race must remain bound up with the evolution of the earth as it progresses through the further evolutionary stages of Jupiter, Venus, and Vulcan. Were Lucifer to succeed, humanity would not be treading its appointed path, but would instead became part of a cosmos that was pure intelligence through and through.

Physiologically, Lucifer is continuously active in us in such a way that he sends up out of the rest of our organism the life forces intended to permeate the head. Psychologically, Lucifer is constantly trying to give our intelligence, which contains only thoughts and images, a substantive content. When we form a mental picture of an artistic nature—I am now stating from a psychological perspective what I just stated from a physiological one—Lucifer constantly tends to give this mental picture a truly substantial content, that is, to suffuse our thoughts and images with ordinary, earthly reality. Were Lucifer successful, the goal of making us lose that other, spiritual reality would be achieved. We would pass over into a kind of thought reality that, instead of remaining "mere" thoughts, would become "real." This tendency to want our fantasies to become realities is always bound up with our humanness, and we make the greatest imaginable effort to achieve it.

Now, all the various internal causes of illness and disease suffered by the human race are related to this Luciferic tendency. Indeed, the detection of Lucifer's efforts to introduce vitalizing forces into the dying forces of the head actually provides the basis for diagnosing all cases of internal illness. The progress of medical science therefore must move in the direction of developing insight into this Luciferic influence. To give medicine such an impetus is one of the hallmarks of the Michael influence beginning to affect human evolution today.

Ahriman's influence is exactly the reverse of this. Ahriman works from the eighth sphere, out of which the rest of our organism, apart from the head, is created. This part of us teems with vitality, and was created and organized for this vitality. Precisely here is where the

Ahrimanic forces work. They strive in the opposite direction, to introduce forces of death, intended by divine evolution for the head, into the vital forces of the rest of our organism. So through Ahriman's agency we receive the forces of death from the eighth sphere. Again, I am speaking here from a physical point of view.

Speaking psychologically—from the point of view of the soul—I would have to say that everything affecting us from the eighth sphere works on the human will, not upon the intelligence. But human willing is based on wishing: the wish element is always involved. And Ahriman is continually trying to introduce a personal element into the wishes that motivate our will. Since this personal bias is concealed in our wishing, the will activity of the human soul is an expression of our cooperation with death. Instead of letting ourselves be imbued by divine ideals that we then carry over into our wishes, and hence into our willing, a personal orientation enters our wishing and willing.

Hence we exist truly at a balancing point between Luciferic and Ahrimanic elements. Together, these elements bring us illness and death on the physical level, while psychologically they bring the illusion that develops when we mistake things that belong only to the realm of thought, mental picturing, or fantasy for reality. Spiritually speaking, this is how egotistic desires enter our being.

Thus we see how the duality of Lucifer-Ahriman is bound up with our humanness. Using the examples of Milton's *Paradise Lost*, Klopstock's *Messiah*, and Goethe's *Faust*, I have shown you how deluded modern civilized humanity is, or can be, regarding this duality. Now, the fact is that we human beings have reached a point that we may characterize as already past the midpoint of earthly evolution.

We know the following. At first, the earth's evolution was on a rising plane; then it reached a peak; and since then it has been descending—though, for certain reasons we need not go into now, there was a plateau up to the end of the Greco-Latin period in the fifteenth century. Since that time, however, the evolution of earthly humanity has really been on the decline.

From a physical standpoint, of course, evolution has been on a descending plane for a good deal longer. Physically considered, it began declining as far back as the period preceding the last ice age, in other words, before the Atlantean catastrophe. This is a fact that Anthroposophists do not need to tell the world, for it is already well-known to geologists.[22] I have often remarked that, as we walk the soil of the earth, in many places we are treading on a disintegrating crust. You only need to consult good geological texts to confirm, as a discovery of physical science, that the earth is now in a declining phase of its evolution. But what lives in us as human beings is also in a declining phase of development. We must not count on any upward trend arising in our bodily development. An upward trend has to come from learning to view humanity from the perspective of progress from our present earthly phase of evolution to other, further evolutionary stages. We must learn to envision the human being of the future: that is Michaelic thinking.

Let me characterize this Michaelic thinking more exactly. When you encounter a fellow human being today, your conscious impression is really an entirely materialistic one. You tell yourself (not aloud of course, and perhaps not even as a conscious thought, but on a deeper level of awareness), "This is a person made of flesh and blood, composed of earthly substances." And you say the same of animals and plants. But this attitude is justified only insofar as the mineral substances you face in a human being, plant, or animal are concerned.

Let us take the most extreme case, human beings, and look at them purely from the standpoint of their external form. [Rudolf Steiner draws on the blackboard.] You do not really "see" the outer form, you do not actually confront it with physical perception, for this outer form consists of more than ninety percent fluid, it is more than ninety percent filled with water. What your physical eyes perceive is the mineral element that fills out the structure. You see whatever the person has absorbed from the external mineral world. You do not see the being who did the absorbing, who united with the mineral element. Hence, when we encounter another human

---

22. Rudolf Steiner is referring here to the Austrian geologist Eduard Suess, 1831–1914, author of *The Face of the Earth* [1883–1909].

being, we speak correctly only if we say to ourselves: "What stands before me are material particles that this individual's spirit-form has stored and gathered, thereby making something invisible visible."

Actual human beings are invisible, truly invisible. All of you sitting here listening to this lecture are invisible to physical senses. But a certain number of shapes with a certain capacity to attract particles of matter are sitting here [drawing], and these particles are visible. We see only the mineral element in people; the real individuals sitting here are supersensible beings, hence invisible.

Michaelic thinking brings us to full consciousness of this in every moment of our waking lives. We stop viewing these conglomerations of mineral particles that have simply been arranged in a certain pattern as human beings. Animals and plants also arrange mineral particles in this way. Minerals alone do not do so. To think Michaelically is to be aware that we move among invisible human beings.

We talk of Ahrimanic and Luciferic beings; we speak of beings belonging to the hierarchies of the Angels, Archangels, and Archai, and so on. All such beings are invisible. We learn to know them by their works, their effects, as we have discussed here in days just past. We learn to know them by their actions. Is it any different with human beings? Here in the physical world we come to know human beings—who are actually invisible—as a result of their having arranged and built up mineral particles in a human pattern. But that pattern is simply an activity on their part, an effect that their humanness brings about. If we have to familiarize ourselves in a certain way with the works of Lucifer and Ahriman, and of Angels, Archangels, and Archai, and so on, that just means a given way of getting to know them. But in their invisibility—in that these beings are supersensible—they do not differ in the least from human beings, provided we think about what a human being is.

It is Michaelic, you see, to realize that our essential nature does not differ at all from that of supersensible beings. Humanity could live without this insight as long as it was receiving something from the mineral world. But since the mineral world entered a declining phase of evolution human beings have had no recourse but to gradually acquire a *spiritual* view of themselves and the world. Indeed, the

strength to develop such an awareness has been increasingly available to us since the 1870s. Since then we have been able to find the
inner strength to look upon humans as supersensible beings, whose
presence is indicated, as though by a gesture of the external mineral
world, rather than to continue to mistake these patterned accumula-
tions of mineral particles for human beings. It is only because of the
Ahrimanic influences I characterized here a week ago that we fight
against this inner awareness and do not open our minds to it.[23]

Everything is connected in human life. And just as we labor under
the delusion that we are material rather than supersensible beings,
we are subject to another delusion. We speak of evolution as if it
went steadily forward. It was artistically impossible, you know, to
embody that kind of evolutionary progression in building the Goetheanum. As I sculptured the capitals I had to portray the first, second, and third in an ascending development, the fourth as holding
the balance in the middle, the fifth in declining development, the
sixth again as simpler, and the seventh as the simplest. The rising
evolution had to be balanced by the declining one.[24]

The situation with our heads is the same. While the rest of our
organism is still on an ascending plane, our heads are already in
decline. Hence to believe evolution consists only of ascents is to
ignore the true state of affairs. It is to hold a view similar to Haeckel,
who under a similar delusion maintained that simple organisms
came at the start of the evolutionary process, further development
leading to more complex organisms, and so on, *ad infinitum*—
through ever more complex creatures and more nearly perfect
stages.[25]

This is nonsense! Every advancing evolution undergoes a retrogressive phase too; every ascent is followed by a descent, and
descent is always implicit in ascent. The ignorance of contemporary humanity regarding the connection between evolution and

---

23. See Steiner, *The Influences of Lucifer and Ahriman*, lecture 4.
24. The capitals of the columns in the first Goetheanum. See Rudolf Steiner, *Ways
to a New Style in Architecture;* also Hagen Biesantz and Arne Klingborg, *The Goetheanum: Rudolf Steiner's Architectural Impulse.*
25. Ernst Haeckel, 1834–1919, German evolutionary biologist and philosopher.

devolution, advancing and retrogressing developmental phases, constitutes one of the most insidious deceptions we are prey to. Where there is progressive evolution there must be involutionary retrogression. At the moment an ascending phase starts to turn back into a declining one, what is physical enters into spiritual development. The way to spiritual development is cleared as soon as physical retrogression sets in. Our head can now undergo spiritual development because its physical decline has begun.

But we shall not understand human beings and the rest of the universe until we come to see things in the right light. We must view our intelligence realistically in its relationship to Lucifer's evolution, as I have described it. Then we shall be able to evaluate these matters properly. We shall be able to realize that our intelligence needs a new thrust if it is to bring us to attainment of our goal. The Christ-Impulse must prevent Lucifer from making us faithless to our preordained divine course.

I spoke of things being connected. For instance, under the influence of the same delusion that attributed certain Luciferic characteristics to the divine powers, we are one-sidedly inclined to see an ideal in the portrayal of beauty. Beauty as such may be portrayed. But we must be conscious that if, as human beings, we were to devote ourselves solely to beauty, we would be cultivating forces that would lead us into Luciferic channels. In the real world, beauty exists no more one-sidedly than evolution, which is always accompanied by devolution. The merely beautiful, used by Lucifer to fetter and blind humanity, seeks to free us from earthly evolution and make us independent of it. Beauty in that sense would sever our connection with the earth. In reality what we are actually confronted with in the world is an interplay between beauty and ugliness—indeed, a fierce battle of the beautiful against the ugly— analogous to the interplay of evolution and devolution. Hence, if we really wish to grasp what art is, we must never forget that its fundamental concern must always and forever be to depict the battle between beauty and ugliness. Reality is achieved only by seeking a state of balance between them, and not when we accept the one-sided reality intended for us by Lucifer and Ahriman.

It is very important that such ideals be embodied in our culture and its development. In Greece—you know how enthusiastically I have often spoken here of Greek civilization—people could still devote themselves one-sidedly to beauty. The decline of earthly evolution had not yet taken hold of human beings—at least, it had not affected the Greeks. Since then, however, we cannot afford the luxury of cultivating beauty alone. To do so would be to escape from reality. Human beings today must boldly and confidently face the real battle between beauty and ugliness. We must be able to experience and share the battle between dissonance and consonance in the world.

Experiencing this struggle means strengthening human evolution. And such strengthening will make it possible to achieve the inner awareness that dispels the illusion that the real nature of human beings consists of accumulated matter, mineral particles, that we have merely attracted to ourselves. Indeed, one must say that, even physically considered, human beings today, in their real nature, do not exhibit any characteristics of a mineral nature, of the outer mineral world. Mineral matter in the outer world is heavy. But what enables us to develop as souls—I am not speaking at the moment of intelligence—is not related to heaviness or gravity, but rather to the opposite, to what is called fluid buoyancy. I have shown you on other occasions how the brain floats in the cerebral fluid.[26] If the brain did not float in this way, the tiny blood vessels in it would be crushed. As you learned in physics classes, when Archimedes was in the bathtub, he discovered that he became lighter in water, and this delighted him so much that he shouted out his famous "Eureka!" As souls, we live in an upward-pulling element of lightness or levity, not in the downward pull of gravity. Our soul life is due to the lightness of the brain as it floats in the cerebral fluid. We live by virtue of something that pulls us away from the earth. One can even state this today in physical terms.

What I wanted to point out during these last three days was, and is, that we need to confront life today with a state of soul that is

---

26. See Rudolf Steiner, *Occult Physiology.*

truly aware in every waking moment of the supersensible in its immediate surroundings. We must reject the delusion that human beings are real because we see them, and that spirit-beings are unreal because we do not. In fact, we do not actually see human beings either; we are deluded if we think we do. In this respect, we are no different from the beings of the spiritual hierarchies. It is our task as modern human beings to recognize and understand this similarity between the hierarchies and ourselves, and even the plants and animals.

We say that as a result of the Mystery of Golgotha, the Christ-Impulse entered earthly evolution, entered human evolution to begin with, and is now united with it. People say they do not see Him. Indeed they cannot see Him, and will not see Him, as long as they remain deluded about human beings and view them as some-thing quite different from what they really are. As soon as the spiri-tual nature of human beings ceases to be mere theory and becomes instead a vividly felt soul reality, enabling us to *see* the supersensible in our fellow human beings, then we will begin to cultivate within us the faculty of perceiving the Christ-Impulse everywhere in our midst. Then we will be able to say with conviction, "Do not look for Him externally. He is among us everywhere." But for this to happen, people will have to develop the humility and modesty to realize that some effort is needed to cultivate this awareness which—right from the beginning—sees a supersensible element in the human being. It is no use just accepting this as a theory. Only if we do not believe that what confronts us externally, physically, is the true person, the real being—only if we believe that to think this is an absurdity—will we have reached the state of mind I mean.

If it were possible for you to go out to the [Goetheanum] build-ing site,[27] pick up an assortment of scraps of building materials lying about there, and hold them in front of you in such a cleverly concealing manner that someone encountering you would not see you but only the material scraps, you would not say that this

---

27. The foundation stone of the first Goetheanum was laid on September 20, 1913; the building was destroyed by fire on New Year's Eve, 1922.

arrangement of scraps was a human being. Yet this is what you do with the mineral substances you encounter in a certain arrangement in the fellow human beings you meet. You say that these mineral substances are a human being because your physical eyes perceive them. But, in fact, they are actually only a gesture pointing to the true human being.

If we look back to pre-Christian times, we find that God's messengers came down to earth in visible form, as it were, and revealed themselves to human beings there, made themselves understandable to them. The greatest of these divine Messengers, the Christ, who revealed Himself in the most sublime earthly event, was also the last to be able to do so without human involvement. We are presently living in the age of the Michael-Revelation. This revelation exists in the same way that earlier revelations did. But it does not force itself upon us, because humanity has entered the evolutionary phase of developing freedom. We must approach the Michael-Revelation. We must prepare ourselves so that Michael may imbue us with the strongest forces so that we may become aware of the supersensible in our immediate earthly environment.

Do not fail to recognize what benefits the Michael-Revelation, approached in freedom, might confer upon human beings today and in the near future! Do not fail to see that humanity is currently trying to solve social questions on the basis of outmoded states of consciousness. Anything that could be solved on that basis has already been solved. The earth is now in a declining, descending phase of its evolution. Outmoded ancient ways of thinking will never meet today's challenges—only a new state of mind can do that. Our task is to contribute to the development of this new consciousness, this new soul state. That people do not outgrow concepts that are thousands of years old must be looked upon as a frightful nightmare, weighing down our souls. We can see how the consequences of these antiquated concepts, emptied of all content and really nothing more than empty phrases, today run their course almost automatically. Everywhere we hear talk of human ideals, but there is no reality, no content to them: they are mere talk. What is needed is a new outlook, a new state of soul. Once upon a time, human beings heard a challenge which, expressed in our language, said: "Repent ye, for the kingdom of heaven is at hand."[28] People living then were still able to change their ways on the basis of their old consciousness. Today that possibility no longer exists. If we are to achieve today what was called for then, it must be on the basis of a new awareness. Michael was the mediator of the tradition of Jahve, the influence of Jahve. But since the end of the 1870s—to the extent that we open ourselves to him—Michael has been mediating an understanding of the Christ-Impulse. But we have to do our part. That involves fulfilling two requirements.

We must correct our own approach by changing a mistaken view, by correcting a certain error. I do not want to burden you too heavily with narrow abstractions and philosophical concerns, but one thing must be pointed out as symptomatic of recent human evolution. At the dawn of the modern age, for example, a philosopher like Descartes lived.[29] Descartes still knew something of the spiritual that acts in and through the agency of the dying human nervous system. At the same time, however, he was responsible for the statement "I think, therefore I am," which is the opposite of the truth. When we are thinking is precisely when we "are not"—for thoughts are only pictures of reality. If thinking were not just a mirror image, a reflection of the real, and we were actually in the realm of reality with our thoughts, thinking could give us nothing. We must become conscious of the reflecting, mirror-image nature of mental activity, of our thought life. As soon as we become aware of this mirror-character, we can call upon another source of reality within us. Michael wants to acquaint us with this other source of reality. We must try to recognize the reflecting character of our world of thought. If we do so, then we will counteract the Luciferic course of evolution. Lucifer's whole interest is in introducing substance into our thinking and promoting the delusion that thinking is permeated with substance. There is nothing substantial in thinking; thinking is just picturing.

28. Cf. John the Baptist in Matthew 3:2–3.
29. Rene Descartes, 1596–1650, author of the famous treatise *Discourse on Method* [1637].

Substance derives from another source, from deeper levels of consciousness. That is one requirement.

We need only be aware that our thoughts make us weak. And then we shall turn to Michael for strength. Michael is the spirit charged with pointing out the source in us of something stronger than thought. Recent civilization has taught us to depend on thought, and so made weaklings of us through our belief that thought contains something real. We like to imagine that we shy away from merely abstract intelligence, but that is an illusion. As modern human beings we are abject slaves of intelligence. We never imbue our thoughts with what should rise and fill them from deeper levels of our being.

The second requirement for encountering Michael is that we imbue our wishes—and hence our will—with a content that can be obtained only from the kind of reality we must recognize as supersensible. I have often stressed that the failure to take the supersensible nature of the Mystery of Golgotha absolutely seriously has had bitter consequences. I have, for instance, called your attention to the views of people such as Adolf Harnack, the liberal theologian.[30] There are many such liberal theologians, and they readily admit that they can find no proof of the Mystery of Golgotha in historical documents. In fact, the existence of Christ Jesus cannot be proved historically, as Caesar's or Napoleon's can be. And why? Because the Mystery of Golgotha was intended to confront us with an event to which we should have supersensible access only. In order that human beings might learn, precisely by means of the Mystery of Golgotha, to raise themselves to a supersensible perspective, there could be no external, physically documented proof of the event.

These are two goals toward which we must strive. The first is to familiarize ourselves with the supersensible in the immediate world of the senses, that is to say, in the world of human beings, animals,

---

30. Adolf Harnack, 1851–1930, German theologian and historian, author of *The History of Dogma* [1886–90]. Steiner is referring here to *The Essence of Christianity* [1899–1900].

and plants. This is the path of Michael. Its continuation is to find the Christ-Impulse in this world we recognize as supersensible.

In telling you this, I am describing the deepest impulses underlying the social issues of our time. The abstract League of Nations is not going to solve international problems. The abstractions it offers won't bring people together. But the spirit beings about whom we have been speaking these past days, who guide us to supersensible realms, will do so.

Outwardly, modern humanity faces hard struggles. No economic or spiritual remedies are available from the pharmacy of past historical evolution to help us face such serious battles, which are only beginning, and which will lead the outworn evolutionary impulses they stem from to absurdity. The ferments that have brought Europe to the edge of the abyss, that will pit Asia and America against each other, engendering worldwide conflict, are products of the past. The path of human evolution to absurdity may be countered only by traveling the path that leads to the spirit: the Michael path, which becomes the path of Christ.

LECTURE FOUR

The Mystery of Golgotha, the central point in earthly evolution, prepared for in Greek thinking, the last remnant of ancient Mystery culture—Scholasticism, the continuation of Greek thinking—Since the fifteenth century: the preparation of a new Mystery culture—The need to penetrate the heart organization with the Christ-Impulse (to balance Lucifer penetrating the head and Ahriman working in the limbs)

November 28, 1919

Following up some things that I presented in last week's lectures, today I would like to make some preparatory remarks that I shall amplify tomorrow and the day after. This will involve reminding you, in a different way than before, of various things needed if we are to pursue our theme further.

One can best understand the course of earthly evolution if one focuses and orders the events of that evolution in relation to its focal point or center of gravity. To do this introduces a certain structure and perspective into everything having to do both with individual development and with human evolution as a whole. For within human evolution, every individual stands within his or her own evolution. The center of gravity, as you know, is the Mystery of Golgotha. With this event, the earth's whole evolution was given its meaning, its true inner content.

When we go back in the development of Western humanity, which received the impulse of the Mystery of Golgotha from the Orient like an explosion, we must note a kind of preparation occurring some five centuries before the event actually took place. This preparation started in Greek culture. One can say that Greek thinking, feeling, and willing show a certain homogeneity during the period of some four-and-a-half centuries before the Mystery of Golgotha. This unifying trend begins with the figure of Socrates, and then continues through all of Greek culture. It is also evident in the arts. Begun by Socrates, the trend is taken up by the tremendous, towering personality of Plato, and then assumes a more scholarly aspect in Aristotle.

From various lectures that I have given, you will recall that, in the period of the Middle Ages following St. Augustine, people were especially careful to apply what they had learned from Aristotle's way of thinking when they tried to understand everything involved in the Mystery of Golgotha, its preparation and its after-effects. Greek thinking became so important for Christian development right up to the end of the Middle Ages because it was used for an understanding of the real nature of the Mystery of Golgotha. We would do well, therefore, to examine what actually occurred in Greece during the last centuries before the Mystery of Golgotha.

What went on in the thinking, feeling, and willing of the Greeks was really the final dying-out of a primeval culture. This culture is no longer accorded proper recognition in our time. The modern study of history cannot see things in their proper light, since it does not reach back to those times when a worldwide culture, emanating from the Mysteries, was the dominant influence on all human will and feeling. To discover the true nature of this primeval culture, we must go back to millennia that are beyond the reach of history—which we can do, using methods such as those outlined in my book *Occult Science.*

This primeval culture had its source in the ancient Mysteries. Individuals who were found to be objectively qualified for direct initiation were admitted to these ancient Mysteries by great, guiding personalities. The knowledge thus imparted to these initiates of the Mysteries then flowed out, through them, to other human beings. It is really impossible to grasp any aspect of the culture of ancient times without taking into account its native soil in the Mysteries. To open minds, that foundation is still quite obvious in the work of Aeschylus. Plato's philosophy, too, still bears its traces. But the actual divine revelations that humanity received through the Mysteries have been lost to history. Remnants of these revelations may be found only in primitive, historically documented traces of that culture. We can best judge what occurred if we realize in what form the primeval Mystery culture, which was the native soil of Greek civilization, still remained in the post-Socratic age. What remained, in fact, was a certain way of thinking and conceiving.

External history reports how Socrates founded the art of dialectics, and how he was the great teacher of the kind of thinking later developed by Aristotle in a more scientific way.[31] But this typically Greek way of thinking and conceiving was only a final echo of a Mystery culture that once teemed with meaning and content. In the Mysteries, spiritual facts—the fundamental causes of the cosmic order—were absorbed cognitively into humanity's whole view of the universe. These great, sublime Mystery contents faded, but the whole manner and configuration of the thinking developed by the Mystery pupils remained. It became a part of history, first in Greek thought, and later in medieval thinking, in the thinking of the

---

31. Cf. also Rudolf Steiner, *The Riddles of Philosophy.*

Christian theologians of the Middle Ages. They adopted the Greek way of thinking essentially for use in their theology. By training themselves in thought-forms, ideas, and concepts that were actually a carry-over of Greek thinking, they learned to grasp what the Mystery of Golgotha had poured into the world. The philosophy of the Middle Ages, so-called Scholasticism,[32] is clearly a merging of the spiritual truths of the Mystery of Golgotha with Greek thinking. The working out, the conceptual elaboration of the Mystery of Golgotha was, if I may use a trivial term, achieved with the tools of Greek thinking and dialectics.

Approximately four-and-a-half centuries passed between the time when the content of the Mysteries was lost, with only a purely formal, purely cognitive remnant remaining, and the Mystery of Golgotha. So we must picture the following. In a prehistoric time, the culture emanating from the Mysteries extends over the entire civilized world. It continues on until, in the course of evolution, all that remains is a distillate of it, namely, Greek thought and dialectics. Then the Mystery of Golgotha occurs. In the West this was understood at first with the help of Greek dialectical thinking. Hence if we really wish to feel our way into the science, which of course included the theology, of the period, let us say, between the tenth and fourteenth centuries, we must resort to a kind of thinking that is quite different from that which people today, with their natural-scientific orientation, are accustomed to. Modern critics of Scholasticism cannot do it justice, for they are all basically science-oriented, and Scholasticism (deriving from Greek dialectics) presupposes an entirely different kind of schooling of thought than modern natural science.

Today we are living at a time when another four-and-a-half centuries have elapsed—this time since natural-scientific thinking took hold of humanity. This began about the middle of the fourteenth century. At that time human beings in the West began to think in a way that was already brought to considerable brilliance by such men as Galileo Galilei and Giordano Bruno.[33] This natural-scientific way

---

32. See Rudolf Steiner, *The Redemption of Thinking*.
33. Galileo Galilei, 1564–1642, and Giordano Bruno, 1548–1600.

of thinking has continued to develop up to the present, and although its logic may seem the same as that practiced by the Greeks, it is actually wholly different. The logic of natural science was derived gradually from nature and natural processes, while Greek logic derived from what pupils beheld in the Mysteries.

We need to clarify the difference between the four-and-a-half centuries that passed before the Mystery of Golgotha entered the civilized world of that time—which was almost exclusively Greek—and the four-and-a-half centuries preceding our own time, during which humanity has been trained by natural-scientific thinking. The best way to do that is with a drawing. [He begins to draw on the blackboard.] Picture the ancient Mystery culture as a kind of Chimborazo in the spiritual culture of those early times.[34] This culture of the Mysteries —its dying echo—then becomes logic in Greece and continues to develop in the four-and-a-half centuries up to the Mystery of Golgotha. Greek logic then continues on into the Middle Ages in the form of Scholasticism. Then, with the fifteenth century, we have the beginning of the new way of thinking—we might call it Galilean, after Galileo. Now the length of time that elapsed between the appearance of the Greek way of thinking and the Mystery of Golgotha is the same as that between the starting-point of "Galilean" thinking and today. We are at about the same distance in time from the start of this period in the fifteenth century as the onset of Greek thinking was from the Mystery of Golgotha. But the period of Greek thinking was a final resonance, a twilight era, whereas we of the present age are dealing with a prelude, something that still has to be evolved and brought to a certain peak. Greek culture marks an end, ours a beginning.

This association or constellation of an ending and a new beginning can be fully understood only if we consider human evolution from a certain spiritual-scientific point of view.

I have said repeatedly that those who seek human self-knowledge through anthroposophical spiritual science do not do so in vain.

---

34. Chimborazo is an extinct volcano and the highest peak (20,702 feet) in the Cordillera Real range of the Andes in west-central Ecuador.

Indeed, the vast majority of humanity is now confronted by a significant future possibility. We must take seriously the fact that humanity as it evolves through history is a developing organism. Just as puberty and other significant developments occur in individual organisms, so equally epoch-making transitional phases occur in the history of humankind.

People still object to the idea of reincarnation on the grounds that we do not remember our past lives. But if we look at the matter realistically, if we consider the evolutionary development of humanity through history *as the evolution of a single organism*, we should not be surprised at our failure to remember earlier incarnations with our ordinary consciousness. I ask you, what do people actually remember of the ordinary course of life? They remember only what they have thought. One cannot really recall anything that one has not yet thought. Just consider how many events in a day go unobserved. We don't recall them because we haven't thought about them, despite their having taken place in our presence. We can remember only what we have actually given thought to.

Now, human evolution in earlier centuries and millennia was not such that people could attain any clarity regarding human nature. "Know thyself" has certainly been experienced as a kind of longing following the onset of Greek thinking, but to know oneself is an injunction that only genuine spiritual insight can satisfy. Only when we use our lives to grasp our own selves in thought—and humanity has only recently become mature enough to do this—will we have prepared ourselves, our memories, to remember past lives in our next incarnation.

To prepare ourselves in this way we will need first to think about what we will want to remember. Only those who, as a result of initiation—but not necessarily initiation attained in a Mystery training— have really been able to behold their own selves can look back today on their past earthly lives. Such individuals are by no means rare. However, even as regards purely bodily development, human beings are subject to change—which may be observed by spiritual-scientific means, though not physiologically.

In fact, our physical constitution is no longer what it was two thousand years ago, and two thousand years hence it will be different again from what it is today. I have often mentioned this. We are moving toward a future when, if I may put it bluntly, the brain will be differently constructed, externally considered, than it is today. In the future, the brain will have the ability to remember back to previous earthly lives. But those who have not prepared for this by reflecting on the self will possess this ability only mechanically—in the form of what we would call today a kind of "inner nervousness," a sense of something missing. Such people, however, will not find what they are missing, because in the meantime human beings will have progressed to a state of bodily maturity such that they will be able to look back on their past incarnations. But those who have not prepared themselves for this backward view will be unable to look backward in this way. And they will experience the capacity that would have allowed them to do so only as a lack. This is why a proper understanding of humanity's own present powers of transformation includes the fact that anthroposophically oriented spiritual science can bring human beings to self-knowledge.

Indeed, today it is already possible to describe the special experience that will persuade people to concern themselves with their earlier incarnations. We live in an era when nuances of feeling that will eventually appear in more and more human beings are already beginning to be experienced by a few individuals. These nuances of feeling are not yet recognized for what they are. Let me describe what they will be like when they eventually emerge. People then will be born into the world with the inner sense: "Insofar as I live with other human beings, consciously or unconsciously I am being educated with them into a certain way of thinking. Thoughts surface in me. I have been born and brought up to think in a certain way. At the same time, however, I look upon what surrounds me, and realize that my thinking and conceiving do not truly fit this outer world." This nuance of feeling is already present today in a few individuals. Such human beings find themselves having to think in a way that seems quite contrary to the voice of outer nature—as if outer nature demanded something quite different. Whenever people have appeared who have revealed that they felt this discrepancy between what they must think and what outer nature says, they have been laughed at. Hegel is a classic example.[35] He expressed certain thoughts about nature—not all of them were nonsense—and built them into a system. Then some pedestrian philistines came and said, "Well, so those are the ideas you have about nature. But if you just look at this or that natural process you'll see that you are mistaken. Nature does not agree with your ideas." To which Hegel replied, "Then all the worse for nature!"

That may seem paradoxical. But there is a solid, if subjective, basis for such feelings. It is fully possible to surrender quite naively to one's inborn way of thinking, telling oneself that where thinking contradicts nature, nature should revise itself accordingly. Of course, such thinkers do eventually become accustomed to what nature teaches. But most people, once they have matured to the point of truly observing nature, fail to notice what amounts to a double soul, or two sets of truths, within them. This can cause considerable suffering in those who become aware of it, because it introduces an element of discrepancy into their soul lives. What I am describing here is now present in only a few individuals, and even they may not be aware of it. But it is something that will become increasingly prevalent. People will increasingly find that their heads follow an inborn tendency to view nature in a way that is counter to its reality. Then they will mature and gradually also learn to see nature as it actually is. This dilemma calls for a solution.

Our souls will experience these divisive feelings above all when they return to life on earth. We will experience an inner surge of thinking and feeling. This surge will be clearly felt. It will cause us to realize that we can sense clearly how the world ought to be, but is not: that it is different. Then we will gradually accustom ourselves to the way it is; we will recognize a second set of laws and be forced to look for an adjustment or balance. But what will that balance be based upon?

---

35. G.W. F. Hegel, 1770–1831, *The Philosophy of Nature* constitutes the second part of his *Encyclopedia* [first appeared 1817].

Let us assume that human beings are born and enter physical existence through birth. [Rudolf Steiner draws on the blackboard.] They bring with them a way of thinking and feeling that is the outgrowth of their previous earthly lives. During the time they spent away from the earth, outer life changed in certain ways. Hence they sense a discrepancy between their thinking as conditioned by a previous life and the way things have developed on earth while they were absent from it. They then gradually live into the new incarnation, by no means fully conscious of what they might learn from their surroundings. They perceive, or as it were absorb, their surroundings as if through a veil. Only after death can they really digest their experiences, and then once again carry them into their next earth life.

As human beings, we will always experience this duality in our soul life. We will always become aware that we have brought something into the world with us at birth compared to which the world into which we are born is always a new experience. As physical human beings we absorb something from this world that our souls cannot immediately digest, something that we will be able to work through again only after death.

As human beings today we must live this way of experiencing life fully and intensely, for that is the only way to become aware of the forces pulsing through our existence which otherwise completely escape our attention. We are knit up in these forces, but unless we try to penetrate them consciously, they remain unconscious and tend to make our souls unhealthy. People will become ever more aware of the discrepancy between what comes over with us from a past life and what is currently being prepared for the next one. And because we will become increasingly aware of this duality, a real means of bridging it—some kind of inner mediation—will become essential. The great question of how to accomplish this will become ever more burning.

We can find an answer to this question of inner mediation only if we consider the following.

I have often described how, in ordinary life, between waking and falling asleep, human beings are only fully awake when engaged in mental activity—in conceptual life. [Here Rudolf Steiner begins to write on the blackboard.] Only when we are mentally active in this way are we fully awake. On the other hand, we are not fully awake in our feeling lives, even in the midst of otherwise waking activities. In fact, even when we are fully awake in our thinking and conceptualizing, our feelings remain on the same level of consciousness as our dreams. Anyone who researches this area knows from direct perception that feelings have no more life than dreams; only the mental images, the concepts, used to represent them give them the appearance of life. The life of our feelings surges up from depths of consciousness in the same way that our dream lives do. As for our will, even when we are awake our actual will life is in a sleeping condition—in matters of will, we are asleep. We walk around during the day, awake in our conceptual lives and deceive ourselves into believing that we are also awake in our will lives as well, simply because we have mental images of the acts it performs. What the will actually experiences does not enter consciousness; only the mental image does. In other words, we dream our feelings and are asleep in our willing. But when imaginative cognition brings the dreaming content of our feelings to full, clear consciousness, we realize that there is *wisdom* not only in our thoughts and concepts but also in our feelings and our willing. (We shall call it wisdom because that is what it "technically" is, even though in many cases it may be the opposite.) Wisdom is not only in our thoughts, therefore, but also in our feelings and our will.

Conceptual activity	Completely awake	Wisdom
Feeling	Dreaming	Wisdom
Will	Sleeping	Wisdom

As human beings living today we can make clear statements only about the content of our mental lives. Of the world of feelings we usually know scarcely more than we know about our dream lives, though it, too, has wisdom in it.

Those who seriously school their own souls using the exercises described in my book *How To Know Higher Worlds* will most quickly develop the ability to become aware of a certain stirring of the soul that most people experience as dreamlike. Indeed, in most people, this soul-stirring is scarcely more orderly than ordinary dreaming, but a degree of order can be introduced into it comparatively soon, so that a person notices that this inner, dreamlike experience is not governed by normal logic. Sometimes, indeed, the logic of this dream experience is quite grotesque, a great variety of rags and tags of thought coming together and running their course in a dream-like way. Truly, there is a strange logic in it. But individuals who apply to their own soul lives even a little of what *How To Know Higher Worlds* describes can recognize that something is going on here—a first, still-very-primitive, inner experience.

When we plunge into this heaving sea of waking dreams, a new reality emerges that is very different from the ordinary reality of external life. In fact, we may notice this new reality emerging comparatively soon. At the same time, however, we will also notice that there is wisdom in all this, but wisdom of a kind we cannot grasp, that we feel we are not ready or mature enough to bring to full consciousness. This wisdom keeps escaping us, and we do not understand what it is about. Gradually, we notice not only that wisdom pours through the upper level of consciousness, permeating our ordinary day-waking lives, but that another level of awareness exists beneath it that appears illogical only because, in our inability as yet to grasp the wisdom of it, we call it illogical. But once we have fully acquired imaginative cognition, these waking dreams cease to seem as grotesque as they do in ordinary life. They become filled with a wisdom that points to another reality, a different world from the sense world we perceive with ordinary wisdom.

In ordinary life, only the world of feeling surges out of this deeper level of awareness into everyday consciousness. At the same time, the world of the will surges up, similarly permeated by wisdom, out of a still deeper level of awareness. Though we are not at all aware of it in ordinary consciousness, we are connected with this wisdom also.

Therefore we may say that we are actually governed by three different levels or strata of consciousness. The first is our conceptual consciousness, in which we live every day; the second is an imaginative consciousness; and the third is an inspired consciousness, which, while remaining at a very deep level, is certainly active in us even though its real nature goes unrecognized in ordinary life:

I. Conceptual consciousness (Luciferic)
II. Imaginative consciousness
III. Inspired consciousness (Ahrimanic)

If only contemporary philosophers were less confused, they would be intensely struck by the difference between what is recognized as truth on the basis of the external observation of nature and what is discovered in mathematics and geometry, for example, when these are applied to an understanding of nature. I am not referring here to people unconcerned with philosophy, but to philosophers who ought to be able to grasp something like this, and don't.

We can say with some justification that we can never really speak of absolute certainty regarding truths arrived at by external observation. This has been noted so often in the history of philosophy that it should not require analysis by philosophers. Kant and Hume have elaborated particularly clearly, even going to the grotesque lengths of saying, "We do indeed observe that the sun rises, but that doesn't give us the right to assert that it will rise again tomorrow. We can only assume that, since it has always risen, it will probably do so tomorrow." That is the way it is with facts or truths drawn from external observation. But this is not the case with mathematical findings, for example. Once we have understood a mathematical truth, we know that it applies for all time. Someone who knows, and can offer reasoned, internal proof, that the square of the hypotenuse of a right triangle is equal to the sum of the squares of the other two sides knows that it is impossible to draw a right triangle to which this formula does not apply.

Such mathematical truths differ from those reached by external observation. That is a recognized fact, although current research does not have the means to grasp the reason for it. The reason is that mathematical truths issue from the inner depths of human nature. They spring out of the third, lowest level of consciousness and shoot, without our having the least understanding how, into our uppermost consciousness, where we perceive them inwardly. Mathematical truths are derived from our own mathematical behavior. We move about, we stand, and so on, describing lines as we do so. This relationship of our will to the world around us is the real source of our mathematical perception. Mathematics comes into existence down there at the third level of consciousness, and then surfaces.

Thus we arrive at very clear concepts of at least a part of this lowest level of consciousness, even though in this case its source is not ordinarily apparent. Mathematical and geometric truths rise up from that level. The middle level of consciousness, on the other hand, has a rather dreamlike, chaotic character. But in our "upper story," where our mental, day-waking life takes place, clarity again prevails, and what rises out of this third level of consciousness is clear to us. What surfaces from the in-between realm reaches most people in the aspect of confused waking dreams. It is very important that we be clear on this point. For this conceptual consciousness is the consciousness that prevailed among the Greeks during the four-and-a-half centuries before Golgotha. They absorbed this first-level, conceptual consciousness which was left to them as a remnant of the Mystery culture. But this consciousness is purely Luciferic, a purely Luciferic element. I described it to you recently. It is intellectualistic culture. Our heads are very clear; they are imbued with wisdom, a generally applicable wisdom. Yet this element in us is Luciferic. [Rudolf Steiner adds the word "Luciferic" on the blackboard.]

And down below, in the third stratum, is something very dear to modern scientists and so dear to Kant in his day that he said that a science of nature exists only to the extent that mathematics is in it. This is a purely Ahrimanic element, coming to the surface through our human nature. [Rudolf Steiner adds the word "Ahrimanic" on the blackboard.]

It is not enough just to know that something is correct. We know that what we grasp intellectually with our heads is correct, but this correctness is a gift from the Luciferic element. And we know, too, that mathematics is correct, but we owe this tremendous correctness to the Ahriman lodged there in us. The most uncertain element occupies the middle region, a region churning with seemingly illogical dreams.

To help you grasp the full importance of this question, I will now characterize another aspect of it. The whole mathematical understanding of the world, as it arose with Galileo and Giordano Bruno, springs essentially from this deeper level of consciousness. Four-and-a-half centuries have now passed since we began to acquire this way of thinking. In other words, for four-and-a-half centuries, we have been working to establish this Ahrimanic element in human thinking and sensing. At the same time that the last rays of the Mystery culture were bringing consciousness to brightest luminosity in Greek thinking, a capacity that will reach its peak only in the future was dawning in the deepest, darkest level of human consciousness. And reach its peak it must. It must still emerge.

Our human soul life resembles the beam of a scale. It must achieve a balance between the Luciferic element on the one side and the Ahrimanic element on the other. The difference between these is that the Luciferic element lies above, in our clear heads, while the Ahrimanic element lies down below, in the wisdom that permeates our will. We must seek the balance in something that at first appears to have no content.

How does wisdom enter this middle realm? For the time being human beings are in the world in such a way that Lucifer supports our head, while Ahriman supports the wisdom inherent in our metabolic-limb system. Now, just as our intellectuality or conceptual consciousness is connected with the head, what we have called the middle state of consciousness depends upon the heart organization and its human rhythm, as you can read in my book *The Riddle of the Soul (The Case for Anthroposophy)*. This middle sphere of our existence—the heart—must now become as ordered as our head-wisdom is ordered by the head's logic, and as Ahrimanic knowledge is ordered by mathematics, geometry, and the rational, external observation of nature.

But what can bring an inner logic, an inner wisdom, an inner capacity of orientation into this middle realm of our human constitution? Why, only the Christ-Impulse that impregnated the earth's culture through the Mystery of Golgotha.

There is a spiritual-scientific anatomy that shows us what head-culture is and what metabolic culture is, and that also shows us the nature and needs of the organizational sphere that lies in-between. That is, permeation with the Christ-Impulse is part of our human nature.

Let us for a moment hypothesize that the Mystery of Golgotha did not enter earthly evolution. If, in fact, the Mystery of Golgotha had not occurred, human beings would still possess their head wisdom. They would also therefore still have all that has developed since the fifteenth century. But, as regards their central being, their human center, they would be desolate and empty. They would increasingly feel a split, a discord, between the two inner spheres I have just described. They would find it impossible to bring about a state of balance. For such balance can be brought about only if we permeate ourselves ever more fully with the Christ-Impulse which calls forth the balance between the Luciferic and Ahrimanic elements.

Thus we may say that in the four-and-a-half centuries preceding Christianity the last remnant of the old Mystery culture was given to humankind as a preparation for the Mystery of Golgotha. It then persisted as a "head-memory" of that culture. And then, again, in the modern period, for four-and-a-half centuries humankind has been undergoing preparation for a new spiritual direction, a new kind of Mystery culture. And the Mystery of Golgotha had to occur as an objective fact in humanity's development in order that these two Mystery cultures could be connected in human historical evolution.

Viewed externally, the course of human evolution is such that the Mystery of Golgotha is incorporated into it as an objective fact. Viewed internally, however, human evolution is such that human beings develop in the interim to the point where, from the fifteenth century onward, they receive the new impetus I have just characterized as Ahrimanic. It is one that will cause them to feel keenly that they need the possibility of building a bridge from one period to the other.

Thus we can begin to form an inner concept or understanding of the human being as threefold. And that concept will be more complete if we connect what I said today with something else that I have often emphasized. Namely, that it was almost impossible for the ancient Greeks, who retained the remnants of ancient Mystery culture, to become atheists—except in the case of a few degenerates, but even then not to the degree that we witness today. Atheism, at least in its more radical forms, is basically a recent phenomenon. The Greeks, who were true masters of dialectics, still sensed the role of the Divine in thinking, even in contentless thinking.

When we realize this and then examine the emergence of atheism, of the complete denial of the existence of any divine element, we discover what it really springs from. Spiritual-scientific methods are, of course, required for this discovery. Atheists are simply human beings in whom something organic is out of order. It can be a matter of a very subtle structural disturbance, but nevertheless atheism is an actual illness.

We must start by realizing that atheism is an illness. If our organism is completely healthy, then its various parts and organs must function together in a way that makes us sense our divine origin: *Ex deo nascimur.*[36]

The second point is quite different, however. Someone may have a feeling for the Divine, but have no possibility to feel the Christ. People are not apt to make fine distinctions about such questions these days; they are too easily satisfied with mere words. If we were to examine the actual spiritual content of the views of a great many people in the West today—discounting their professed belief in the freedom of the will, and so on—we would find that the whole configuration of their thinking contradicts their assertions. They are

---

36. *Ex deo nascimur* [from God we are born] is the first of the three foundational Rosicrucian meditations. The other two are: *In Christo morimur* [in Christ we die] and *Per spiritum sanctum reviviscimus* [through the Holy Spirit we come to life again]. See Rudolf Steiner, *The Inner Nature of Man and Our Life Between Death and Rebirth.*

merely culturally conditioned to speak of Christ or of freedom and the like. A great many of our contemporaries are no more than Turks. Their faith is as fatalistic as the Muslims', even though they describe it as "natural necessity." Islam is more prevalent than we think. If we disregard their words and consider their soul-spiritual content, many a Christian is actually a Turk. People call themselves Christians even though they cannot find the transition between the God they sense and the Christ.

I need only mention Adolf Harnack, the classic example of a modern theologian, who wrote *The Essence of Christianity*. Just try striking out the name of Christ wherever it occurs in this work and substitute the name of God. The content of the book will remain completely unchanged. In fact, there is not the slightest need to refer to the Christ in anything Harnack says. For what he is saying he needs only a universal Father God who created the world. His assertions are inwardly and outwardly untrue, for though he takes his quotes from the Gospels, his use of them requires no connection with the Christ. It must become possible to conceive of Christ without identifying Him with God the Father. Many modern evangelical theologians are particularly incapable of distinguishing between the concept of a universal God and the concept of Christ. Failure to find Christ in life is different from failure to find God, that is, the Father God.

You know that it is not a question here of doubting the Divinity of Christ. What matters is making an exact distinction, in the sphere of the Divine, between God the Father and God the Christ. This affects human soul life. Not to find God the Father is an illness; not to find the Christ is a disaster. For we human beings are so connected with the Christ that we are inwardly dependent on Him. That is to say, we are dependent on an event that took place historically. We must therefore find a relationship to the Christ here on earth, in our outer lives. To fail to do so is disastrous. To be an atheist, to fail to find the Father God, is an illness. It is a calamity not to find the Son God, the Christ.

What does failure to find the Spirit involve? It means to lack the possibility of grasping one's own spirituality so as to discover its

connection with the spirituality of the world. To fail to acknowledge the Spirit is spiritual weakness, feeble-mindedness. It is a soul
deficiency.

Please remember these three deficiencies of the human soul;
then tomorrow we will be able to continue this contemplation in
the right way. Remember what I have said today about the three
levels of consciousness. Remember that to be an atheist is an illness—if we fail to discover the God who gives us birth, we cannot
possess a sound and healthy organism. Remember that failure to
find the Christ is a disaster, and failure to find the Spirit is weak-
mindedness.

These are the different ways humankind approaches the Trinity.
It will become ever more necessary for humanity to concern itself
with these concrete aspects of soul life instead of always being
caught in generalized, vague, nebulous views. People today have a
marked tendency toward the nebulous. To replace this tendency
with one which enters into the concrete aspects of soul life is an
essential task of our age.

LECTURE FIVE

The evolution of the human soul—The problem of necessity
and human freedom—the evolution of the God concept from
the fourth to the sixteenth centuries—Michael's deed influence
as the counterpole to Ahriman—The necessity of the Christ-
Impulse

November 29, 1919

We can develop a consciousness that truly upholds the soul only if
we open ourselves to the most important and essential laws of
human evolution. We must familiarize ourselves with what went on
in that evolution and make it part of the content of our inner lives.
That is the task confronting modern humanity.

To fulfill this task requires that we take most seriously that, as I said recently, the evolution of humanity resembles the evolution of a living being. Just as a single human individual undergoes a lawful development, so does humankind as a whole. This means that we must begin to become conscious that we have participated, in our repeated earthly lives, in the various phases of human evolution. At the same time, we also need to develop an understanding of the variety of soul moods that characterize the different epochs of that evolution.

I have often stated that what is called history today is actually a *fable convenue*, a fiction, because in the abstract listing of events and the highly superficial search for cause and effect in historical research no attention is paid to the transformations and metamorphoses that have occurred in human soul life. If, in fact, we investigate history from this point of view—namely, from the perspective of an evolving, metamorphosing soul life—we would discover that to believe that the soul mood of people today is more or less the same as it was in the time of the earliest recorded historical documents is an unwarranted prejudice. This is just not the case.

Even the simplest, most primitive people living in the ninth or tenth centuries after Christ had an entirely different configuration of soul than those who lived after the middle of the fifteenth century. This can be noted in both the higher and lower level of human culture.

Acquaint yourselves with Dante's *De Monarchia*, a curious work on monarchy.[37] When you read something of this sort, and read it not as a curiosity, but with a certain sense for cultural history, you will find things in it that could be written only by a representative person of the time, things that could never come from the soul of a modern author. Let me give just one example.

De Monarchia is a serious treatise about the civil or political basis of monarchy. Dante tries to prove that the Romans were the world's most outstanding people, and that it was their absolute right to conquer the whole known world. He tries to prove that the Roman conquest was based upon a more profound right than the right to

37. Dante Alighieri, 1265–1321.

independence of various smaller peoples, on the grounds that God had ordained the Romans to rule over smaller nations for their own good. Dante offers many arguments, quite in the spirit of his time, to support the right of Roman rulership. In one argument, for instance, he says that Romans are the offspring of Aeneas.[38] Aeneas married three wives in succession. The first was Crusa, and this marriage entitled him to rule Asia. His second marriage was with Dido, through whom he acquired the right to rule Africa. Finally, he married Lavinia, who gave him—and thereby the Romans—the right to rule Europe. Hermann Grimm,[39] commenting on this, remarked, not inappropriately I believe, that it was lucky indeed that America and Australia had not yet been discovered!

However, Dante's reasoning was entirely natural for an enlightened—indeed, the most enlightened—spirit of his time. It had the force of legal argument. Now I ask you to try to imagine a contemporary jurist coming up with such reasoning. One simply cannot imagine it. Indeed, it is impossible to imagine this way of thinking, which Dante also applied in other areas, emerging from the frame of mind, the soul constitution, of people today.

An example as obvious as this is shows how urgent it is to note the way soul attitudes change over time. Up to the present, it was perhaps permissible to disregard such matters. But today we can no longer disregard them, and this will be especially true for humanity in the future. That is simply because up to our time, or at least up to the end of the eighteenth century, humankind possessed certain instincts.[40] Since the French Revolution everything has been gradually transformed, although some remnants of the former soul configuration did persist. Out of these instincts, human beings were at one time able to develop a consciousness capable of supporting the soul. But these instincts vanished in the course of humanity's ongoing evolution as an organism, and today individuals must develop their connection with the whole human race quite consciously.

---

38. Legendary founder of Rome as described in Virgil's great epic of the founding of Rome, the *Aeneid*.
39. Hermann Grimm 1828–1901 German art historian.
40. See: Rudolf Steiner, *Michaelmas and the Soul Forces of Man*.

This, after all, is the whole meaning, the deeper significance, of the social question! What party-minded people say is mostly only superficial talk. What is really moving in the depths of people's souls is not expressed by such superficial formulae. What moves people today is their feeling that they must forge a conscious connection between the individual and the whole of humanity—that is what developing a social impulse means.

But this cannot be achieved without paying attention to the law of evolution. Let us therefore now do again as we have done so often in the past when considering other kinds of questions. Let us consider, for example, the period from about the fourth century A.D. to about the sixteenth century. During this period, we find Christianity spreading all over civilized Europe. We find this expansion imbued with the characteristics I mentioned yesterday and have often spoken of before. A central concern of the period, therefore, was to develop an understanding of the secrets of Golgotha with the help of ideas and concepts inherited from Greek culture. But then evolution began to take a different turn. We know that this started somewhat earlier, about the middle of the fifteenth century, although it first became clearly apparent in the sixteenth century when scientifically oriented thinking began to take hold among more advanced people, and it went on to find ever wider acceptance.

Scientifically oriented thinking has many interesting aspects, but let us today look at one in particular. It is characteristic of someone who is a dyed-in-the-wool, up-to-date thinker that he or she cannot deal with the problem of necessity of nature and human freedom. Modern, natural-scientific thought tends increasingly to view human beings as part of nature, and to conceive of nature herself as a chain of interrelated causes and effects. Granted, many people still see clearly that freedom, the experience of freedom, is a fact of human consciousness, but this does not prevent those who enter deeply into a particular kind of natural-scientific thinking from being unable to deal with the question of freedom. For a person who thinks about human nature in modern scientific terms cannot apply that type of thinking to thinking about human freedom.

Some people treat freedom and responsibility very lightly. I knew a professor of criminal law who began his lectures by saying, "Ladies and Gentlemen, it is my task to lecture you on criminal law. We shall begin with the axiom that human freedom and responsibility exist. For if human freedom and responsibility did not there could be no criminal law. However, criminal law exists, since I am to lecture to you on the subject. Therefore, freedom and human responsibility also exist." This line of argument is a bit primitive, but it nevertheless indicates how hard it is for people today to know where to look for an answer when they want to know how natural necessity can be reconciled with freedom. In other words, no matter how we express it, the reality is that in the course of the last few centuries human beings have been compelled in their thinking to concede a certain omnipotence to natural necessity. People do not exactly put it thus, but their thinking is along these lines. They conceive of natural necessity as omnipotent.

What, actually, is this omnipotence?

The best way to proceed will be to remind you of something I have often discussed. When modern thinkers assert that human beings consist of only a body and a soul, they believe they are acting or, rather, thinking in a quite unbiased, purely scientific manner as befits scientific researchers. At least up to the time of Wilhelm Wundt,[41] a philosopher held (but only by grace of his publisher) to be a great man, people maintained that anyone thinking without prejudice or bias had to consider that a human being consisted of body and soul alone—that is, provided that the existence of the soul was granted at all. Any attempts to advance the truth that the human being is actually composed of body, soul, and spirit have been very timid.

Modern philosophers who believe they are unbiased in their belief that humans consist of only soul and body are unaware that their view is simply the result of a historical process that started with the Eighth Ecumenical Council of Constantinople. At this Council, the Catholic Church abolished the spirit and established the dogma that henceforth orthodox Christians must conceive of a human

---

41. Wilhelm Wundt, 1832–1920, founder of experimental psychology.

being as comprised of body and soul alone, the soul possessing some spiritual characteristics. That was a commandment of the Church. Modern philosophers still teach this dogma today, unaware that where they believe themselves to be furthering unbiased science, they have merely accepted a church dogma. Such is the situation today in various matters held to be "pure science."

The case of natural necessity is similar. The whole course of evolution between the fourth and the sixteenth centuries tended toward an increasing crystallization of a particular understanding of God. If we look into the subtleties of spiritual evolution during that time, we see that a quite particular concept of God was being elaborated in human thinking. This culminated in the saying "God the Almighty." Almost no one realizes today that it would have made no sense for someone who lived before the fourth century A.D. to speak of "God the Almighty." We are not talking of the catechism here. Naturally, in the catechism, you find it stated that God is almighty, all wise, all good, and so on. But none of this has anything to do with reality. Prior to the fourth century, no one with any understanding of such matters would have thought of attaching "almightiness" to God as a basic attribute of the divine nature. People still felt the influence of the Greek concepts. When people thought of God's essence, they would not in the first place have called it "almighty," but rather "all-wise," or "omniscient." [Rudolf Steiner starts to draw on the blackboard.]

Wisdom, then, was considered the fundamental attribute of God's Being. The concept of omnipotence was attached only gradually to the idea of God, starting in the fourth century. Then further developments occurred. The concept of a personal deity was abandoned in favor of an ever more mechanically conceived natural order. The more recent concept of natural necessity, of the omnipotence of nature, is nothing but the outcome of the evolution of the God-concept from the fourth through the sixteenth centuries. The personal attributes of the Divine were simply abandoned, and what had earlier been the concept of God became the way one thought about nature.

Any genuinely modern scientist would, of course, fiercely object to such a statement. Just as those philosophers who believe they are exercising unbiased thinking when they assert that human beings possess only a body and soul are, in fact, merely following the dicta of the Eighth Ecumenical Council of 869 and enslaving themselves to a historical dogma, so all these scientists—Haeckelians, Darwinists, and all the rest, including the physicists with their natural order—are simply disciples of the theological trend that developed in the period from St. Augustine to Calvin.[42] This must be recognized.

It is characteristic of every evolutionary development that it undergoes both an evolutionary and an involutionary or devolutionary phase. While the concept of God as "Almighty" was developing, a similar undercurrent in the subconscious depths of the human soul was unfolding that eventually surfaced as the accepted doctrine of natural necessity. And ever since the sixteenth century a new subconscious undercurrent has been developing. It is preparing itself right now, precisely in the present era, to surface as the accepted doctrine of a later time.

It is a characteristic of the Michael age that what has been forming as an undercurrent of natural necessity must henceforth emerge as a surface current. But we must grasp the inner spirit of earthly evolution if we wish to arrive at any adequate concept of what is being prepared in this way.

I pointed out recently that the trend of earthly evolution—and hence of human evolution—is in a declining phase. Earthly humanity and earthly evolution are both actually decadent. I showed you that this is even a recognized geological fact—that knowledgeable geologists recognize that the earth's crust is in a process of decay. But not only the earth is decaying; humankind itself is especially involved in this process through the influence of forces of an earthly-sensory nature. Humanity as it evolves must begin to adopt a course of absorbing spiritual impulses that counteract this decadence. Conscious spiritual life must be nurtured. We must be clear that we have already passed the peak of earthly development. For earthly evolution to have a future, the spirit must be taken up ever more clearly and distinctly.

---

42. i.e., from the fourth to the sixteenth centuries.

At first hearing, this may sound abstract. But for spiritual investigators—for the spiritual researcher—it is not at all abstract. You know that we can trace the evolution of what is now the earth through Saturn, Sun, and Moon phases of development. You know, too, that the evolutionary developments through which contemporary humanity passed in the Saturn, Sun, and Moon phases of evolution were preliminary, preparatory stages for the earthly phase. In fact, only upon reaching the earthly stage and receiving the I did human beings actually attain their humanness. And it is as human beings, as we pass through future stages of earthly evolution, that we will continue to pour more and more content into our humanness.

Now you know that the so-called Archai, the Time Spirits of the present who are also known as Spirits of Personality, were at the same stage of evolution during the Saturn period as human beings are today, though in an entirely different form and with a totally different outer aspect. In my books I have said that the beings we now refer to as Archai were human beings in the Saturn period, while the Archangels were human beings during the Sun period, and the Angels were human beings in the Moon evolution. During the period of earthly evolution it is *we* who are human beings.

We have of course continued to evolve, always preparing ourselves for further evolution. If we look back to the Moon phase of evolution, we can see that the Angeloi then were at the human stage, though due to the entirely different conditions prevailing on the ancient Moon their appearance was quite different from ours. But at the same time, alongside these Moon-stage human beings or Angeloi, we ourselves were there, developing in such a way as to prepare us for the earthly phase of evolution. Indeed, that preparatory stage was already sufficiently advanced for us to have had some actual, even troublesome, significance for the Angeloi when the Moon had entered its declining phase.

We face an exactly similar situation in this period of the earth's decline. Since the earth entered its declining phase, other beings have advanced. It is a significant finding of spiritual-scientific research, one that needs to be taken very, very seriously, that we have entered the phase of earth's evolution when those beings will assert themselves who, in the subsequent Jupiter phase of earth's evolution, will have advanced to human form. Their form, though it will differ from ours, will nevertheless be comparable to the human. We ourselves, of course, will be different on Jupiter. But these Jupiterian human beings are already here, just as we were present on the Moon. They are here, though naturally they are not externally visible. I have spoken to you recently about what it means to be externally visible, and described human beings also as supersensible beings. Supersensibly considered, these beings are indeed very definitely present.

Let me emphasize again how extremely serious it is that certain beings are actually asserting themselves in our environment, as they have been doing increasingly since the middle of the fifteenth century. Until now they have chiefly developed the stimulus for a force very similar to that of the human will, the will-force I described yesterday as inhabiting the deeper levels of human consciousness. These invisible beings are bound up with a content that, at present, ordinarily remains unconscious, although it already exerts a very strong influence on the development of modern humanity.

This is an enormous problem for anyone directly involved in spiritual research. I felt its challenge most strongly in 1914 when this catastrophic war broke out, as I reported then in one form or another to some of our friends. One had to wonder how to account for an event that broke like a storm over European humanity, stemming from causes impossible to assess in the ordinary way of judging historical events. Anyone who is aware that scarcely more than thirty or forty people in all of Europe were involved in the decisive events of 1914, and is aware too of the state of mind of those few individuals, faces a really significant problem. For strange as it may sound today, most of those individuals were in a state of dimmed, darkened consciousness. Indeed, in recent years a great deal has happened as the result of just such a condition of dimmed consciousness. We see the most important decisions issuing from positions of authority at the end of July and the beginning of August, 1914—decisions taken by individuals in a state of beclouded consciousness. This has continued since then, right up to the present. It is a particularly frightening problem. Spiritual-scientific research reveals that the darkened consciousness of these individuals was like an open door: the will-beings took possession of the consciousness of these individuals by means of their dimmed awareness, seizing control of their veiled, darkness-enwrapped consciousness and acting through it out of their own consciousness.

Who are the beings responsible for this, these as-yet subhuman beings? We must ask this question with utmost seriousness. What kind of beings are they?

We have considered the origin of human intelligence, of intelligent behavior, which, to put it simply, makes use of our head as its instrument. And we saw that an intelligent soul state is attributable to the deed of the Archangel Michael, a deed usually pictured as the overthrowing of the Dragon. That is actually a very trivial symbol for it. To portray Michael and the Dragon correctly we have to first imagine the Michael Being, and then the dragon as everything that is involved with our so-called reason, our intelligence. It was into our human heads rather than down into some hell that Michael hurled the hosts of his enemy. The Luciferic impulse lives on in our heads. Therefore I describe human intelligence as a truly Luciferic impulse. Looking back on the earth's development, we come to the deed of Michael, and we can say that the illumination of human nature with the power of reason is bound up with that Michaelic deed.

Something different is happening now. The subhuman beings whose chief characteristic is an impulse similar to our human will are now emerging from below as it were, whereas the hosts cast down by Michael came down from above. And where the latter beings laid hold on human *mental* capacity, the former seize on the human *will*, uniting themselves with it. These are beings from the realm of Ahriman.

Ahrimanic influences were at work in the darkened consciousness of the individuals I mentioned. Indeed, we will lack true insight into nature as it includes human beings—nature as Goethe sets it forth in his prose "Hymn to Nature"[43]—until we recognize that these

---

43. See Goethe's *Scientific Writings.*

Ahrimanic forces are just as *objectively* present in the world as, say, magnetism and electricity and so on are. For nature as conceived by modern scientific research has no place for human beings, only for their physical vehicle.

We must realize that beings who envision an ascent of the Ahrimanic hosts similar to the descent of the Luciferic hosts that occurred at the start of earth evolution are now entering human evolution. They represent an influence upon human willpower analogous to the Luciferic influence upon human mental capacity.

We must realize that these beings are definitely emerging and that we must reckon for the time being with a concept of nature that involves only the human being, because animals developed only later in earthly evolution and these beings have as yet no influence on them. But we cannot understand human beings without including these beings in the picture. These actually subhuman beings are controlled as a group by higher Ahrimanic beings, and are thus powerful far beyond their own nature. The Ahrimanic element gives them their strong willpower and directs their activity. Their effect is so compelling that those whom they enslave are unable, in their human weakness, to resist unless they strengthen themselves spiritually.

What are these hosts trying to achieve? Just as the Luciferic hosts that Michael cast down sought to illuminate human reason, so these other hosts intend to permeate the human will. What are they trying to accomplish there? They burrow, so to speak, in the deepest layer of consciousness where human beings of today, even when they are awake, are still asleep. People do not notice these beings entering their souls, and even their bodily natures. Once within us, these beings attract to themselves all that has remained Luciferic and unpermeated by Christ in us. They can successfully seize hold of those elements.

These things are very real! I have already mentioned a phenomenon which, in a higher sense, is of particular cultural and historical significance. Nowadays we are being treated to all sorts of books of "self-justification," as they are called. Everybody you can think of, from Theobald Bothmann to Jagow—they're all writing them.

Clemenceau and Wilson[44] will get around to it later; they'll be writing too; everybody's doing it.

Now we need only take one or two individual examples, let's say the two thick volumes by Tirpitz and Ludendorff.[45] It is intensely interesting for thoughtful people—people who think in the spirit of the time—to examine the way such people write. These two books are very different, for neither person could tolerate the other, and they held widely differing views. But we need not go into their views here—it is the spiritual configuration we want to discuss. The books are in contemporary German, more or less. But the thought-forms! We have to cultivate a sense for such matters, as they otherwise go unnoticed. Since the date 1919 is printed on their title pages, we tend to think of these books as current. But the thought-forms are the product of a mentality that prompts the reader to ask what they actually are. I asked myself this question in all seriousness, and examined both books to find the answer. It is simply totally untrue that they are written in German. Externally speaking they are written in German, of course. But in fact they are just translations, for the thought-forms are those of the time of Imperial Rome, of Caesar. The whole way these men think is exactly the same as the way Caesar thought.

Once we have gained an understanding of the metamorphosis of humankind I have just described, we begin to notice how behind the times such souls are, for they have not participated in that metamorphosis. It is mere chance that the Tirpitz and Ludendorff

---

44. Theobald von Bethmann-Hollweg, 1856–1921, the German Reich's chancellor, author of *Observations on the World War* [1919–21]; Gottleib von Jagow, 1863–1935, Prussian minister of state, author of *The Cause and Outbreak of World War* [1919]; Clemenceau, 1841–1929, French Prime Minister, 1917–20; Woodrow Wilson, 1856–1924, President of the United States, author of *The Fourteen Points* that are the foundation of the Treaty of Versailles.

45. Alfred von Tirpitz, 1849–1930, German naval commander. After the fall of the German Empire he took refuge in Switzerland where he published his *Memoirs,* 1919. He returned to Germany where he became a member of the Reichstag. Erich Ludendorff, 1865–1937, German general and politician. After the German defeat he fled to Sweden. He returned to live in Munich [1919] and took part in reactionary conspiracies. Nationalist Socialist member of the Reichstag [1924–28]. He supported Hitler, then deserted him. He wrote *My War Memoirs* {1914–18}.

memoirs deal with current events. They could equally well be reports of Caesar's campaigns. Any knowledgeable person could prove this. Another way of describing the situation is to say that Christianity has passed these men by, they have absorbed none of it. If it were just a matter of words, then, yes, perhaps they even prayed in Christian churches when they were young. I say perhaps, because I don't know. In fact, I don't believe that is true in Tirpitz's case, and I have my doubts in Ludendorff's too, not that it matters. What matters is that neither carries the true Christian impulse in his heart and soul. Their development stopped short at an earlier stage of humanity's evolution.

The spirits I have described can approach and subjugate mentalities or spiritual configurations that Tirpitz and Ludendorff represent. Such a mentality attracts these spirits: it is their means of gaining control. And thereby an alien element, coming from a spiritual sphere, can enter into the decisions such individuals make.

In Ludendorff's case this can be historically proven. Although there is not yet such a thing as historical psychopathology, it won't be long before there is. Then it will be proven in Ludendorff's case. The town of Lüttich (Liège) was captured on the sixth of August. An entire army corps, including Ludendorff, who was then still a colonel, was jammed into its streets. All the decisions were his to make: the command was his. What occurred was solely due to his own swift decision. In this action, Ludendorff lost his normal consciousness. His state of mind became that of Caesar, a darkened consciousness that opens the door for the Ahrimanic world to enter.

The times pose these problems for us and we may not ignore them. Of course they are not comfortable. What is comfortable nowadays is to think differently about human beings—in fact, not to think about human beings at all, not to get involved with them. Indeed, it is dangerous to talk about things as they really are when so many people have no love for a sense of the truth. Besides, out of a misplaced sentimentality, people might find these things emotionally abhorrent.

Nevertheless, the kind of outlook I am proposing will result in a thorough recognition of the need for the Christ-Impulse. We must note all the places where the Christ-Impulse cannot be found. Yesterday, we saw that the Christ-Impulse must take hold of the middle level of consciousness. Today we can add to this that when the Christ-Impulse takes hold of the middle level of consciousness—when human beings have become thoroughly enchristed—then the Ahrimanic forces cannot get through this middle stratum, cannot make their way up through the middle level and use their spiritual forces to drag down the powers of the intellect. Everything depends upon this.

Today it is of vital importance to realize that the influences that nonhuman, subhuman beings exert upon us—beings who in turn are influenced by still other beings—are just as important as those originating in the human world.

Last week I characterized the Michael influence. It is a very essential one. For just as it is true that the Luciferic influence on human intelligence resulted from Michael's deed, so it is true that the opposite process or counterpole, the surfacing of certain Ahrimanic beings, is occurring now. Only the continuing activity of Michael will arm us against these hosts.

It is thoroughly dangerous, physiologically speaking, to continue clinging to the idea of natural necessity, to the kind of fatalism implicit in the doctrine of necessity. For to be educated—both in school and in the rest of life—by concepts based merely on natural necessity, on the omnipotence of natural necessity, weakens human heads. Thereby human consciousness becomes so passive that other forces take it over. And thus human beings lose the strength they need for the Christ-Impulse in its present form to take its intended place in the human soul.

In a certain way I am under an obligation to speak at this time on the subject which I have begun to discuss today, namely, the intrusion of certain Ahrimanic beings with whom we are going to have to reckon. Tomorrow, I will continue on the subject. Many people living on our earth today are already aware of this intrusion, but they interpret it wrongly because either they know nothing, or they want to know nothing, of the real triad of Christ, Lucifer, and Ahriman. Instead they lump Lucifer and Ahriman together. They fail to discriminate between Lucifer and Ahriman and therefore fail to recognize the basic nature of the Ahrimanic beings. Only by clearly distinguishing the Ahrimanic and becoming aware of its contrast to the Luciferic can we judge the nature of the supersensible influences that are now surfacing as the counterpart to Michael's casting down the Dragon. It is as if certain beings were being lifted up out of Ahrimanic depths. These beings find vulnerable areas to attack in human beings when the latter yield to unbridled instincts and impulses and fail to strive to understand them clearly.

There is actually a method now—perhaps I should say, an anti-method—for veiling our instinctual understanding by setting up one concept and then sliding another over it, so that it is impossible to assess anything accurately. Just think of the battle cry of the modern proletariat—"Workers of the world, unite!" [46] This is based, as I have often shown, on absolutely justified demands. But the slogan is not based on these demands. Our threefold concept[47] actually deals with these demands for the first time. Behind the slogan, in fact, lies something of a fundamentally different nature. For what does this slogan really mean? It means: Nurture antipathy, as proletarians, against the other classes, nurture something similar to hate as single individuals, and then to unite, which is to say, love one another. Unite your feelings of hatred, develop love of your class—a love for comrades of a common class—born out of hate. Love each other out of hatred!

Here we see two opposing conceptual poles established, making human understanding so nebulous that our instincts are suppressed. The result is that we do not know what we are dealing with. If I may use so paradoxical an expression, something actually exists in the nature of an anti-method that uses our own modern way of thinking to veil the sway of our instinctual life, making it especially vulnerable to attack by the Ahrimanic beings I have been describing.

---

46. See the *Communist Manifesto*.
47. See Rudolf Steiner, *Towards Social Renewal.*

SIX

The ancient yoga culture and the new yoga will—The achievement of a new knowledge of pre-existence as Michael culture in
the future—the evolution of the God concept from the fourth to
the sixteenth centuries—Michael's deed influence as the counterpole to Ahriman—The necessity of the Christ-Impulse

Dornach, November 30, 1919

You will have gathered from the lectures over the last few days how
essential it is—to gain a complete understanding of the essence of a
human being—that we penetrate the structure of our human
organism and recognize above all the far-reaching difference
between what we may call the human head organization and what
we have called the rest of the organism. You know too, of course,
that we then further divide this latter section into separate parts, so
that we have a threefold membering there. For the moment, however, if we are to understand the most significant impulse in human
evolution facing us in the present and in the immediate future, the
distinction between the head and the remainder of the body is the
important one.

Now, when we speak in this spiritual-scientific way of "the head
organization and the rest of the body," these "organizational"
aspects of the human organism should be thought of, to begin with,
more as images—as symbols or pictures, created by nature, of the
soul and spiritual elements whose expression or revelation they are.
We can really understand the role of human beings in earthly
humanity's overall evolution only if we take into consideration the
different participation in it of the head and the remaining organism. Everything having to do with the head, with conceptual life that
uses the head as its tool, is something that, if we stay within post-
Atlantean evolution, reaches far back in it. If we contemplate the
period immediately following the great Atlantean catastrophe, that
is, the eighth to sixth millennia B.C., we find a very different human
soul-mood from our own in those areas that constituted the then
civilized world. The content of people's consciousness at that time,

their characteristic view of the world, can scarcely be compared with
our present sense-based and thought-filled approach to the world
around us. In my book *Occult Science* I called this culture, reaching
so far back in time, the ancient Indian civilization. It is fair to say
that the human organization, which at that time was primarily head-
related, was so different from our own that our present way of reckoning time and space would have been totally foreign to that
ancient people. Their experience of the world was more one of
looking out over an immeasurable immensity of space and their perception of time was a non-linear one in which different temporal
moments interpenetrated. There was nothing resembling our distinct emphasis on time and space in that period.

The first suggestion of time and space as we know them appears
only toward the onset of the fifth and fourth millennia before
Christ—the epoch we designate as that of ancient Persian culture.
But the whole mood of soul life at that period was still such as to
make comparison with our own difficult. People of that time were
chiefly concerned with perceiving shades of light and darkness in
their surroundings. The abstractions in which we live today would
still have been completely alien to their natures. They still had a unified comprehensive perception, an awareness that the whole visible
world was simultaneously both permeated with light and shading off
into darkness. The moral world order was viewed in the same way. A
kindly, benevolent individual was experienced as a person of light
and brightness; someone who was mistrustful and self-seeking was
experienced as a person of darkness. People were still seen surrounded by an aura in which their morality was reflected. And if
someone had spoken to people of that ancient Persian period about
what we call the natural order, they would not have had the least
understanding of it. For them, in their world of light and shadow, a
natural order in the sense we mean today did not exist. Their world
was a world of light and shadow. In the world of tones, for instance,
they distinguished certain nuances as bright and others as dark or
shadowy. The world for them was simply one of light and shadow;
and what found expression in these qualities were spiritual beings
and natural forces, between which no distinction was made. These

people would have felt our distinguishing between natural necessity and human freedom to be insanity; for them, no such duality as free choice and natural necessity existed. They saw everything in their world of light and darkness as a single spiritual-physical unity. If I were to make a drawing of the character of that ancient Persian view of things (its meaning will be clear only after a further commentary), I would have to draw a line resembling the world-serpent, the symbol of the All, which encompasses the unity of humanity's vision.

After this soul-mood had lasted a little over two thousand years, a period began whose traces we can still perceive in the Egypto-Chaldean world view and also, in a special form, in the world view whose reflection is preserved in the Old Testament.

During this epoch something appeared on the scene that was closer to our present way of seeing things. A certain nuance or inkling of natural necessity entered human conceiving, though it was a far cry from the concept of what we call today mechanical or even vital natural order. During this period natural events and Divine Will or Providence were still sensed as inseparable. Providence and natural happenings were still one and the same. When people moved their hands or arms, they knew that it was the divine element permeating them that moved them. And when a tree shook in the wind they saw the shaking as no different from the movement of their hands: both motions were felt to be expressions of the same divine power of Providence. They did not see any distinction between the God acting within them and the God without. The God in nature and the God within were the same Divinity. People of that time were aware that something existed in human nature whereby the Providence in nature and the Providence in humanity could meet each other.

This was how the people of that time experienced the process of human breathing. When a tree shook, they said that it was a deed of the God without; and when they themselves moved a limb, they said it was a deed of the God within. They said that when they drew a breath, worked it over within them, and then exhaled it again, this was the God without who entered and left them, the same divine element experienced in both phases of the breathing process. They felt that, as breathing creatures, they were simultaneously beings of outer nature and their inner selves.

If I were to characterize the world view of the third post-Atlantean epoch as I did the ancient Persian period, I would have to do so in this way:

This line represents, on one pole, nature outside, and on the other, human existence, the two meeting and crossing one another in the breathing process.

In the fourth post-Atlantean period, the Greco-Latin, this changes. In this epoch, the contrast between inner and outer, between natural existence and human existence, confronts humanity in all its starkness. Human beings begin to feel themselves in contrast to nature. And if I were to characterize the feeling humanity developed in the Greek age, I would have to do so thus:

That is to say, the Greeks began to feel what was external as one category, and what was internal as another, with no crossing point between them.

In a certain way what people had in common with nature remains outside consciousness. It disappears from consciousness. Indeed, in the Indian yoga that arose at this time, the aim was to restore this commonality to consciousness. Hence this yoga was a kind of "atavistic" going-back to earlier evolutionary stages that sought to bring back into consciousness the process of breathing which, as late as the third epoch, was still the natural state by which people felt themselves to be at once both inside and outside. This fourth, Greco-Latin epoch began in the eighth century B.C. This was the period when people began practicing the late-Indian yoga exercises as a means of regaining what they had once possessed, especially in the ancient Indian culture, but then had lost.

Thus, in the Greco-Latin epoch, awareness of the breathing process was lost. And if we ask why people then tried to revive ancient Indian yoga culture, and what they hoped to acquire thereby, we must answer: they sought a true understanding of the outer world. By understanding the breathing process, the people of the third post-Atlantean culture had an understanding of something within themselves that was simultaneously also outside.

This understanding of the outer world in relation to the inner is certainly something that must be recovered, though by a different method, another path. The fourth post-Atlantean (Greco-Latin) epoch ended only around 1413—really not until the middle of the fifteenth century—and today we are still experiencing its aftereffects in the form of a double element in our souls. Our head organization gives us an incomplete view of nature, of what we call the external world, while our internal organization, the rest of our organism, gives us an incomplete knowledge of ourselves. Between these two lies an empty space in which, were it present, we could see a representation of both a world process, nature, and an inner process, our own.

What we must do now is regain what has been lost, but this time consciously. This means regain the ability to take hold of an inner element in our being that belongs to both the soul and to the outer world, something that again overlaps, reaches into both:

This must be the striving of the fifth post-Atlantean epoch: to rediscover in our inner being the element in which an external process is also occurring.

You will probably remember that I already mentioned this important need in my last article for the *The Social Future*.[48] I was ostensibly discussing the significance of such matters for social life, but I made a point of specifically stating that we must discover a place in ourselves where we can take hold of something within us that we recognize at the same time to be a process of the external world. As people

---

48. *The Social Future* was a journal. Rudolf Steiner is referring to his article in the third issue, *Geistesleben, Rechtsordnung, Wirtschaft* [Spiritual life, the organization of rights, economy]; there were four issues. See GA 24.

today we will not succeed in doing this by reverting to ancient Yoga culture; that culture belongs to the past, and, what is more, the breathing process itself has changed. Of course, this cannot be clinically demonstrated. But the human breathing process has nevertheless undergone a change since the third post-Atlantean period. Crudely put, human beings of the third post-Atlantean culture still breathed soul, whereas now we breathe air. It is not just our concepts that have become materialistic; reality itself has lost its soul.

I beg you not to view what I have just said as something insignificant. Just think what it means that the very reality in which we exist has changed so much that the air we breathe is different than it was approximately four millennia ago. It is not just our consciousness that is different. No indeed! There was once soul in the earth's atmosphere. The air itself was soul. It is now soul no longer, or at least not in the same sense. The spiritual beings of an elementary nature about whom I spoke yesterday are again permeating the air, and we can breathe them if we practice yoga. But what could be achieved in normal breathing three thousand years ago cannot be artificially revived. What can be revived is only the great illusion in which the person of the ancient Orient lived. The description I am giving you is entirely realistic. The ensoulment of the air, once experienced by human beings, is no longer present. Therefore the spirits about whom I spoke yesterday and whom I shall call the anti-Michaelic beings are able to penetrate the air and so to enter human beings as I described. Only by replacing yoga-type practices with the proper methods can they be driven out. We must realize that these right methods must be striven for and attempted, which can happen only if we establish a much subtler consciousness of our relationship to the external world, so that we become increasingly aware of something resembling a breathing process taking place in our etheric bodies. Indeed, a process similar to breathing—the inhaling of freshly oxygenated air and the exhaling of carbon dioxide—goes on in all our sense perceptions.

Just consider how we see objects. Let us take a radical case, that of seeing a flame. You gaze at a flame, and something happens that is similar to breathing in, only it is a much subtler process. Then if you close your eyes—and you can make a similar experiment with all your senses—you will see an afterimage of the flame, which gradually changes, or, as Goethe said, fades away.[49] Quite aside from the purely physiological aspect of the perceptual process, therefore, the etheric body is deeply involved in absorbing a light-impression and its subsequent fading. But a tremendously important element is concealed here: namely, the soul element that, three thousand years ago, was breathed in and out with the air. And we must develop insight into the ensoulment of the sense processes, similar to the insight into the ensoulment of the breathing process possessed by humanity three millennia ago.

This relationship between then and now is connected with the fact that we could call the culture in which people of that period lived a kind of night-culture. Jahve made himself known through his prophets by night-time dreams. But now we must develop a delicacy of intercourse with the world such that we perceive it not merely in the form of sense impressions, but also with spiritual content. We must make sure that we enter into a communicative soul relationship with the world in our experience of every ray of light, of every tone and perception of warmth. Indeed, such soul-intercourse must become a matter of significance to us.

We can help ourselves achieve this. I have explained to you that the Mystery of Golgotha occurred in the fourth post-Atlantean epoch, which, if we wish to be entirely precise, began in 747 B.C. and ended in A.D. 1413. The Mystery of Golgotha took place in the first third of that period. But it was the echoes of an older outlook that provided people with the first means of grasping that Mystery. This way of understanding the Mystery must be replaced by a new one. New methods must be developed, for the old way of understanding is outmoded; it no longer suffices. And many attempts to make human thinking adequate to grasp the Mystery of Golgotha have proven inappropriate to achieving that goal.

You see, all outwardly material phenomena have a soul-spiritual aspect, and all soul-spiritual phenomena have an outward material

---

49. See Goethe's Color Theory in *Scientific Writings*.

aspect. Thus the fact that the earth's air was denuded of its soul element, with the result that human beings no longer had ensouled
air to breathe, had an important spiritual consequence in human
evolution. For this breathing-in of soul—the soul with which
human beings had been endowed from the beginning (the Old
Testament puts it, "And God breathed into his nostrils the breath
of life, and man became a living soul"[50])—made it possible for people to be conscious of the pre-existence of the soul element, of the
existence of the soul before the descent into the physical world
through birth or conception. Human beings lost this consciousness
of the soul's pre-existence to the degree that the breathing process
ceased to be ensouled. Thus, already during Aristotle's lifetime,[51]
in the fourth post-Atlantean epoch, it was no longer possible for
human beings to grasp the pre-existence of the soul. The means
were no longer available.

Looked at historically, it is a curious fact that, although the Christ
event, the greatest of all events, broke into the evolution of the
earth, humanity must mature to understand it. At first, human
beings were still able to grasp rays streaming from the Mystery of
Golgotha with the help of remnants of the cognitive capacity stemming from the old primeval culture. But this capacity was then lost,
and dogmatics—doctrinal theology—deviated further and further
from any grasp of it. The Church forbids people to believe in pre-
existence, not because pre-existence and the Mystery of Golgotha
are incompatible, but because the de-ensouling of the air made it
impossible for human understanding to possess the energy of soul
needed to develop a consciousness of pre-existence. So pre-existence disappeared from what became head-consciousness.

But once we are again endowed with ensouled sense perceptions,
a crossing-point will be re-established, and in that intersection we
will all take hold of the human will that streams up out of the third
level of consciousness that I have been describing these past several
days. At the same time, this will provide us with the subjective-

---

50. Genesis 2:7.
51. See Rudolf Steiner, *Anthroposophy, Psychosophy, Pneumatosophy,* lecture 9.

objective element that Goethe so longed for.[52] And so we shall once again have the possibility of a first sensitive inkling of how truly remarkable the process of human sense perception is in its relationship to the outer world. Regarding sense perception, we have for the moment only crude conceptions—conceptions that picture the outer world affecting us, and ourselves merely reacting to it. These conceptions are crude and clumsy. The reality is rather that a soul process enters us from without and is taken hold of by a profoundly unconscious inner soul process, so that the two—the outer and the inner soul processes—overlap. Cosmic thoughts enter us from without, the human will works outward from within, and that will and the cosmic thoughts meet and overlap at a crossing point, just as once upon a time an objective element met and crossed a subjective element in the breathing process. We must learn to feel how our will works through our eyes, and how true it is that the activity of the senses delicately mingles with the passivity, whereby cosmic thoughts and human will meet. Indeed, we must develop a new yoga-will. This will provide us with something analogous to what was given human beings in the breathing process three thousand years ago. Our conceiving must become far more soul-like, much more spiritual.

That was the direction Goethe's striving took. Goethe wanted to arrive at pure phenomena, to which he gave the name primal phenomena [*Urphänomenon*]. He admitted only those elements of the outer world that work upon human beings without any interference on the part of Luciferic thought issuing from the human head itself. Thought was to be allowed to serve only in the activity of relating phenomena to one another. Goethe was looking for primal phenomena, rather than for laws of nature; that was the significant thing about his striving. In the case of a pure or primal phenomenon[53] we have something in the external world that enables us to perceive the activity of our will as we observe it. This allows us to lift

52. See Goethe's *Scientific Writings*: "The Experiment as Mediator between Subject and Object."
53. See Goethe, *Italian Journey*.

ourselves again to the objective-subjective level typical, for example, of ancient Hebrew teaching. We must learn not to speak all the time merely of the contrast between the material and the spiritual, but to recognize the interplay of the material and the spiritual as a unity experienced particularly in sense perception. Once we no longer see nature as material and do not, as Gustav Theodor Fechner did, merely "fantasize" something of a soul nature into it,[54] something resembling the Jahve culture of three thousand years ago will come about. Once we have learned to take in the soul element in nature along with the sense perceptions of it, we will live in a Christ relationship to outer nature, and this Christ relationship will be a kind of spiritual breathing process.

We can help ourselves to do this if we realize more and more—simply on the basis of healthy human reason—that pre-existence is a reality on which the existence of the soul is founded. Here we must balance the purely egoistic conception of the soul's post-existence—which springs only from our desire to continue living after death—with knowledge of the soul's pre-existence. We must lift ourselves again to a perception of the true eternity of the soul, but in a different way than before. This is what we may rightly call Michaelic culture. We will have achieved what humanity needs for the future when we go about in the world aware that in all we see and hear—with every perception and tone—a soul-spiritual element flows into us, while we at the same time send a soul element flowing out into the world.

Let us go back again to our image. You see a flame. Then you close your eyes and you see an afterimage that gradually disappears. Is this just a subjective process? Modern physiologists say it is, but that is not correct. The afterimage is an objective process in the cosmic ether, in the same sense that the presence of carbon dioxide in the air we exhale is an objective process. You imprint an image upon the cosmic ether. You yourself experience it only as a gradually disappearing afterimage. But it is not just a subjective process; it

54. G. T. Fechner, 1801–1887, German physicist, psychologist, philosopher. Among others, author of *A Little Book of Life after Death*.

is an objective process. Here you have something objective. You have the possibility of recognizing how something that takes place within you is simultaneously a subtle cosmic process once you realize; "When I see a flame, close my eyes, and let the afterimage disappear, this is something that doesn't just take place in me, it is something going on in the world as well."(Of course, it disappears too if you keep your eyes open, but then you don't notice it.)

But it is not only in relation to a flame that this happens. If I say to a person that somebody told me something or other (it doesn't matter whether it is true or not), that constitutes a judgment, a moral or intellectual act, performed inside me. That too, fades away like the image of the flame. It is an objective process in the universe. When you think a good thought about someone, and it then fades away, it exists in the cosmic ether as an objective process. And when you have a bad thought, it too is an objective process that fades away. You can't close off what you perceive of the world, or your judgments about it, in some private inner space. Your own view of the world may be that it is happening inside you, but it is equally an objective process taking place simultaneously in the universe. Just as people of the third epoch were aware that the breathing process both went on inside human beings and was an objective cosmic process too, the humanity of the future must become aware that the soul processes I have described are simultaneously objective cosmic processes.

This transformation of consciousness is something that requires the development of greater soul strength than people are used to developing today. To imbue ourselves with such an awareness is to open the door to the Michael culture. If we take light as generally representing sense perception, we must go forward to an understanding of light as ensouled, just as it was wholly a matter of course for people of the second and third millennia B.C. to conceive of the air as ensouled, simply because it was. We must completely cease to see light as our materialistic age is used to seeing it; we must cease believing that light is only vibrations rayed out by the Sun, as modern physics and the ordinary human consciousness hold. We must become aware that soul is moving through cosmic space on wings of light, and we must realize, too, that this was not the case in the epoch that preceded our own. In that epoch, air brought us the same element that light now brings us. This is an objective distinction in earth-process. Broadly speaking, we may picture it thus:

MYSTERY OF GOLGOTHA

| Air-soul-process | Light-soul-process |

We can observe this difference in earthly evolution. And midway between these two processes, effecting the transition from one to the other, the Mystery of Golgotha occurs. For the present and future of the human race, it will not suffice to talk about the spirit in abstract terms, nor will it suffice to lapse into nebulous pantheism or the like. Human beings must begin to recognize the ensoulment of something that heretofore they have experienced only as a material process.

The important thing is to learn to say: There was a time before the Mystery of Golgotha when the earth possessed an atmosphere filled with soul that was part of the human soul; but that atmosphere has become empty of soul, of the soul element shared by human beings; for the element of soul that formerly lived in the air has taken up its habitation in the light which surrounds us during the daylight hours. It was Christ's uniting Himself with the earth that made this possible. Thus both air and light have undergone a soul-spiritual change in the course of the evolution of the earth.

It is a childish idea to think of air and light as purely material elements that have remained unchanged through the millennia of earthly evolution. Air and light have undergone inner changes. We are now living in a different atmosphere and a different light than our souls did in their earlier incarnations on the earth. The important thing is to learn to see—to cognize—external-material reality as soul-spiritual reality. We will never achieve true spiritual science by describing things as purely material in the way we do today, and then adding, as a kind of decorative detail, the casual statement that a spiritual element also inheres in everything material. People really behave very strangely with regard to such matters; they really are determined to resort to abstractions. But for the future the essential thing is not to make an abstract distinction between the material and the spiritual, but to look for the spiritual itself in the material, so that one can describe it as spiritual, and recognize in what is spiritual its transition into matter and its way of working there. Only when we can do this will we really have succeeded in regaining a true understanding of human nature. Blood is "a very special fluid" indeed.[55] But the blood that is talked about today in physiology is by no means a very special fluid; it is just a fluid whose chemical composition is analyzed like that of any other aspect of the material world. It is nothing special. But if we can begin from the standpoint of real soul-insight into the metamorphosis of air and light, then we will be able to rise to a soul-spiritual grasp of ourselves too, in all the members of our being; we will not be left with abstract matter and abstract spirit, but will become familiar instead with the interplay of spirit, soul, and body. That will be Michael culture.

This is something that our age demands, something that those who want to understand our epoch should realize with every fiber of their soul-life. For some time now, anything of an unusual nature requiring introduction into human experience has met with resistance. I have often cited the delightful example of a rather crass case. In 1835, not quite a century ago, a learned medical faculty in Bavaria was asked, when the building of a first railroad from Furth to Nuremberg was being planned, whether it was a good idea from a medical perspective. The medical faculty answered—the document exists, I'm not making this up—that the railroad ought not to be built, because it would make people nervous to cover ground in this manner. And, moreover, they added that if people actually insisted on demanding railroads, then high walls would have to be built along both sides of the tracks so that witnesses to the passing trains would not be stricken with concussions of the brain. As you see, an informed opinion of this kind is one thing, and the actual course of evolution quite another.

---

55. The original phrase comes from Goethe's *Faust*. See also lecture of October 25, 1906.

Today, we laugh at a document such as the one composed by the Bavarian medical faculty. Yet perhaps we have no right to laugh, for given similar circumstances we still have exactly the same sort of attitude today. Nor can we really criticize the Bavarian medical faculty. If we compare the nervous state of modern humanity with that of two centuries ago, we do see that people have become nervous. The Bavarian medical faculty may have taken a somewhat exaggerated stand, but people have become nervous.

But matters of this kind are not the important thing in human evolutionary progress. What is important is that certain impulses intended to enter earthly evolution really do enter it and do not meet with rejection. Such impulses that have to enter cultural evolution from time to time do not contribute to our love of comfort. Therefore we must undertake an objective reading of what our duty is with respect to human cultural evolution, rather than considering comfort, even comfort of a higher kind.

I am concluding my remarks with these words because it is quite obvious that a sharp conflict is already looming between anthroposophical knowledge and the various religious confessions. Because they wish to remain stuck in old established ruts, rather than advance to new insight into the Mystery of Golgotha, these confessions will continue to sharpen the hostile position they have already taken. And it would be extremely careless of us not to be aware that this battle has already started.

As you can imagine, I am not in the least eager for such conflicts—and I especially do not wish for a battle with the Catholic Church such as it seems so intent on pursuing. Those sufficiently familiar with the profounder historical impulses underlying the confessions extant today are very loathe to engage in warfare with their ancient and venerable values. But if a battle is forced, there is no avoiding it. And the priesthood today is thoroughly unwilling to let enter what must enter: namely, spiritual science.

We can also foresee that we shall be engaged in the grotesque but necessary combatting of things of the kind I recently spoke to you about—things like the fact that Catholics will have to seek information about anthroposophically oriented spiritual science in hostile literature, since any reading of my own books has been forbidden to Catholics by the Pope. This is no laughing matter; it must be taken very seriously! Any conflict that surfaces in so grotesque a manner, and that is capable of broadcasting such judgments, cannot be treated casually.

This is particularly true when such conflicts are not welcomed. Let us consider the example of the Catholic Church, not because Protestant churches are any different, but because the Catholic Church is more powerful. These churches are based on venerable and ancient practices. We need only realize what surrounds a priest as he reads the Mass, what is behind every aspect of his vestments, what lies in every act in the celebration of the Mass, to be aware of the presence of venerable and ancient sacred practices there—practices more ancient than Christianity. For the Christian sacrifice of the Mass is a transformed ancient cult, carried over from the primeval Mysteries and adapted to Christianity. Such is the background of the modern priesthood that employs such means of warfare! If one has the deepest veneration for both the cult and the symbolism it contains, and yet also sees with what evil means those values are protected and new values attempting to enter human evolution are attacked, it becomes clear how seriously these matters must be taken. Certainly they must be well studied and thoroughly penetrated.

What is announcing itself in this way is only just beginning. This is no time for being asleep to such issues; rather, we must sharpen our sights to them. It is no longer right to remain asleep. During these first two decades of the Anthroposophical Movement in Middle Europe we could allow ourselves to carry on in the sleepy sectarian way that has been so hard to combat in our circles and is still deeply lodged in the attitudes of those in the movement. But the time is over when we could allow ourselves such sleepy sectarianism. It is profoundly true, as I have often emphasized, that we must be absolutely clear about the world-historical significance of the Anthroposophical Movement, ignoring pettinesses, and yet considering even little impulses seriously and at length.

PART

3

ONE

MICHAEL'S MISSION: THE SPIRITUALIZATION OF THE KNOWLEDGE OF SPACE [1]
Dornach, December 17, 1922

...Only since the first third of the fifteenth century have human concepts and ideas become purely human. And since this period began, humanity has concerned itself chiefly with what is *spatial*.

But if one goes still further back—to the cultures we have called Old Indian, Old Persian, Egypto-Chaldean—one finds everywhere conceptions of the world referring to World *Ages*. These point back to an ancient time, the "Golden Age," when human beings still interacted with the Gods. And they point back, too, to another epoch, when human beings still experienced the earthly sun-reflection of the Divine, which we call the Silver Age, and so on. Time and the course of Time play a conspicuous role in the world pictures of these early evolutionary phases. Likewise, if we consider the Greek epoch, and the picture of the world that was simultaneously current in more Northern and Middle European regions, we find everywhere that the idea of Time plays an essential role. The Greeks pointed back to a primeval Age when cosmic happenings were the outcome of relations between Uranus and Gaia. After this, they pointed to the next Age of Chronos and Rhea, and then to the Age of Zeus and the other Gods known to Greek Mythology who ruled the cosmos and the earth. Germanic Mythology is the same. Time plays the essential role in all these world pictures.

Space plays a much less important part. The spatial element is still obscure in the Norse and Germanic world pictures—those

---

1. From: Rudolf Steiner, *Man and the World of Stars*, pp. 82–93.

containing images like the Yggdrasil, the World Ash, and the Giant Ymir, and so forth. It is quite clear in these that something is taking place in Time, but the idea of Space is still only dimly dawning—it is a factor of no great importance. It is not until the age of Galileo, Copernicus, and Giordano Bruno, in fact, that Space actually begins to play its great role in our picture of the universe. Even in the Ptolemaic system, which is admittedly concerned with Space, Time is still a much more essential element than it is in the picture familiar to us since the fifteenth century, where Time plays only a secondary role. For instance, today the present distribution of stars in cosmic space is taken as the starting-point for research and then through calculation conclusions are reached as to what the world picture was like in earlier times. Today the concept of Space, the spatial picture of the world, has become the most important. All human judgments are based on the principle of Space. Modern humanity has elaborated this spatial element in its picture of the external world, as well as in all its thinking. Indeed, today such spatial thinking has reached its zenith.

Think how difficult it is for people today to follow an exposition in terms of Time. They are happy as soon as Space is brought in—at least to the extent of drawing something on the blackboard. And if the feeling of Space is conveyed by means of photographs, then they are truly in their element! "Illustration"—and by this I mean something expressed in terms of *Space*—is what our contemporaries strive to achieve in every exposition. Time, inasmuch as it is in perpetual flow, has become something that causes us discomfort. We still attach value to it in music; but even there the tendency towards the spatial is quite evident. . . .

This orientation of the soul to the spatial is certainly very characteristic of our present time. Whoever observes modern culture and civilization with open eyes will find it everywhere.

On the other hand, in anthroposophical Spiritual Science, we strive, as you know, to get away from what is spatial. To be sure, we meet the desire for what is spatial in that we, too, try to give tangible form to the spiritual—but we do this to strengthen the faculty of ideation. But we must always be conscious that this is only a means of illustration and that what is essential is to strive, at least to strive, to transcend the spatial....

Inwardly considered, what is it we are seeking to achieve? If we transfer ourselves in thought into the position of the divine-spiritual Beings in whose ranks we live between death and rebirth, discerning how they direct their gaze downward, and observe (through the various means I have described) the course of events on earth, then we find that these divine-spiritual Beings looked down to the earth in the earlier ages of human evolution—in the Old Indian, Old Persian, Old Egypto-Chaldean epochs—and beheld what human beings were doing, their view of nature and of their social life. At that time—if I may put it so—these divine spiritual Beings could still say to themselves about human deeds and thoughts: "The deeds and thoughts of human beings come from their memory of—or they are an echo of—what they experienced with us in our world." Certainly, in the case of the Chaldeans or Egyptians it was still quite evident that the primary wish of human beings on the earth was to carry out what the Gods above had thought or were thinking. When the gods looked down to the earth, they saw events occurring that were in keeping with their intentions; and it was the same when they looked into human thoughts—as Gods are able to do. Since the first third of the fifteenth century, however, all this has changed. Since then, when divine-spiritual Beings look down to the earth, especially when they look down at the present time, they find things everywhere fundamentally alien to them: they find that human beings are doing things on earth which they themselves planned solely in accordance with the phenomena and processes of earthly existence. To the Gods with whom we live between death and rebirth, this is an entirely alien attitude.

When an alchemist in his laboratory sought to ascertain the divine-spiritual will by combining and separating the Elements, a God would have beheld something akin to his own nature in what the alchemist was doing. If a God were to look into a modern laboratory, the methods and procedures adopted there would be intensely alien. It may be said with absolute truthfulness that since the first third of the fifteenth century, the Gods have felt as if the whole human race has in a certain respect fallen away from them, as if human beings below on the earth were engaged in self-made trivialities, in things which the Gods cannot understand—certainly not the Gods who still guided human hands and minds in the pursuit of science in Greco-Latin times. These divine-spiritual Beings can take no active interest in what is done in modern laboratories, let alone modern hospitals.

I was obliged on a previous occasion to say that when the Gods look down through windows, as I called them, what interests them least of all on earth is the kind of work carried out by professors. It goes to the very heart of those who have genuine insight into modern Initiation Science that they must say to themselves: "In recent times human beings have become estranged from the Gods. We must therefore seek for bridges to reconnect us with the divine-spiritual world." This is what quickens the impulse for our anthroposophical Spiritual Science. Its desire is to transform scientific ideas and concepts that are unintelligible to the gods in such a way that they are spiritualized and are thus able to provide a bridge to the Divine-Spiritual. . . .

A cosmic truth of great significance underlies these things. The conception of Space is an entirely human conception. The Gods with whom human beings live together in the most important period of their lives—the period between death and a new birth—have a vivid conception of Time, but no conception of Space such as human beings acquire on earth. This earthly conception of Space is entirely human. A human being really enters into Space for the first time when he or she descends from the divine-spiritual world into the physical, earthly world. True, as seen from here, everything appears in spatial perspective. But dimensional thinking, if I may put it so, is something that is entirely earthly.

This conception of Space has become ingrained in Western civilization since the fifteenth century. But once bridges to the divine world have been found again by spiritualizing purely spatial knowledge, then all that humanity gained from the science of Space during the period when human beings emancipated their thought

most drastically from the divine world—i.e., since the fifteenth century—all this will become important for the divine-spiritual world.
If human beings will but bring the spirit into the conception of
Space once more, humanity can conquer a new portion of the universe for the Gods.

You see, what I described in *Occult Science*—the periods of Old
Saturn, Old Sun, Old Moon, Earth and the future periods of Jupiter, Venus, Vulcan—is only present to the Gods in *Time.* Here on
earth, however, it lives itself out in terms of space. Today we are living in the "Earth" period of evolution, but in events on the earth
there still linger echoes of the periods of Old Moon, Old Sun and
Old Saturn.

If you steep yourselves in the description of the Old Saturn period
given in *Occult Science,* you will say: The Saturn period is past, but the
effect of its warmth is still present in our earthly existence. Saturn,
Sun, Moon, Earth are within one another; they exist simultaneously.
The Gods see them in *Time.* Although in earlier ages, even during
Chaldean times, they were seen in their temporal succession, now
we see them within one another, spatially within one another.
Indeed this leads very much further and if we study these things in
detail, we shall discover what really lies behind them.

Imagine that you stretch out your left hand. The Divine lives in
everything terrestrial. The Divine lives in your muscles, in your
nerves. Now, touch the fingers of your right hand with the fingers of
your left hand. This is something which the divine-spiritual Beings
cannot follow. They follow the left and right hands up to the point
of contact, but the feeling, the touch, that arises between the two is
an experience which the faculties possessed by the Gods do not
make possible: it is something that arises only in Space. Just as little
as the Gods behold Saturn, Sun, Moon and Earth simultaneously,
but only in succession, in Time, so they have none of the purely spatial experiences known to human beings. When you look with your
left and right eyes and have the lines of vision from right and from
left, the activity of the Gods is present in the vision from the right
eye and again in the vision from the left eye, but a purely human
element lies in the meeting of the two lines of vision. Because we

have been placed into the world of Space, this is the way we experience as human beings. It is something that we experience in a state of emancipation from the activity of the Gods.

You need only extend this imagery of the right and left hands to other domains of earthly life, and you will find a great many human experiences that fall right away from the field of vision of the Gods. It is really only since the first third of the fifteenth century that humanity has brought ideas of a purely human kind into these domains. Hence human thinking has become less and less intelligible to the Gods when they look down to the earth. And with this in mind we must turn our attention to that most important event in the last third of the nineteenth century, which may be characterized by saying that the rulership of the Spiritual Being known as Gabriel was succeeded by the rulership of the Spiritual Being known as Michael.

In the last third of the nineteenth century, the Spiritual Being we call Michael became the Ruler, as it were, of everything of a spiritual character in human events on the earth. Whereas Gabriel is a Being oriented more to the passive qualities of human beings, Michael is the active Being, the Being who, as it were, pulses through our breath, our veins, our nerves, to the end that we may actively develop all that belongs to our full humanity in connection with the Cosmos. What stands before us as a challenge from Michael is that we become active in our very thoughts, working out our view of the world through our own inner activity. We belong truly to the Michael Age only when we do not sit down inactively and seek to let enlightenment come to us from within and from without. We must co-operate *actively* in what the world offers us by way of experiences and opportunities for observation. If a person carries out an experiment, this does not fundamentally involve activity; he or she is not necessarily *active*. The experiment is just an event like any other event in Nature, except that it is directed by human intelligence. But all happenings in Nature have also been directed by intelligence! How is human mental life nowadays affected by experiments? There is no active participation, for the experimenters simply look on and try to eliminate activity as much as possible.

They want to let the experiment tell them everything and regard as fanciful anything that is the outcome of their own inner activity. It is precisely in its scientific ideas that humanity is least of all in the Michael Age.

But humanity *must* enter the Michael Age. If we ask ourselves, "What does it actually mean, in the whole cosmic context, that Gabriel passed the scepter on to Michael?" we must answer: It means that of all the Beings who spiritually guide humanity, Michael is the Spirit who is the first to draw near to what human beings on earth are doing as the result of the emancipation of knowledge that began with the first third of the fifteenth century. Gabriel stands in utter perplexity before the ideas and notions of a cultured person of the modern age. But Michael, who is closely connected with the forces of the Sun, can at least allow his activity to penetrate the human thought that can impel the free deeds of human beings. Michael can work, for instance, into what I have called in *Occult Science*, free, pure thinking which must be the true impulse for the individual human will acting in freedom in the new age. Michael has his own particular relationship to human deeds that spring from the impulse of love.

Michael, therefore, is the messenger whom the Gods sent down to receive what is now being spiritualized out of the knowledge that has been emancipated from the spirit. The science which, in the form of anthroposophical Spiritual Science, re-spiritualizes spatial thinking, lifting it again into the supersensible, works from below upward, stretching out its hands, as it were from below upward, to grasp the hands of Michael stretching down from above. Once these hands meet, the bridge can be created between human beings and the Gods. Michael became the Regent of the Age because he is to receive what the Gods wish to receive from what humanity can add to the understanding of Time by the understanding of Space—for this augments the knowledge the Gods already possess.

The Gods picture Saturn, Sun, Moon, and Earth phases of evolution in temporal succession. When human beings develop the latest phase of human thought life in the right way, they view this evolution spatially. The Gods can picture the outstretching of the left and of the right hand, but the actual contact between the hands is a purely human affair. The Gods can live in the line of vision of the left eye and in the line of vision of the right eye, but human beings alone see how the vision of the left eye meets the vision of the right eye *spatially.* Michael directs his gaze upon the earth. And by entering into connection with what human beings develop in pure thought and objectify in pure will, he is able to take cognizance of what is acquired by the citizens of earth, by human beings, as the fruit of spatial thinking. He is able to carry it into the divine worlds.

If human beings were merely to develop spatial knowledge and not spiritualize it, if they were to stop short at Anthropology and were unwilling to advance to Anthroposophy,[2] then the Michael Age would pass them by. Michael would retire from his rulership and would bring the Gods the message: "Humanity wants to separate itself from the Gods." If Michael is to bring the right message to the world of the Gods, he must be able to say: "During my Age, human beings raised into the Supersensible what they had developed as purely spatial thinking. Therefore we can accept humanity once more. Human beings have re-united their thought with ours." If human evolution proceeds in the right way, Michael will not have to say to the Gods: "Human beings have become used to staring at everything spatially. They have come to despise what lives only in time." But if human beings are resolved to achieve their earthly goal, Michael will have to say: "Human beings have taken pains to reintroduce Time and the Supersensible into the Spatial." Therefore those may be regarded as having linked their lives directly to the life of the Gods who are not content merely staring at the Spatial and cannot accept things in so material a form as was customary at the beginning of the twentieth century. . . .

---

2. See Rudolf Steiner, *The Case for Anthroposophy* (*Riddles of the Soul*), Chapter One.

TWO

MICHAEL, THE DRAGON, AND THE HUMAN SOUL
OR GEMÜT [3]
Vienna, September 27, 1923

When Anthroposophy is discussed in certain circles today, one of the many misstatements made about it is that it is intellectual, that it appeals predominantly to the scientific mind, that it does not sufficiently consider the needs of the human *Gemüt*[4]....

Today, in what I might call a sort of historical retrospect, we shall discuss first how, in earlier periods of human evolution, this *Gemüt* was granted a voice in the search for knowledge. It was permitted to conjure up grandiose and mighty images before the human soul, intended to illuminate the efforts of human beings to realize their incorporation into the body of world events and the cosmos, as well as their participation in the changing times. In those days when the human *Gemüt* was still allowed to contribute its share to the creation of world views, these images it conjured up really constituted their most important element. They represented vast and comprehensive cosmic relationships and assigned humanity its place in them.

To create a basis for further study of the human *Gemüt* from the perspective of Anthroposophy, I should like to present you today with one of those grandiose, majestic images that used to function in the way I have indicated. At the same time, this image is one of those that is especially appropriate to bring before our souls in a new manner. With this appropriateness, we shall also deal. I should like to talk to you, then, about an image with which you are all familiar, but whose significance for human consciousness has gradually

---

3. From Rudolf Steiner, *Michaelmas and the Soul-Forces of Man*, pp.1–17.
4. The German word, *Gemüt*, is almost untranslatable. Rudolf Steiner says of it "this *Gemüt* lives in the center of soul life." The dictionary defines *Gemüt* as "heart, soul, or mind." But these must be thought of as one, not as separate. Hence the original translator proposes: "the mind warmed by a loving heart and stimulated by the soul's imaginative power."

or partly faded and partly suffered from misconception. I refer to the image of *Michael's conflict or battle with the Dragon.* Many people are still deeply affected by this image, but its more profound content is either only faintly understood or misunderstood. At best, the image makes no close contact with the human *Gemüt,* as it did once, even as late as the eighteenth century. People today have no understanding of the changes that have taken place in this respect, of how great a proportion of what so-called intelligent people today call fantastic visions constituted the most serious element of ancient world views. This is the case, above all, with the image of Michael's combat with the Dragon.

Nowadays, most people when they reflect on human evolution on the earth are inclined by a materialistic world view to trace the relatively more perfect human form further and further back to less perfect forms, to physical-animal forebears. In this way, they actually move away from contemporary human beings who can experience their own natures in an inner, psycho-spiritual way to arrive at far more material creatures from whom human beings are supposed to have descended—creatures standing much closer to material existence. In other words, people assume that matter has gradually evolved upward to the point where it experiences spirit. But that was not the view even in comparatively recent times. In fact, it was really the exact opposite.

Even as late as the eighteenth century, when those who had not been infected by the materialistic mentality and perspective cast their inner gaze back to prehistoric humankind, they saw their ancestors not as beings who were less human than themselves but as beings who were more spiritual. In fact, most people at that time were not yet materialistic. Looking back, they saw beings in whom spirituality was so inherent that they did not take on physical bodies as people on earth do today. Indeed, for them the earth as we know it did not even exist then. That is, looking back to their forebears, people in the eighteenth century still beheld beings who lived in a higher, more spiritual way than human beings of their time. These beings had bodies of much finer, more spiritual substance than we know today. They did not assign beings who were like present day humans to such a sphere, but more exalted beings —beings having at most an etheric body, but not a physical one. Such, approximately, were our ancestors as people in the eighteenth century still conceived them.

People used to look back to a time when there were no so-called higher animals either, when at most there existed only animals whose descendants of the jelly-fish kind live in the oceans today. On what was the ancestor of our earth, therefore, they imagined, so to speak, an animal kingdom on the plane below that of human beings; and, above this, a kingdom embracing only beings with at most an etheric body. In other words, what I enumerated in *Occult Science, an Outline*, as Beings of the higher Hierarchies would still be today, though in a different form, what was then considered in a certain sense the ancestry of humanity.

These beings—*Angeloi, Archangeloi,* and *Archai*—were not destined in their then stage of evolution to be free beings in the sense in which we speak of freedom in relation to human beings. These Beings did not experience the will in a way that could give them the unique feeling we humans express when we speak of "desiring something arbitrarily." These Beings desired nothing arbitrarily. They willed what flowed into their being as divine will, for they had completely identified their will with the divine will. The divine Beings ranking above them and signifying, in their interrelationships, the divine guidance of the world—these beings willed, in a sense, through the lower Spirits, the Archangels and Angels; so that the latter willed absolutely according to the purpose and in the sense of superior, divine-spiritual will.

The world of ideas of this older humanity was as follows. It was believed that in that ancient epoch the time had not yet come when beings could develop who would be conscious of the feeling of freedom. The divine-spiritual world-order had postponed to a later epoch the moment when a number of the Spirits, identified with the divine will, were to receive a free will of their own. This would occur when the right moment in world evolution was reached....

But then—as this ancient humanity saw it—a certain number of beings arose among these Spirits, who wanted to dissociate their will, as it were, emancipate it, from the divine will, although their true cosmic destiny was to remain identified with the will of the divine spirit. In superhuman pride, certain Beings revolted because they desired freedom of will before the time had come for their freedom to mature; and the most important of these beings, their leader, was conceived of as the Being who took shape in the *Dragon* that *Michael combats*—Michael, who remained above, in the realm of those spirits that wanted to continue molding their will to the divine-spiritual will above them.

By thus remaining steadfast within the divine-spiritual will, Michael received the impulse to deal adequately with the Spirit that grasped at freedom prematurely, if I may put it that way; for the forms possessed by Beings of the Hierarchy of the *Angeloi, Archangeloi*, and *Archai* were simply not adapted to beings destined to have a free will, that is, emancipated from divine will, as I have described. Such forms, namely, the human form were not to come into being until later in world evolution. All this is conceived as happening in a period when cosmic development of the human form was not yet possible; nor were higher animal forms possible—only the low ones I mentioned.

Thus a form had to come into being that might be called cosmically contradictory, and the refractory Spirit had to be poured into this mold, so to speak. It could neither be an animal form of the kind destined to appear only later, nor an animal form of that time, made of the then prevalent softer matter, so to speak. It could only be an animal form that differed from any that was possible in the physical world. At the same time, in order to represent a cosmic contradiction, it had to resemble an animal. And the only form that could be evolved out of what was possible at that time was the form of a Dragon. Naturally, when painted or otherwise represented, this Dragon has been interpreted in various ways throughout history— more or less suitably interpreted, according to what artists were able to cognize with inner imagination of a being that had developed a refractory will. In any case, this form is not to be found among those that became possible in the physical world in the animal range up to the human: it had to remain a supersensible being. As such, it could

not exist in the realm inhabited by the Beings of the higher Hierarchies—Angels, Archangels, and so forth. It had to be transferred, as
it were, and placed among the beings that could evolve in the
course of physical development. This is the story of "The Fall of the
Dragon from Heaven to Earth." It was Michael's deed to bestow this
form that is *supra-animalistic*—i.e., supersensible, but intolerable in
the supersensible realm. For although the Dragon is supersensible,
it is incompatible with the realm of the supersensible where it
existed before it rebelled.

Thus this Dragon form was transferred to the physical world, but as
a superphysical, supersensible form. It lived thereafter in the realm
where the minerals, plants, and animals live: in what became the
earth. But it did not live there in a way that a human eye could perceive it as it does an ordinary animal. When the soul's eye is raised to
those worlds for which provision was made, so to speak, in the plan
of higher worlds, it beholds in its imaginations the Beings of the
higher Hierarchies. And when the human physical eye observes the
physical world it sees simply what has come into being in the various
kingdoms of nature, up to the form of the physical-sensible human
being. But when the soul's eye is directed to what physical nature
embraces, it beholds this inherently contradictory form of the Adversary, of the one who is like an animal and yet not like an animal, the
one who dwells in the visible world, yet is himself invisible: it beholds
the form of the Dragon. And in the whole genesis of the Dragon
human beings of old saw the act of Michael, who remained in the
realm of spirit in the form appropriate to that realm.

The earth then came into being, and with it, humanity; and
human beings were meant to become, in a sense, twofold beings.
With one part of their being, with their psycho-spiritual part, they
were to reach up into what is called the heavenly or supersensible
world; and with the other, with their physical-etheric part, they were
to belong to that nature which came into being as the nature of the
earth, a new cosmic body—the cosmic body to which the apostate
Spirit, the Adversary, was relegated. This is where human beings
had to come into being. They were the beings who, according to the
primordial decree that underlies all, belong in this world. Humanity

belongs on the earth. The Dragon did not belong on the earth, but had been transferred thither.

And now consider what humans encountered on the earth as they came into existence with it. They encountered what had evolved as outer nature from the previous kingdoms of nature, which tended toward and culminated in our present mineral, plant, and animal kingdoms, up to our own physical form. This is what humanity encountered—what we are accustomed to call extra-human nature. But what was this? It was, and still is today, the continuation of what was intended by the highest creative powers in the ongoing plan for the world's evolution. That is why as human beings, experiencing it in our *Gemüt or soul*, we can look out upon external nature—upon the minerals and all that is connected with the mineral world, upon the wondrous crystal formations, upon the mountains, the clouds, and all the other forms—and behold this outer nature in its condition of death, as it were, its condition of not being alive. But we see all this that is not alive as something that an earlier divine world discarded—just as the human corpse, though with a different significance, is discarded by the living person at death.

Although the visible aspect of the human corpse is not something that can impress us positively at first sight, yet in a certain sense it is a divine corpse, a corpse on a higher plane, that arose in the mineral kingdom and may be regarded as reflecting, in its form and shape, the originally formless-living Divinity. Indeed, what then comes into being as the higher kingdoms of nature can be regarded as further reflections of what originally existed as the formless Divine. In other words, someone can gaze upon the whole of nature and feel that this extra-human nature is a mirror of the Divine in this world.

And that, after all, is what nature is supposed to give to our human *Gemüt*: a mirror of the Divine. Naively, and not by means of speculation, we must be able to feel joy and harmony at the sight of this or that manifestation of nature. We must be able to feel inner jubilation and enthusiasm when we experience creative nature in its sprouting and blossoming. And our very unawareness of the cause of this elation, this enthusiasm, this overflowing joy in nature, should evoke deep down in our hearts the feeling that our *Gemüt* is so intimately related to nature that we can recognize, dimly, "All this nature the Gods have taken out of themselves and established in the world as their mirror—the same Gods from whom my *Gemüt* derives, from whom I myself spring but in a different way." All our inner elation and joy in nature, all that rises within us as a feeling of release when we participate vividly in the freshness of nature, all this should be attuned to the feeling of relationship between our human *Gemüt* and what lives out there in nature as a mirror of the Divinity....

Such was the feeling still cherished by many enlightened people even in the eighteenth century. They still felt vividly the difference between outer nature and what nature becomes after humans have devoured, breathed, and perceived it. They felt the difference between naive outer nature, as it is perceptible to the senses, and human, inwardly surging sensuality. This difference was still lovingly clear to many in the eighteenth century who experienced nature and humanity and described them to their pupils, described how nature and humanity are involved in the conflict between Michael and the Dragon.

Considering that this radical polaric contrast of outer nature in its essential innocence and inner, human nature in its corruption or guilt still occupied human souls in the eighteenth century, we must not forget the Dragon that Michael relegated to the world of nature because he found it unworthy to remain in the world of spirituality. Out in the world of minerals, plants, even of animals, the Dragon, whose form is incompatible with nature, assumed none of the forms of nature beings. It assumed the dragon form which today must seem fantastic to many of us, a form that must inevitably remain supersensible. It cannot enter a mineral, a plant, or an animal, nor can it enter a physical human body. But it can enter that which outer, innocent nature becomes, in the form of guilt in the upwelling life of instincts in the physical human body. Thus, as late as the eighteenth century, many people still said, "And the Dragon, the Old Serpent, was cast down out of heaven to earth, where it had no home; but then it built its bulwark in human nature, and now it is entrenched there."

In this way the mighty image of Michael and the Dragon was still an integral part of human cognition in those times. An anthroposophy appropriate to that period would have explained that by taking outer nature into oneself through nourishment, breathing, and perception, one creates within oneself a sphere of action for the Dragon. The Dragon lives in human nature. This idea lived clearly in the souls of people in the eighteenth century. Indeed, one can easily imagine that if they asked some clairvoyant being on another planet to draw a picture of the earth, this clairvoyant would have shown everything existing in the mineral, plant, and animal realms—in a word, in the extra-human realm—as bearing no trace of the Dragon, and to represent the earth-being the clairvoyant would have drawn the Dragon coiling through the animality in human beings.

Thus the situation had changed relative to what it had been in pre-human times. For pre-humanity, the conflict between Michael and the Dragon was located in outer objectivity, so to speak. But now the Dragon was *outwardly* nowhere to be found. Where then was it? Where would one have to look for it? Anywhere there were human beings on earth—that's where the Dragon was. If Michael wanted to carry on his mission, which in pre-human times lay in objective nature, when his task was to conquer the Dragon, the world-monster, externally, then he had to continue the struggle *within* human nature. This change from outward to inward occurred in the remote past and persisted into the eighteenth century. Those who held this view knew that they had transferred to the inner human being an event that formerly had been a cosmic one. In effect, they said: "Looking back to olden times, you must imagine that Michael cast the Dragon out of heaven down to earth—an event occurring in extra-human worlds. But now look at more recent times. Human beings come to earth, they take outer nature into themselves and transform it, and so help the Dragon take possession of it. Thus the conflict between Michael and the Dragon must now be carried out upon the earth."

Such trends of thought were not as abstract as people today would like thoughts to be. Today people like to get along with thoughts that are as obvious as possible. They put it this way: "Well, formerly an event like the conflict between Michael and the Dragon was simply thought of as external, but in the course of evolution humanity has turned inward; hence such an event is now perceived only inwardly." Truly, those who are content to stop at such abstractions are not to be envied, and in any case they fail to envision the course of the world history of human thought. For it happened as I have just presented it: *the outer cosmic conflict of Michael and the Dragon was transferred to the inner human being, because only in human nature could the Dragon now find its sphere of action.*

This moving of the Dragon into the human being brought the germination of human freedom into Michael's task. For if the conflict had simply continued within human beings in the same way that it had formerly taken place outside them, then human beings would have become complete automatons. By being transferred into the human interior, the struggle becomes, in a sense, to express it in an outer abstraction, a battle between higher and lower human natures. Now, the only form higher nature could assume for human consciousness was that of Michael in the supersensible worlds, to whom human beings were led to lift their gaze. As a matter of fact, in the eighteenth century, numerous guides and instructions still existed, all providing ways by which people could reach the sphere of Michael and, with the help of Michael's power, fight the Dragon dwelling in their animal natures.

A person, able to see into the deeper spiritual life of the eighteenth century, would have to be pictured somewhat as follows. Outwardly, there is the human form, in whose lower, animalistic portion the Dragon is writhing, even coiling, about the heart. And then as it were *behind* the person—for higher things are seen with the back of the head—there is the outer cosmic figure of Michael, towering, radiant, both retaining his cosmic nature and reflecting it into higher human nature, so that the person's etheric body etherically reflects Michael's cosmic figure. And then, in the head—but working down into the heart—one can see Michael's power or force crushing the Dragon and causing its blood to flow from the heart down to the limbs.

Such was the picture of the inner human struggle between Michael and the Dragon that many people still harbored in the eighteenth century. It was also the picture that suggested to many people that, as they put it, it was their duty to conquer the "lower" with the help of the "higher." In other words, it was a picture that taught people that they needed the power of Michael for their own lives.

Scientific intellect, on the other hand, sees the Kant-Laplace theory of the origin of the universe; it sees the Kant-Laplace primal vapor—perhaps even a spiral vapor. And out of this, the planets evolve, leaving the sun in the middle. And then, on one of these planets, the kingdoms of nature gradually arise; humanity comes into being. And, looking into the future, intellect sees all this passing over again into the great graveyard of natural existence. The intellect cannot help imagining the matter in this way; and because intellect has increasingly become the sole recognized authority on human cognition, philosophy has gradually become what it is today for humankind in general. But in all the earlier peoples of whom I have spoken the eye of the soul, as I might call it, was active. We can be isolated from the world in our intellects, for everyone has his or her own head and in that head his or her own thoughts. But in our *Gemüt* or soul, we cannot become isolated in this way, for the soul is not dependent on the head, but upon our rhythmic organism. The air I have within me at the present moment, I did not have within me a moment ago: it was the general air; and in another moment when I exhale it will be the general air again. It is only the head that isolates human beings, making of them *hermits on the earth*. In fact even in relation to our souls' physical organization, we are not isolated in this way, but rather belong to the cosmos, indeed are merely figures in the cosmos.

But gradually the *Gemüt*—the soul—lost its power of vision, and the head alone became seeing. The head by itself, however, develops only intellectuality: it isolates people. When human beings still saw with their souls, they did not project abstract thoughts into the cosmos with the object of interpreting or explaining it: they still saw great images into it, like that of Michael's battle with the Dragon. Such people saw what lived in their own nature and being, something that had evolved out of the world, the cosmos, as I described it today. They saw the inner struggle of Michael come to life in the human being, in the *anthropos*. They saw this inner Michael struggle take the place of the outer cosmic Michael struggle. They saw *anthroposophy* develop out of *cosmosophy*. Whenever we turn from the abstract thoughts that affect us as cold and matter-of-fact, whose intellectuality makes us shiver and look back to an older world view, we find ourselves guided to *images*, one of the greatest of which is Michael's war with the Dragon—Michael, who first cast the Dragon to earth where (I may say) the Dragon could take up his human fortress; Michael, who then became the fighter of the Dragon in humanity, as I have described.

In the picture that I have evoked for you today, Michael stands cosmically behind us, while within us is an etheric image of Michael. This image carries out the real struggle by which human beings themselves, participating in Michael's battle, can gradually become free. For it is not Michael himself who wages the battle, but human devotion and the image of Michael that it calls forth. In the cosmic Michael there still lives that Being who engaged in the original cosmic struggle with the Dragon. We can look toward this Being. Truly, not upon earth alone do events take place—in fact earthly events remain incomprehensible to us unless we can see them as images of events in the supersensible world and to find their causes there. In this regard a deed was performed by Michael in the supersensible realm shortly before our time, a deed I should like to characterize in the following way. In doing so I must speak in a way that is discredited today as being anthropomorphic—and yet how could I relate what occurs in the supersensible world other than by using human words to describe it?

The epoch during which Michael cast the Dragon down to earth may be thought of as lying far back in pre-human times. But then, when humanity appears upon the earth, the war between Michael and the Dragon becomes ever more an inner struggle, until, at the end of the nineteenth century, Michael could say, "My image in humanity is now sufficiently condensed for human beings to be aware of it within themselves: they can now feel the Conqueror of the Dragon in their souls—or, at least, the image means something to them." The last third of the nineteenth century stands for something extraordinarily important in human evolution. In ancient times only a tenuous image of Michael existed in human beings; but this image condensed more and more, and in the last third of the nineteenth century the situation changed. In earlier times, the invisible, supersensible Dragon was predominantly active in the passions and instincts, desires and animal lusts. For ordinary consciousness, this Dragon remains subsensible. It lives in humanity's animal nature. It lives in all that tends to drag human beings down, in all that incites human beings to become more and more sub-human. This condition was such that Michael always intervened in human nature in order that humanity should not fall too low.

In the last third of the nineteenth century, however, Michael's image in human beings became so strong that now it depended as it were upon people's good will to consciously feel themselves upward and raise themselves to Michael's image—in order that, on the one hand, they might see the image of the Dragon in their unenlightened experience of the feelings while, on the other, the radiant figure of Michael may stand before their soul's eye: radiant in spiritual vision, yet within the reach of ordinary consciousness. Thus the content of the human soul can be this: "The power of the Dragon is working within me, trying to drag me down. I do not see it. I *feel* it as something that would drag me down below myself. But in the spirit I *see* the luminous Angel whose cosmic task has always been the vanquishing of the Dragon. I concentrate my soul upon this glowing figure, I let its light stream into my *Gemüt,* and thus my soul, illumined and warmed, will bear within it the strength of Michael. Hence, out of my own free resolution, I shall be able, through my alliance with Michael, to conquer the might of the Dragon in my lower nature."

If the good will necessary to raise such a conception to a religious force and so inscribe it in every human soul were widely available, then we would not have all the vague and impotent ideas such as prevail in every quarter today—plans for reforms, and the like. Rather, we would have something that could once more seize hold of the whole inner being, because something that can seize the inner being can be inscribed in the living *Gemüt,* which enters into a living relationship with the whole cosmos the moment it really comes to life.

Then those glowing thoughts of Michael would be the first harbingers of our ability to penetrate once more into the supersensible world. The striving for enlightenment would become inwardly and deeply religious. And thereby human beings would be prepared to celebrate the festivals of the year, whose understanding only glimmers faintly across the ages—but at least it glimmers. They would be prepared to celebrate in full consciousness the festival the calendar sets at the end of September, at the beginning of autumn, the Michael Festival, Michaelmas. For Michaelmas will regain its significance only when we are able to experience in our souls such a living vision. When we can feel this vision in a living way and can make it into an instinctive contemporary social impulse, then this Michael Festival—because the impulses spring directly from the spiritual world—could well be regarded as the crowning impulse of our time—indeed, even the initial impulse we need to find our way out of the present disaster. For it would add something real to all the talk about ideals, something not originating in human heads or hearts but in the cosmos.

And then, when trees shed their leaves and blossoms ripen into fruit, and nature sends us her first frost and prepares to sink into her winter death, we would be able to feel the burgeoning of spirit with which we should unite ourselves at Michaelmas, just as we feel the Easter Festival in sprouting, budding spring. Then, as citizens of the cosmos, we would be able to carry impulses into our lives which, because they are not abstract, would not remain ineffective but would reveal their power immediately. Indeed, until we can develop such cosmic impulses in our *Gemüt or soul,* life will not have a soul content again.

THREE

THE MICHAEL IMAGINATION [5]
Dornach, October 5, 1923

Today, I would like begin by reminding you how events that take place behind the veil of appearances, outside the physical, sense-perceptible world, can be described in pictorial terms. One has to speak in this way of these events, but the pictures correspond throughout with reality.

With regard to sense-perceptible events, we live in a time of hard tests for humanity, and these tests will become harder still. Many old forms of civilization, to which people still mistakenly cling, will sink into the abyss, and there will be an insistent demand that humanity must find its way to something new. In speaking of the course that the external human life will take in the near future, we cannot—as I have often said—arouse any kind of optimistic hopes. But a valid judgment as to the significance of external events cannot be formed unless we consider also the determining, directing cosmic events that occur behind the veil of the senses.

If we look attentively at our surroundings with our physical eyes and other senses, we perceive the physical environment of the earth, and the various kingdoms of nature within it. This is the milieu in which all that manifests as wind and weather in the course of the year comes to pass. When we direct our senses toward the external world, we have all this before us. These are the external facts. But behind the atmosphere, the sun-illuminated atmosphere, lies another world, perceptible by spiritual organs, as we may call them. Compared with the sense-world, this other world is a higher world, a world wherein a kind of light, a kind of spiritual or astral light, in which spiritual existence and spiritual deeds shine out and run their course. And these are truly no less significant for the whole development of the world and humanity than historical events taking place in the external environment of the earth and on its surface.

---

5. From: Rudolf Steiner, *The Four Seasons and the Archangels*, pp. 9–23.

Anyone today who is able to penetrate into these astral realms, wandering through them as one may wander among woods and mountains and find signposts at crossroads, may find "signposts" there in the astral light, inscribed in spiritual script. But these signposts have a quite special characteristic: they are not comprehensible without further explanation, even for someone who can "read" in the astral light. In the spiritual world and in its communications, things are not made as convenient as possible: anything one encounters there presents itself as a riddle to be solved. Only through inner investigation, through experiencing inwardly the riddle and much else, can one discover what the inscription on a spiritual signpost signifies.

Thus at this time—indeed for some decades now, but particularly at this time of hard trials for humankind—one can read in the astral light, as one goes about spiritually in these realms, a remarkable saying. It sounds like a prosaic comparison, but in this case, because of its inner significance, the prosaic does not remain prosaic. Just as we find notices to help us find our way—and we find signposts even in poetical landscapes—so we encounter an important spiritual signpost in the astral light. Time and time again, exactly repeated, we find there today the following saying, inscribed in highly significant spiritual script:

> O Humanity,
> You mold it to your service,
> You reveal it according to the value of its substance
> In many of your works.
> Yet it will bring you healing
> Only when it reveals to you
> The lofty power of its spirit.

Injunctions of this kind that point to facts significant for humanity are inscribed, as I have said, in the astral light. They present themselves first as a kind of riddle to be solved, so that human beings may bring their soul-forces into activity. Today we will contribute something to the solving of this verse—which is actually a simple saying, but an important one for humankind today.

Let us recall how in many of our studies here the course of the year has been brought before our souls.[6] In the beginning we observe it quite externally: when spring comes we see nature sprouting and budding; we see how plants grow and come to flower, how life everywhere springs up out of the soil. All this is enhanced as summer draws on; and in summer it rises to its highest level. Then, when autumn comes, it withers and fades away; and when winter comes it dies into the lap of the earth.

This cycle of the year—which in earlier times, when a more instinctive consciousness prevailed, was celebrated with festivals—has another side, which we have also mentioned here.[7] During winter the earth is united with the elemental spirits. They withdraw into the earth's interior and live there among the plant roots that are preparing for new growth, and among the other nature-beings who spend the winter there. Then, when spring comes, the earth breathes out its elemental being, as it were. The elemental spirits rise up as though from a tomb and ascend into the atmosphere. During winter they accepted the inner order of the earth, but now, as spring advances and especially as summer approaches, they receive more and more into their being and activity the order imposed upon them by the stars and the movements of the stars. Then, when high summer comes, there is a renewed surging of life in the earth's periphery among these elemental beings who had spent the winter in quiet and silence under the earth's mantle of snow. In the swirling and whirling of their dance they are governed by the reciprocal laws of planetary movement, by the pattern of the fixed stars, and so on. Then when autumn comes, the elemental beings turn towards the earth. As they approach it, they become subject more and more to its laws, so that in winter they can be breathed in again by the earth, once more to rest there in quietude.

Those who can experience the cycle of the year in this way feel that their whole human life is wonderfully enriched. Today—and it

---

6. See, for instance, *The Cycle of the Year as Breathing-Process of the Earth*; also, more generally, *The Festivals and their Meaning*.
7. For example, *Michaelmas and the Soul-Forces of Man*; also *Mystery Knowledge and Mystery Centers*.

has been so for some time past—we normally experience, and then but dimly and half-consciously, only the physical-etheric processes of the body occurring within the skin. We experience our breathing, the circulation of the blood. Everything that takes its course outside, in wind and weather, during the year; all that lives in the sprouting of the seed-forces, the fruiting of the earth-forces—all this is no less significant and decisive for the whole of human life, even though we are not conscious of it, than the breathing and blood-circulation which go on inside our skin.

When the sun rises over any region of the earth, we share in the effects of its warmth and light. And when we accept Anthroposophy in the right sense, reading it not like a sensational novel but so that what it imparts becomes the content of our mind, then we gradually educate heart and soul to experience all that goes on outside in the course of a year. Just as in the course of a day we experience early freshness, and readiness for work in the morning, and then the onset of hunger and of evening weariness, and just as we can trace the inner life and activity of the forces and substances within our skin, so, by taking to heart anthroposophical ideas—entirely different from the usual descriptions of sense-perceptible events—we can prepare our souls to become receptive to the activities that go on outside in the course of the year. We can continually deepen this sympathetic participation in the cycle of the year, and we can enrich it so that we do not live sourly—as one might say—within our skin, letting the outer world pass us by. On the contrary, we can enrich our experience so that we feel ourselves living in the blossoming of every flower, in the breaking open of the buds, in that wonderful secret of the morning, the glistening of dew-drops in the rays of the sun. In these ways, we can get beyond the dull, conventional way of reacting to the outer world that merely puts on an overcoat in winter and lighter clothes in summer and takes an umbrella when it rains. Only by going out of ourselves so that we experience the interweaving activity, the flow and ebb, of nature, do we really understand the cycle of the year.

If we do that, then, when spring passes over the earth and summer is drawing near, we will be in the midst of it with our heart and soul; we will discern how the sprouting, budding life of nature unfolds, how the elemental spirits fly and whirl in a pattern laid down for them by planetary movements. Then, in high summer, we will go out of ourselves and share in the life of the cosmos. Certainly this will dampen down our own inner lives, but at the same time our experience of summer will lead us out—in a cosmic waking sleep, we might say—to enter into the doing of the planets.

Today, generally speaking, people feel they can enter into the life of nature only in the season of growth—of germination, budding, flowering, and fruiting. Even if they cannot fully experience all this, they have more sympathy and perception for it than they have for the autumnal season of fading and dying away. In truth, however, we earn the right to enter into the spring season of growth only if we can also enter into the time when summer wanes and autumn draws on: the season of sinking down and dying that comes with winter. And if, during high summer, we rise inwardly, in cosmic waking sleep, with the elemental beings to the region where planetary activity in the outer world can be inwardly experienced, then we ought equally to sink ourselves down under the frost and snow-mantle of winter, so that we enter into the secrets of the womb of the earth during midwinter. And we ought, too, to participate in the fading and dying-off of nature when autumn begins.

If we are to participate in nature's waning, as we do in nature's growing, we can do so only if in a certain sense we can experience the dying away of nature in our inner being. For if we become more sensitive to the secret workings of nature, and thus participate actively in nature's germinating and fruiting, it follows that we will lovingly experience also the effects of autumn in the outer world. But it would bring us no comfort if we were to experience this only in the form it takes in nature, if we were to come only to a nature-consciousness of the secret of autumn and winter—as we readily do regarding the secrets of spring and summer. When the events of autumn and winter draw on, when Michaelmas comes, we certainly must enter sensitively into the processes of fading and dying; but we must not, as we do in summer, give ourselves over to a nature-consciousness. On the contrary, we must then devote ourselves to *self-consciousness.* When external nature is dying, we must oppose nature-consciousness with the force of self-consciousness.

Then the form of Michael stands before us again. If, under the impulse of Anthroposophy, we enter thus into the enjoyment of nature, the consciousness of nature, but also awake in ourselves an autumnal self-consciousness, then the image of Michael and the Dragon will stand majestically before us, revealing pictorially how nature-consciousness is overcome by self-consciousness when autumn draws near. This will happen if we can experience not only an inner spring and summer, but also a dying, death-bringing autumn and winter. This will make it possible for the picture of Michael and the Dragon to appear again as a forcible Imagination, summoning us to inner activity.

For those of us who out of present spiritual knowledge wrestle our way through to an experience of this picture, it expresses something very powerful. For when, following St. John's Tide,[8] July, August and September draw on, we realize how we have been living through a waking-sleep of inner planetary experience together with the earth's elemental beings, and we become aware of what this really signifies.

It signifies an inner process of combustion, but we must not picture this as being like external combustion. All the processes which take a definite form in the outer world occur also within the human organism, but in a different guise. And so it is a fact that these inner processes reflect the year's changing course.

The inner process which occurs during high summer is a permeation of the organism by what is represented crudely in the material world as *sulphur.* When we live with the summer sun and its effects, we experience a sulphurizing process in our physical-etheric being. The sulphur that we carry within us as a useful substance has a special importance for us in high summer, an importance quite different from its importance at other seasons. It becomes a kind of combustion process. It is natural for humans that the sulphur within

---

8. See Rudolf Steiner, "The St. John Imagination" in *The Four Seasons and the Archangels.*

us should thus rise at midsummer to a specially enhanced condition. Material substances in different beings have secrets not dreamt
of by materialistic science.

Everything that is physical-etheric in human beings is thus glowed
through at midsummer with inward sulphur-fire, to use Jacob Boehme's expression.[9] It is a gentle, intimate process, not perceptible
by ordinary consciousness, but—as is generally true of other such
processes—it has a tremendous, decisive significance for events in
the cosmos.

This sulphurizing process in human bodies at midsummer,
although it is so mild and gentle and imperceptible to us, has a
great importance to the evolution of the cosmos. A great deal happens out there in the cosmos when in summer human beings shine
inwardly with the sulphur-process. It is not only the physically visible
glow-worms (*Johannis Käferchen*[10]) which shine out around St. John's
Day. Seen from other planets, the inner being of humans then
begins to shine, becoming visible as a being of light to the etheric
eyes of other planetary beings. That is the sulphurizing process. At
the height of summer, human beings begin to shine out into cosmic
space as brightly for other planetary beings as glow-worms shine
with their own light in the meadows at St. John's Tide.

From the standpoint of the cosmos, this is a majestically beautiful
sight, for human beings shine out into the cosmos in glorious astral
light during high summer, but at the same time it gives occasion for
the Ahrimanic power to draw near to humanity. For this Ahrimanic
power is closely related to the sulphurizing process in the human
organism. We can see, on the one hand, how human beings shine out
into the cosmos in the St. John's light, and on the other how the
Dragonlike serpent-form of Ahriman winds its way among the human
beings shining in the astral light, trying to ensnare and embrace
them, to draw them down into the realm of half-conscious sleep and

---

9. Jacob Boehme, 1575–1624, German mystic and Hermetic cosmologist, was a
central figure in the development of esoteric philosophy, idealism, Romanticism
and protestant theology (from the Quakers and Pietists to Paul Tillich). See Rudolf Steiner, *Mysticism at the Dawn of the Modern Age.*
10. Literally, "John's bugs."

dreams. There, caught in this web of illusion, human beings would become world-dreamers, and in this condition they would be a prey to the Ahrimanic powers. All this is significant for the cosmos also.

And when in high summer, from a particular constellation, meteors fall in great showers of cosmic iron, then this cosmic iron, which carries an enormously powerful healing force, is the weapon which the Gods bring to bear against Ahriman, as he seeks Dragonlike to coil round the shining human forms. The force which falls on the earth in the meteoric iron is truly a cosmic force whereby the higher Gods endeavor to gain a victory over the Ahrimanic powers, when autumn approaches. And this majestic display in cosmic space, when the August meteor showers stream down into the human being shining in the astral light, has its counterpart—so gentle and apparently so small—in a change that occurs in the human blood. This human blood, which is in truth not such a material thing as contemporary science imagines, but is permeated throughout by impulses from soul and spirit, is rayed through by the force which is carried as iron into the blood and wages war there on anxiety, fear, and hate. The processes which are set going in every blood corpuscle when the force of iron shoots into it are the same, on a minute human scale, as those which take place when meteors fall in a shining stream through the air. This permeation of human blood by the anxiety-dispelling force of iron is a meteoric activity. The effect of the raying in of the iron is to drive fear and anxiety out of the blood.

And so, while the Gods with their meteors wage war on the Spirit who would like to radiate fear over all the earth by his coiling serpentine form, and while they cause iron to stream radiantly into this fear-tainted atmosphere, which reaches its peak when autumn approaches or when summer wanes—so the same process occurs inwardly in humans, when their blood is permeated with iron. We can understand these things only if, on the one hand, we understand their inner spiritual significance and, on the other, if we recognize how the sulphur-process and the iron-process in human beings are connected with corresponding events in the cosmos.

Those who look out into space and see a shooting star should say to themselves with reverence for the Gods: "That occurrence in the great expanse of space has its minute counterpart continuously in myself. There are the shooting stars, while in every one of my blood corpuscles iron is taking form. My life is full of shooting stars, miniature shooting stars." And this inner fall of shooting stars, pointing to the life of the blood, is especially important when autumn approaches, when the sulphur-process is at its peak. For when people are shining like glow-worms in the way I have described, then the counter-force is present also, for millions of tiny meteors are scintillating inwardly in their blood.

This is the connection between the inner human being and the universe. And then we can see how, especially when autumn is approaching, there is a great raying-out of sulphur from the nervous system toward the brain. The whole person can then be seen as a sulphur-illuminated phantom, so to speak.

But raying into this bluish-yellow sulphur atmosphere come the meteor swarms from the blood. That is the other phantom. While the sulphur-phantom rises in clouds from our lower parts toward our head, the iron-forming process rays out from our heads, pouring itself like a stream of meteors into the life of the blood.

Such are human beings, when Michaelmas draws near. We must learn to make conscious use of the meteoric-force in our blood. We must learn to keep the Michael Festival by making it a festival for the conquest of anxiety and fear, a festival of inner strength and initiative—*a festival for the commemoration of selfless self-consciousness.*

Just as we celebrate the Redeemer's birth at Christmas and at Easter we celebrate His death and resurrection, and as at St. John's Tide we celebrate the outpouring of human souls into cosmic space, so at Michaelmas—if the Michael Festival is to be rightly understood—we must celebrate that which lives spiritually in the sulphurizing and meteorizing process in human beings. Especially at Michaelmas we should stand before human consciousness in its whole soul-spiritual significance. Then we will be able to say to ourselves: "You will become lord of this process, which otherwise takes its natural course outside your consciousness, if (just as you bow thankfully before the birth of the Redeemer at Christmas and experience Easter with deep inner response) you now learn to experience how during this autumn festival of Michael there should grow in you all that goes against love of ease, against anxiety, and makes for the unfolding of inner initiative and free, strong, courageous will." The Festival of Strong Will: that is how we should conceive of the Michael Festival. If that is done, if the knowledge of nature becomes true, spiritual human self-consciousness, then the Michael Festival will shine out in its true colors.

But before human beings can think of celebrating the Michael Festival, there will have to be a renewal in human souls. It is the renewal of the whole human soul-disposition that should be celebrated at the Michael Festival—not as an outward or conventional ceremony, but as a festival which renews the whole inner person.

Then, out of all I have described, the majestic image of Michael and the Dragon will arise once more. But this picture of Michael and the Dragon paints itself out of the cosmos. The Dragon paints itself for us, forming its body out of bluish-yellow sulphur streams. We see the Dragon shaping itself in shimmering clouds of radiance out of the sulphur-vapors; and over the Dragon rises the figure of Michael: Michael with his sword.

We shall picture this rightly only if we see the space where Michael displays his power and his lordship over the Dragon as filled not with indifferent clouds but with showers of meteoric iron. These showers take form from the power that streams out from Michael's heart; they are welded together into the sword of Michael, who overcomes the Dragon with his sword of meteoric iron.

If we understand what is going on in the universe and in human beings, then the cosmos paints out of its own forces. Then in our paintings we will not lay on this or that color according to human ideas, but will paint, in harmony with divine powers, the world which expresses their being, the whole being of Michael and the Dragon, as it can hover before us. Ancient pictures and images can be renewed if we can paint in this way out of direct contemplation of the cosmos. Then our pictures will show what is really there, and not what fanciful individuals may somehow portray in images of Michael and the Dragon.

Then humanity will come to understand these things, and to reflect on them with understanding, and will bring mind and feeling and will to meet the autumn in the course of the year. Then at the beginning of autumn, at the Michael Festival, the picture of Michael with the Dragon will stand there to act as a powerful summons, a powerful spur to action, which must work on human beings in the midst of the events of our times. And then we shall understand how this impulse points symbolically to something in which the whole destiny, perhaps indeed the tragedy, of our epoch is being played out.

During the last three or four centuries we have developed a magnificent natural science and a far-reaching technology, based on the most widely-distributed material to be found on earth. We have learned to make out of iron nearly all the most essential and important things produced by humankind in a materialistic age. In our locomotives, our factories, on all sides we see how we have built up this whole material civilization on iron, or on steel, which is only iron transformed. And all the uses to which iron is put are a symbolic indication of how we have built our whole life and outlook out of matter and want to go on doing so. But that is a downward-leading path. We can rescue ourselves from these impending dangers only if we start to spiritualize life in this very domain where iron is used, if we penetrate through what surrounds it to the spiritual. We must turn from the iron which is used for making engines and look up again to the meteoric iron which showers down from the cosmos to the earth and is the outer material from which the power of Michael is forged. Humanity must come to see the great significance of the following words: "Here on earth, in this epoch of materialism, you have made use of iron, in accordance with the insight gained from your observation of matter. Just as you must transform your vision of matter through the development of natural science into Spiritual Science, so must you rise from your former idea of iron to a perception of meteoric iron, the iron of Michael's sword. Then healing will come from what you can make of it."

This is the content of the saying:

O Humanity,
You mold it (iron) to your service,
You reveal it (iron) according to the value of its substance
In many of your works.
Yet it will bring you healing
Only when it reveals to you
The lofty power of its spirit.

That is, the lofty power of Michael, with the sword he has welded together in cosmic space out of meteoric iron. Healing will come when our material civilization proves capable of spiritualizing the power of iron into the power of Michael-Iron, which gives human beings self-consciousness instead of mere nature-consciousness.

FOUR

THE TASKS OF THE MICHAEL AGE[11]
Dornach, January 13, 1924

The Michael period into which the world entered in the last third of the nineteenth century, and into which humanity must now enter with increasing consciousness, is very different from former periods of Michael leadership. You know, of course, that as evolution goes forward, the seven great Archangelic Spirits enter human life from time to time, one after another. Thus, after a certain time has elapsed, a particular guidance of the world—the guidance of Gabriel or Uriel, Raphael, or Michael—is repeated. Our present Michael period is, however, essentially different from the preceding periods of Michael. This is due to the fact that, since the first third of the fifteenth century, humanity has been standing in a quite different relation to the spiritual world than ever before. And this new relation to the spiritual world necessarily alters the character of a

11. From: Rudolf Steiner, *Rosicrucianism and Modern Initiation*, pp. 83–98.

human being's relation to that Spirit now guiding the destinies of humankind, whom we call by the ancient name of Michael. Recently I have spoken to you again of the Rosicrucian Movement. Rosicrucianism, as I have shown you, degenerated in many quarters into charlatanry. Indeed, most of what has come down to us under that name is pure charlatanry. Nevertheless, as I have explained on many former occasions, an individuality did exist who may rightly be described by the name of Christian Rosenkreutz.[12] And he may be said, in a sense, to have set the example of how an enlightened individuality—a person who had knowledge of the spirit—could, at the dawn of the new phase of human evolution, enter into relation with the spiritual world.

Christian Rosenkreutz was allowed to ask many questions, to inquire concerning deeply significant riddles of existence in a way that was quite new when compared with earlier human experiences. For you must remember that *at the same time as* Rosicrucianism was arising and directing human minds—with "Faustian" endeavor, as it was sometimes called in later times—toward the spiritual world, abstract natural science was also arising. The bearers of this modern stream of spiritual life—people like Galileo, Giordano Bruno, Copernicus, or Kepler—worthy as they are of our fullest recognition, were in a different situation from the Rosicrucians, who wanted to foster, not a merely formal or abstract, but a true knowledge of the world. The Rosicrucians perceived how completely times had changed for the whole of human life, and therewith how completely the relation of the Gods to humankind had also changed. We might describe it as follows.

Until the fourth century A.D., and indeed as late as the twelfth or thirteenth century, human beings were still able to draw forth from themselves real knowledge of the spiritual world, even if this was only rudimentary. By practicing the exercises given in the ancient Mysteries, they could draw forth from themselves the secrets of

---

12. See Rudolf Steiner, *The Temple Legend*; *Theosophy of the Rosicrucian*; *Esoteric Christianity and the Mission of Christian Rosenkreutz*; also *A Christian Rosenkreutz Anthology* (edited by Paul M. Allen).

existence. For it really was the case in ancient humanity that what Initiates had to say to their fellow human beings, they drew forth from the depths of their own souls, brought it up to the surface of thought, to the world of ideas. They were quite conscious that they were drawing forth their knowledge from the inner being of the human soul. The spiritual exercises they undertook were intended, as you know, to shake the human heart to its depths, to induce in the heart and mind experiences a person does not undergo in the ordinary round of life. Thereby the secrets of the world of the Gods were, one might say, drawn forth from human depths, from the innermost being of humanity.

One cannot, however, *see* these secrets in the act of drawing them forth. In the old instinctive clairvoyance human beings did, it is true, behold the secrets of the world; they saw them in Imagination, heard them in Inspiration, united with them in Intuition. But all this is impossible as long as we stand there *alone*—just as little as it is possible for me to draw you a triangle without a blackboard to draw it on. The triangle I draw on the board portrays to me what I carry in a purely spiritual way within me. The triangle as a whole—all the laws of the triangle—are in me; and when I draw the triangle on the board, I bring home to myself what is really already there all the time within me. That is what happens when we draw diagrams. And it is the same when it is a question of deriving real knowledge out of our being—the being of humanity—as was done in the ancient Mysteries. This knowledge too must, in a sense, be *written* somewhere. Every such knowledge, if it is to be seen in the Spirit, must be inscribed in that which has been called from time immemorial the "astral light," i.e., in the fine substantiality of the Akasha. Everything must be written there; and human beings must be able to develop the faculty of writing in the astral light.

This faculty has depended on many different things in the course of human evolution. I do not intend to speak here of far-off pristine ages, and will leave on one side the first post-Atlantean epoch, the ancient Indian. At that time things were somewhat different. Let us begin then with the ancient Persian epoch, as you will find it described in *An Outline of Occult Science*. That time was one of instinctive clairvoyance. There was knowledge of the divine-spiritual world; and—inasmuch as the *earth,* the solid earth, afforded *resistance*—this knowledge could be written into the astral light for humanity to behold it. Such writing itself is done, needless to say, with spiritual organs; but even spiritual organs require a basis of resistance. The things that are seen in the Spirit are not, of course, inscribed onto the earth itself. Rather, they are written into the astral light, and the earth acts as a ground of resistance. In the old Persian epoch seers could feel the resistance of the earth; and only thereby could the perceptions they drew forth from their inner being grow into actual visions.

In the next epoch, the Egypto-Chaldean, all the knowledge that the Initiates drew forth from their souls was able to be written into the astral light with the help of the *fluid* element. One must have a clear and correct picture of this development from epoch to epoch. Initiates of the Old Persian epoch looked to the solid earth. Wherever they saw plants or stones around them, the astral light reflected the inner vision back to them. Initiates of the Egypto-Chaldean epoch, for their part, looked into the sea or the river—into the falling rain or the rising mist. Looking into the river or the sea, they saw the secrets that endure. But the secrets relative to the transient—to the creations of the Gods in things that are transient— these they beheld in the downpouring rain or the ascending mist. You must familiarize yourselves with the idea that the ancients did not look at mist and rain in the prosaic, matter-of-fact way that we do today. Rain and mist said a great deal to the Egypto-Chaldeans— revealed the secrets of the Gods to them.

Then, in the Greco-Latin period, the visions were like a *Fata Morgana* in the *air.* The Greeks saw Zeus, saw the Gods, in the astral light, but they had the feeling that the astral light only reflected the Gods under certain conditions. Hence the Greeks assigned their Gods to special places—places where the air could offer the resistance required for inscription in the astral light. Thus it remained until the fourth century after Christ. Even among the early Church Fathers, and above all among the Greek Fathers, there were many who—by means of the resistance of the air—saw this Fata Morgana of their own spiritual visions in the astral light. (You may find it confirmed in their writings.) Thus they had clear knowledge of the fact that the Logos, the Divine Word, revealed Himself out of human beings—through Nature. But in the course of time this knowledge faded, although feeble echoes of it still continued in a few specially gifted persons, even as late as the twelfth or thirteenth century. But when the age of abstract knowledge came—when human beings became entirely dependent on the logical sequence of ideas and the results of sense observation—then neither earth, water, nor air afforded resistance to the astral light, but only the element of the *warmth ether.* This is not known, of course, to those who are completely wrapped up in abstract thoughts. Such people have no idea that these abstract thoughts of theirs are written into the astral light. But indeed they are; and it is the element of warmth ether alone that affords them the resistance they need. And now we find the following.

Remember what I said, that in the ancient Persian epoch people had the solid earth as a resistance to behold what they had inscribed into the astral light. And what is thus received into the astral light— everything for which the solid earth is the resistance—rays out, but only as far as the sphere of the Moon. Further it cannot go. Thence, it rays back again. Hence it remains, so to speak, with the earth. Humans behold the secrets reflected by virtue of the earth; the secrets remain, however, because of the pressure of the lunar sphere.

Now let us look at the Egypto-Chaldean epoch. Here it is the water on the earth that reflects. What is thus reflected goes out as far as the Saturn sphere. And now it is Saturn that "presses," and so makes it possible for humans to "hold" on earth what they behold in Spirit. And if we go on into the Greco-Latin period—extending as it does right into the twelfth or thirteenth century—we find the visions inscribed in the astral light by virtue of the air. This time what is inscribed goes right to the boundary of the cosmic sphere before it returns. It is now much more fleeting; yet it is still such that one could remain united with one's visions. The Initiates of all these epochs therefore knew every time that such spiritual vision as they

had enjoyed—through the resistance of earth or water or air—
remained: the visions were there. But coming into modern times,
when only the element of the warmth ether was left to offer resistance, we find that the element of the warmth ether carries all that
is written into it out into cosmic realms, right out of space into the
spiritual worlds. It is no longer there!

It is so indeed, my friends. Take the most pedantic of modern professors with his ideas. He must of course *have* ideas—some of them
have none at all!—but assuming that the professor has ideas, then
through the instrumentality of the warmth ether these ideas are
gathered up in the astral light. But the warmth ether is transient
and fleeting; in it, everything immediately becomes merged and
fused, and goes out into the cosmic distances.

Such a person as Christian Rosenkreutz knew that the Initiates of
old had lived right with their visions. They had fastened and confirmed what they beheld, knowing that it was there, reflected somewhere in the heavens—be it in the Moon sphere or in the planetary
sphere, or at the end of the Universe. But now, nothing at all was
reflected. For the immediate, wide-awake vision of a human being,
nothing at all was reflected. People could discover ideas about
Nature, the Copernican cosmology could arise, all manner of ideas
could be evolved—but in the warmth ether these ideas were simply
scattered abroad and merged into the cosmic vastness.

Then it came about that Christian Rosenkreutz, under the inspiration of a higher Spirit, found a way to perceive the reflected radiation after all, in spite of the fact that one had to work with a
reflection depending on the warmth ether alone. This happened in
the following way. Other states of consciousness—dim, subconscious
and sleeplike—were called into play, states in which a person is *normally* outside the body. Then it became perceptible that what is discovered by means of modern abstract ideas is inscribed after all—
not in space, but written in the spiritual world. This, then, is what we
find in the Rosicrucian Movement. The Rosicrucians, living as they
were in a transitional stage, acquainted themselves with all that
could be discovered about nature in that epoch, received it into
themselves and assimilated it as only a human being can assimilate

it. What for others was science, they enhanced into true wisdom. Holding it in their souls, they then tried, after deep meditation, to pass into sleep in a condition of the highest possible purity. And thus it happened that the divine-spiritual worlds—no longer just the spatial end of the universe, but the divine-spiritual worlds them-selves—brought back to them in a *spiritually real language* what had first been apprehended in abstract ideas.

The Copernican cosmology, for example, was taught in Rosicru-cian schools; but in special states of consciousness the ideas con-tained in it came back in the form I have explained to you. It was the Rosicrucians, above all, who released that what a person receives in the form of modern knowledge must first be carried forth, so to speak, must first be *offered to the Gods,* so that the Gods may translate it into their language and then give it back again to human beings.

This possibility has remained up to the present. It is still true, my dear friends. If you are touched by the Rosicrucian principle of Ini-tiation as understood among us here, study the system of Haeckel, with all its materialism; study it, and at the same time permeate yourselves with the methods of cognition indicated in *How To Know Higher Worlds.* Take what you learn in Haeckel's *Anthropogenesis.*[13] In that form it may very likely repel you. Master it nevertheless; learn all that can be learned about it through studying today's natural sci-ence, and then carry it towards the Gods. If you do this, you will find what is said concerning evolution in *Occult Science.*

Such is the connection between the feeble, shadowy knowledge that we can acquire with the physical body and the knowledge the Gods can give us, if we first duly prepare ourselves by studying this external knowledge in the right spirit. For what a person can learn here on earth a person must first bring to the Gods. The times, you see, have changed!

Another thing has happened. Let people strive as they will today, they can no longer draw anything forth from themselves as an-cient Initiates once did. It all becomes impure, permeated with

---

13. A*nthropogenie oder Entwickelungsgeschichte des menschen* [Anthropogeny or the Evolutionary History of Humanity], 1874.

instincts—as is evident in the case of spiritualistic mediums, and other morbid or pathological conditions. All that arises merely from within becomes impure. The time for such creations from within is over and gone—actually it was already past in the twelfth or thirteenth century. What has happened can be expressed approximately as follows.

The Old Persian Initiates wrote a great deal into the astral light with the help of the resistance of the solid earth. When the first Initiate of the Old Persian epoch appeared, the whole of the astral light destined for humanity was like an unwritten slate.... The whole of Nature, all the elements—the solid, the liquid, the airy, and the warm—was then an unwritten slate and the Old Persian Initiates wrote on this slate as much as could be written by making use of the earth's resistance. This was how, to begin with, the secrets destined to come to humanity from the Gods were inscribed in the astral light. The tablet was then partially inscribed; yet, in another respect, it was still empty. Thus the Initiates of the Egypto-Chaldean epoch were able to continue the writing in their way, gaining their visions by the resistance of water. And so a second portion of the tablet was inscribed. Then came the Greek Initiates; they inscribed a third portion. And now the tablet of nature was fully inscribed. By the thirteenth or fourteenth century, it was fully inscribed.

Then human beings began to write into the warmth ether—the warmth-ether that is spread abroad, that disperses. For a time—until the nineteenth century—people continued to write in the warmth ether; they had, however, no inkling that these experiences of theirs are also inscribed in the astral light. But now, my dear friends, the time has come when human beings must recognize that it is not out of themselves, in the old sense, that they can find the secrets of the world, but only by preparing themselves in heart and mind to read what is written on the astral tablet which is now full of writing. This we must prepare to do today; for this we must make ourselves ripe. No longer have we to draw forth the truth from ourselves like Initiates of old; we must be able to read all that is written in the astral light. If we succeed in doing this, then what we gain from the warmth ether works as an inspiration. It works in such a way that the Gods come to meet us; they bring to us in its reality what we have acquired by our own efforts here on earth. And what we receive in this way from the warmth ether reacts in turn on all that stands written on the tablet by virtue of air, water and earth.

Thus natural science is today the true basis for spiritual seership. Learn first by the study of science to know the properties of air, water and earth. Then, having attained the corresponding inner faculties, you will find that as you gaze into the airy, the watery, and the earthly element, the astral light will stream forth—and not like some vague mist or cloud, but so that we can read in it the secrets of world-existence and the secrets of human life.

What, then, do we read there? We, the humanity of today, read what we ourselves have written in it. For what does it mean, to say that the ancient Greeks, Egyptians, Chaldeans, Persians wrote in the astral light? It means: *we ourselves wrote it there in our former lives on earth!*

You see, my dear friends, just as our own memory of the common things that we experience in earthly life preserves these things for us, so does the astral light preserve for us what we have written in it. The astral light is spread around us—a fully written tablet with respect to the secrets which we ourselves have inscribed. We must read, if we would rediscover the secrets of nature. A kind of *evolution memory* must arise in humankind. A consciousness must gradually arise that such a thing as an evolution memory exists, and that to recover former epochs of culture the humanity today must read in the astral light—just as we, individually, at a later age in life, read in our own youth with the help of our ordinary memory. This reality must come into human consciousness, and it is with this in view that I gave the lectures at Christmas.[14] I wanted you to see how we have to draw forth from the astral light the secrets that we need today. The old initiation was directed mainly to the *subjective* life; the new initiation concentrates on the *objective*. That is the great difference. For all that was subjective—all that the Gods have secreted into

---

14. See Rudolf Steiner, *The Christmas Conference (for the Foundation of the General Anthroposophical Society 1923/24)*.

humanity—has been written into the outer world. What they secreted in the sentient body came out in the Old Persian epoch; what they secreted in the intellectual or mind-soul came out during the Greek epoch. The spiritual soul we are now to evolve is independent; it brings forth nothing more out of itself. The spiritual soul stands over against what is already there. As human beings we must find our true humanity again in the astral light.

That, then, is how it was with the Rosicrucian Movement. In a time of transition, it had to content itself with entering into certain dreamlike conditions and, as it were, dreaming the higher truth of that which science discovers in a dry, matter-of-fact way, out of the nature that is all around us. But since the beginning of the Michael epoch, since the end of the 1870's, the situation has been different. The same thing that was attained in the time of the old Rosicrucians in the way described above, can now be attained in a conscious way. Today, therefore, we can say: We no longer need that other condition, which was half-conscious, what we need is a state of enhanced consciousness. Then, with the knowledge of nature which we acquire, we can dive into the higher world; and the knowledge we have acquired will come to meet us from that higher world. We can read again what has been written in the astral light; and as we do so, it comes to meet us in spiritual reality. We carry up into a spiritual world the knowledge of nature attained here, or we carry up thither the creations of naturalistic art, or again the feelings we develop out of a religion that works naturalistically in the soul—for even religion has become naturalistic nowadays. And as we carry all this up into the spiritual, then, provided we develop the necessary faculties, we do indeed encounter Michael.

So we may say: the old Rosicrucian Movement is characterized by the fact that its most illumined spirits had an intense longing to meet Michael; but they could only do so, as it were, in *dream*. Since the end of the last third of the nineteenth century, human beings can meet Michael in the Spirit, in a *fully conscious* way.

Michael, however, is a Being with this peculiar characteristic: He reveals nothing if we ourselves do not bring him something from our diligent spiritual work on earth. Michael is a silent spirit, silent and reserved. The other ruling Archangels are Spirits who talk a great deal—in a spiritual sense, of course. But Michael is taciturn. He is a Spirit who says very little. At most he will now and then give brief directions. What we have to learn from Michael is not really the word, but, if I may so express it, the *look*; it is the power, the direction, of his gaze that we must learn from.

This is because Michael concerns himself most of all with *what* humanity creates out of the Spirit. Michael lives with the consequences of what human beings have created. The other Spirits live more with the cause; Michael lives with the consequences. The other Spirits kindle in human beings the impulses for what they ought to do. Michael wants to be the spiritual hero of freedom; Michael allows people to act, and then takes what becomes of human deeds, receives it and carries it on and out into the cosmos, to continue in the cosmos what humans themselves cannot yet do with it.

With other Beings of the Hierarchy of Archangels, we have the feeling that impulses are coming toward us from them. In greater or lesser degree, impulses to do this or that come from them. Michael is the Spirit from whom in our time impulses do not come; for the present Michael Age is his most characteristic epoch. It is the epoch, namely, when things are to arise out of human freedom. But when a person has once done something out of his or her own inner freedom, consciously or unconsciously kindled by the reading of the astral light, then Michael carries that human earthly deed out into the cosmos, that it may become a cosmic deed. Michael takes care of the results, the other Spirits are concerned rather with causes.

Michael is, however, not merely a silent, taciturn Spirit. In relation to many things on earth with which a human being still lives today, Michael meets humanity with a very clear gesture of repulsion. For example, we can feel how Michael constantly repels and pushes aside with a gesture of deprecation all knowledge about human, animal, or plant life that tends to lay stress on inherited characteristics, on all that is inherited in physical nature. Michael means to show that such knowledge cannot help human beings at all in relation to the spiritual world. What we can discover in the human and animal and plant kingdoms that is independent of the purely hereditary nature—that alone can be carried up before Michael. *Then* we receive, not the eloquent gesture of deprecation, but the look of approval telling us that it is a thought rightly conceived in harmony with cosmic guidance. For this is what we learn increasingly to strive for: so to direct our thoughts that we may strike through to the astral light and behold the secrets of existence, and then come before Michael and receive his approving look telling us, That is right, that is in harmony with the cosmic guidance.

Michael also sternly rejects all separating elements—such as human languages. So long as we only clothe our knowledge each in our own language, and do not carry it right up into the *thoughts*, we cannot come near Michael. On this account, there is a very significant battle waging today in the spiritual world. On the one hand, the Michael-Impulse has entered the human evolution. The Michael-Impulse is there. On the other hand, there is much in human evolution that does not want to receive the Michael-Impulse, that wants to reject it. Among the things that would reject the Impulse of Michael today are feelings of nationality. They flared up in the nineteenth century, and have become strong in the twentieth—stronger and stronger. Many things have been ordered—or rather, sadly disordered—in accordance with this principle of nationality.

This is in direct opposition to the Michael principle. It contains Ahrimanic forces that strive against the inpouring of the Michael-Forces into the earthly human life. Thus we see this war being waged by upward-attacking Ahrimanic spirits who would like to carry upward what comes from the inherited impulses of nationality, which Michael sternly rejects and repels.

A most lively spiritual conflict is in fact being waged today in this direction—for this is the state of affairs over a great portion of humankind. Thoughts are not present at all; people think only in words, and to think in words is no way to approach Michael. We come to Michael only when we get through the words to real inner experiences of the spirit—when we cease to hang on to words, and come through to real inner experiences of the spirit.

This is the very essence, the secret of modern Initiation: to get beyond words, to a living experience of the spirit. It is in no way contrary to a feeling for the beauty of language. Precisely when we no longer *think* in language, we begin to *feel* it. As a true element of feeling, it begins to live in us and flow outward from us. This is the experience to which a human being today must aspire. Perhaps, to begin with, we cannot attain this experience in speech. Perhaps we can more readily find our way to it through writing. For with regard to writing, too, it must be said that human beings today do not *have* writing; writing *has them.* What do I mean by this? I mean that in our wrist, in our hand, we have a certain train of writing. We write mechanically, out of the hand. This is a thing that fetters us. We only become unfettered when we write as we paint or draw—when every letter as it stands beside the next becomes for us a thing that is painted or drawn. Then there is no longer what is ordinarily called a "handwriting." *We draw* the *form* of the letter. Our relation to the letter is objective; we see it before us—that is the essential thing.

For this reason, strange as it may sound, in certain Rosicrucian schools learning to write was prohibited up to the fourteenth or fifteenth year of age; so that the form, the mechanism which comes to expression in writing, did not enter the human organism. Only when one's intelligence was more developed did one approach the form of the letter, and then it was so arranged that simultaneously with learning the conventional letters, needed for human intercourse, one had to learn other, specifically Rosicrucian letters, which are now supposed to have been a secret script. But that was not intended; the idea was that for an A one should learn at the same time another sign: O. For then, one would not hold fast to the sign, but get free of it and feel the real A as something higher than any mere sign, be it A or O. Otherwise, the *letter* would be identified with that which comes forth from the human being, soaring and hovering around him or her as *sound.*

With Rosicrucianism many things found their way to the people at large. It was one of their fundamental principles, that from the small circles in which they were united, Rosicrucians should go out into the world—generally working, as I have told you, as doctors of medicine. But, at the same time, while they practiced medicine, they spread knowledge of many things in the wide circles into which they came. Moreover, together with such knowledge, certain moods and feelings were spread. We find such moods and feelings wherever the Rosicrucian stream left its traces. Sometimes they even assume grotesque forms. For instance, out of such moods and feelings of soul, people came to regard the whole of our modern relationship to writing—and *a fortiori*, to printing—as a black art. For it is quite true, nothing hinders one more from reading in the astral light than ordinary writing. This artificial fixing hinders one very much from reading in the astral light. One has always first to overcome it when one wants to read in the astral light.

At this point two things come together, one of which I mentioned a short while ago. I told you how in the production of spiritual knowledge the human being must always be present with full *inner activity*. I confess that I myself have a number of notebooks in which I write or record in some way the results I come to. I generally do not look at them again! Only by calling into activity not the head alone but the whole person, one enables these perceptions—which must indeed take hold of the entire being—to come forth, to find expression. A person who does this will gradually grow accustomed not to care so much for what he or she sees physically, and that is already fixed, but will try to remain in the *activity*, in order not to spoil the faculty of seeing in the astral light. It is good to practice this reticence. As far as possible, when fixing things in ordinary writing, one should not adhere to writing as such, but either draw and redraw the letters with a certain aesthetic pleasure (for then it is as though one were painting and it becomes an art). Certainly, one should abstain from reflecting upon what one has written. In this way one learns not to spoil the impressions in the astral light.

If we are obliged to relate to writing in the modern way, we mar our spiritual progress. For this reason, in Waldorf education, great care is taken that the child does not go so far in writing as is usual in the educational methods of today. Care is taken to enable him to remain within the spiritual, for that is essential.

The world today must find the way to accept once more the principle of initiation among the principles of civilization. Only thereby will it come about that human beings, here on earth, will gather in their souls something with which they can go before Michael, so as to meet Michael's approving gaze, the look that says: "That is right, that is cosmically right." Thereby the will is fastened and made firm, and thereby humanity is incorporated in the spiritual progress of the universe. Humanity itself thus becomes a co-worker in what Michael seeks to instill into human earthly evolution—beginning now in this present Michael epoch. . . .

FIVE

FROM THE GABRIEL TO THE MICHAEL AGE[15]
Arnhem, July,19, 1924

. . . In speaking of a happening such as this Michael Event, we must always remember that the world develops by stages. When we study the evolution of the world with the faculties that we possess by virtue of our present human earthly life between birth and death, we see humanity evolving on the earth. We see ancient peoples arising from still earlier peoples. We see the Greeks and the Romans gradually emerge out of a background of very ancient Oriental civilizations—from the Indian, the Chinese, the Arabian and the Egypto-Chaldean- peoples. Then we come to the Middle Ages and finally to our own modern age with all its aberrations, but also with its great technical achievements. And not only is there this external development of peoples but behind it, as it were, evolution is also taking place. We can see, too, that this evolution is being undergone not only by humanity but also by spiritual Beings who are connected in certain ways with human evolution. In their ranks are the Beings

---

15. From: Rudolf Steiner, *Karmic Relationships (Esoteric Studies), Volume VI*, pp. 142–161.

called the *Angeloi*—Angels in Christian terminology. Angels are directly connected with the *individual* human being. Insofar as guidance from one earthly life to another is necessary, they lead or guide each individual. They are Guardians and Protectors whenever and wherever protection is needed. Thus, though supersensible and imperceptible to earthly sight, the *Angeloi* are directly connected with the evolution of humanity.

In the next immediately adjacent spiritual realm, the spiritual Beings whom we call the Hierarchy of the *Archangeloi*, the Archangels, unfold their activity. The *Archangeloi* have to do with much that also plays a part in the evolution of humanity. They have to do, not with the individual human being, but with groups of human beings. Thus, as I have said in many anthroposophical lectures, the evolution of the *peoples* is under the rulership of Archangelic Beings.[16] But it is also the case that certain epochs in earthly evolution receive their essential impulses from individual *Archangeloi*. For example, during the three centuries preceding the last third of the nineteenth century, namely during the nineteenth, eighteenth, seventeenth centuries and part of the sixteenth, we must think of the civilized world as being essentially under the dominion of the Archangel known to Christians capable of speaking of these things, as *Gabriel*. This period was therefore the Age of Gabriel.

This particular Gabriel Age is of great significance for the whole evolution of humanity in modern times. This significance derives from the fact that, since the time of the Mystery of Golgotha, human beings on earth have gradually been able to realize the following: Through the Mystery of Golgotha, Christ, the sublime Being of the Sun, has come down to the earth. He has descended from the Sun to the earth, entering into the body of Jesus and uniting Himself with the earth's destiny. But although the Christ Being has remained united with the earth, it was not possible during the successive Archangelic rulerships from the time of the Mystery of Golgotha to that of Gabriel, for the Christ -Impulse itself to actually lay hold of the inner physical and etheric forces of humanity. This

---

16. See this volume pp. 3–6.

first became possible under the Gabriel-Impulse which began to work about three hundred years before the last third of the nineteenth century. Thus, in reality, it is only since that time that *by way of the forces of heredity themselves* the Christ-Impulse has been able to penetrate humanity inwardly. As yet, this has not been achieved.

Gabriel rules over the whole realm of the physical forces of heredity within humanity. Gabriel is the supersensible Spirit who is connected essentially with the sequence of the generations, who is (if I may put it so) the great Guardian Spirit of mothers who bring the children into the world. Gabriel has to do with births, with the embryonic development of human beings. The forces of Gabriel work in the *spiritual* processes underlying the physical process of reproduction. And so it is only since this recent Gabriel rulership that the physical reproduction of humanity on earth has come into connection in the real sense with the Christ-Impulse.

From the end of the 1870's, the rulership of *Michael* begins. It is a rulership altogether different in character from that of Gabriel. Whereas the rulership of the Archangel in the three preceding centuries comes to expression in spiritual impulses working in the physical, the rulership of Michael has above all to do with the powers of the intelligence in humankind—with everything, therefore, that has to do with human intellectual, spiritual, and cultural evolution. In any study of the earthly circumstances of humanity it is extremely important to realize that Gabriel's rulership, which in the spiritual sphere has an effect upon what is most deeply *physical,* is always followed by the regency of Michael, who has to do with the *spiritual* element in culture. The Archangel Gabriel is the divine Guardian of the process of physical propagation. But the Spirit who has to do with the development of the sciences, the arts, and the cultural element of the epoch, is the Archangel known in Christianity as Michael.

Seven successive Archangelic rulerships rule over the civilizations that are predominant in every epoch. Six other such rulerships have therefore preceded the present rulership of Michael. And if, beginning with Gabriel, we go backwards through these, we come to an epoch when Michael again held sway. Every such rulership, therefore, is always the repetition of earlier, identical rulerships, and the evolution of the Archangels themselves takes place through this cyclic progress. After a period of about two thousand years, the same Archangel always assumes the rulership again within the predominating civilization.

But these periods of rulership, each of which lasts for a little over three hundred years, are essentially different from one another. The difference is not always as great as it is between the rulerships of Michael and Gabriel, but the rulerships are, nevertheless, essentially different. And here we can say: Each reign of Gabriel is preparatory to an age when peoples become more widely separated from one another and more differentiated. In the age following his dominion nationalistic tendencies also become accentuated. So, if you ask why it is that such strong nationalistic feeling is asserting itself today under the rulership of Michael, which has now begun, the answer is that preparation took place spiritually a long time ago; the influence worked on and then began to decline, but the after-effects—often worse than the event itself—continue. Only by degrees can the impulse of Michael make its way into what is, to a great extent, a legacy from the past reign of Gabriel. But always, when an age of Michael dawns, a longing begins to arise in human beings to overcome racial distinctions and to spread through all the peoples living on the earth the highest and most spiritual form of culture produced by that particular age. Michael's rulership is always characterized by the growth of *cosmopolitanism*, by the spread of a spiritual impulse among peoples who are ready to receive it, no matter what language they speak. Of the seven Archangels who send their impulses into the evolution of humanity, Michael is always the one who gives the cosmopolitan impulse—and at the same time the impulse for the spreading of whatever is of most intrinsic value in a particular epoch.

If we turn now to earlier times in human evolution and ask ourselves in what period the previous Michael Age occurred, we come to the epoch which culminated in those cosmopolitan deeds springing from the impulse of the lofty spiritual culture of *Greece*, whose fruits were carried over to Asia through the campaigns of Alexander.

There, developing on the foundations of ancient culture, we see the urge to take the spiritual culture of Greece—the little country of Greece—over to the Oriental peoples, to Egypt. There is an urge to spread a cosmopolitan impulse in this way among all peoples able to receive it. This cosmopolitan impulse, this urge of the earlier Age of Michael, to spread over the world all that the Greek culture had achieved for humanity, was of the greatest possible significance. The crowning triumph of that Age was represented, in a certain sense, by the Egyptian city of Alexandria in its prime.

These things came to pass in the preceding Age of Michael. Thereafter, the other six Archangels assume in time their dominions. And in the last third of the nineteenth century, at the end of the seventies, a new Michael Age begins. But never yet in the whole of earthly evolution has the difference between two Ages of Michael been as great as that between the Michael Age at the time of Alexander and the one in which we have been living since the end of the 1870's. For between these two reigns of Michael falls the event which gives earthly evolution its true meaning: The Mystery of Golgotha.

Let us now consider what it is that Michael has to administer in the spiritual Cosmos. It is Michael's task to administer a power that is essentially *spiritual*, reaching its zenith in the human faculty of *intellectual understanding*. Michael is not the Spirit who, if I may put it so, cultivates intellectuality per se; the spirituality he bestows strives to bring enlightenment to humankind in the form of ideas and thoughts—but ideas and thoughts that grasp the spiritual. Michael's wish is that human beings shall be free beings—but beings who can see revelations from the spiritual worlds in what comes to them as concepts and thoughts.

And now think of the Michael Age at the time of Alexander. As I have so often said, human beings in our day are extremely clever. That is to say, they form concepts, they have ideas. They are intellectual, possessing as it were a *self-made* intellectuality. People were clever, too, in the days of Alexander. But if they had been asked in those times, Whence do you derive your concepts, your ideas? They would not have said, We have produced them out of ourselves. . . .

No, they received into themselves the spiritual revelations, and together with these revelations, the ideas. They did not regard the ideas as something which we evolve out of ourselves, but as something revealed to us by our spiritual nature. The task of Michael at that time was to administer this *heavenly* Intellectuality (intelligence or intellectual ability) in contrast to earthly intellectuality. Michael was the greatest of the Archangels who have their abode on the Sun. He was the Spirit who sent down from the Sun to the earth not only the Sun's physical-etheric rays but, in them, the inspired Intellectuality. And in those past times human beings knew: the power of Intelligence on earth is a gift of the heavens, of the Sun; it is sent down from the Sun. And the one who actually sends the spiritual Intellectuality down to the earth is Michael. In the ancient Sun Mysteries this wonderful Initiation-teaching was given: Michael dwells on the Sun; there he administers the Cosmic Intelligence. This Cosmic Intelligence, inspired into human beings, is a gift of Michael.

Then came the epoch when human beings were to be made ready to unfold intellect out of their own, individual soul forces; they were not merely to receive Cosmic Intelligence through revelation but to evolve Intelligence out of their inner forces. Preparation for this was made by Aristotelianism—that remarkable philosophy which arose in the twilight period of Greek culture and was the impulse underlying the campaigns of Alexander the Great in Africa and Asia.

By means of Aristotelianism, earthly Intelligence emerged as though from the shell of the Cosmic Intelligence. And from what came to be known as Aristotelian logic there arose that intellectual framework upon which the thinking of all subsequent centuries was based and which conditioned human intelligence.

And now you must conceive that through this single deed the Michael-Impulse culminated. earthly-human intelligence was established while, as a result of the campaigns of Alexander, the culture of Greece was imprinted upon those peoples who at that time were ready to receive the cosmopolitan impulse.

The epoch of Michael was followed by that of *Oriphiel.* The Archangel Oriphiel assumed dominion. The Mystery of Golgotha took place. At the beginning of the Christian era, those human souls who had been conscious of the leadership of the Archangel Michael in Alexander's time and had participated in the deeds of which I have just spoken, were gathered around Michael in the realm of the Sun. Michael had relinquished his dominion for the time being to Oriphiel, and in the realm of the Sun, together with those human souls who were to be his servants, Michael witnessed the departure of Christ from the Sun.

This, too, is something of which we must be mindful. Those human souls who are connected with the Anthroposophical Movement may say to themselves: We were united with Michael in the realm of the Sun. Christ, who hitherto had sent His Impulses towards the earth from the Sun, departed from the Sun in order to unite Himself with earthly evolution! Try to picture to yourselves this stupendous cosmic event that took place in realms beyond the earth. It lies within the mighty vistas open to those human souls who at that time were gathered around Michael as servants of the *Angeloi*, after Michael's rulership on earth had ended. In the realm of the Sun these souls witnessed the Christ's departure from the Sun. "He is departing...!" This was their great and overwhelming experience when Christ left in order to unite His destiny with the destiny of earthly humanity.

Truly, it is not only on the earth but in the life between death and rebirth that the souls of human beings receive the impulses for the paths they take. Above all, this was the case among those who had lived through the time of Alexander. A great and mighty impulse went forth from that moment in cosmic history when these souls witnessed the departure of Christ from the Sun. They saw clearly: Cosmic Intelligence is passing over gradually from the Cosmos to the earth! And Michael, together with those around him saw that all the Intelligence, which once streamed through the Cosmos, was now sinking down, stage by stage, upon the earth.

Michael and those who belonged to him—no matter whether they were in the spiritual world or incarnate for a brief earthly life— were able to visualize the rays of the Intelligence arriving, in the eighth century of the Christian era, in the earthly realm itself. And they knew that down upon the earth the Intelligence would unfold and develop further. Now, on the earth, the appearance of the first "self-made" thinkers could be observed. Hitherto, great human beings who were "thinkers" had received their thoughts by way of Inspiration. Thoughts had been inspired into them. Only now, from the eighth century A.D. were there those who could be called "self-made" thinkers—thinkers who produced their own thoughts out of themselves. And within the Archangelic host in the realm of the Sun, the mighty proclamation rang forth from Michael: The power belonging to my kingdom and under my administration in this realm is here no longer; it streams downwards to the earth and must there surge onwards!

This was the view of the earth as witnessed from the Sun from the eighth century onward. And within it was the great mystery: namely, that the forces which are pre-eminently the forces of Michael have descended from the heavens and are now upon the earth. This was the profound secret which was known to Initiates in Schools such as those I spoke of yesterday, for example, the renowned School of Chartres.[17] In earlier times, when men wished to discover the true nature of Intelligence they had been obliged, in the Mystery Centers, to look upward to the Sun. Now Intelligence was upon the earth, though not as yet very clearly perceptible. But, gradually, there was recognition that human beings were now evolving who possessed individual intelligence of their own. One of those in European civilization in whom the first sparks of personal thinking were alight was Johannes Scotus Eriugena.[18] I have often spoken of him. But there had been a few others, even before him, whose thoughts were not merely inspired, who no longer received revelations, but who could be called self-made thinkers. And now this individual thinking became more and more widespread.

---

17. Rudolf Steiner, *Karmic Relationships*, Volume VI, lecture VII; also *Karmic Relationships* generally, but above all volumes III and IV. Also René Querido, *The Golden Age of Chartres*.

18. See Rudolf Steiner, *The Riddles of Philosophy*; also *Occult History*, Lecture 3; *Man in the Light of Occultism, Theosophy and Philosophy*, lecture 4; also GA 204, lecture 15 (June 2, 1921); also Christopher Bamford, *The Voice of the Eagle*.

But the possibility existed of making this self-produced think-ing serve a particular end in earthly evolution. Consider what this self-produced thinking was: it was the sum-total of those impulses that had found their way to the earth from Michael's heavenly realm. And for the time being Michael was called upon to allow this Intelligence to unfold without his participation. Not until the year 1879 was he to re-assume his rulership. In the meantime, the Intelli-gence developed in such a way that he could not exercise dominion over the first stages. Michael could not exert influence over those who were unfolding their own, individual thoughts. His time, his rulership, had not yet come.

This profound secret of the descent of the Intelligence in the evo-lution of humanity was known in a few Mystery Centers over in the East. And so, within these particular Mysteries, a few chosen pupils were initiated into this secret by certain deeply spiritual, highly evolved people. Through dispensations of a nature which it is diffi-cult for the earthly intellect to comprehend, the illustrious Court[19] (of which I have spoken at the Goetheanum and in other places) came into touch with this secret of which certain Oriental Mysteries were fully cognizant. In the eighth and at the beginning of the ninth century, under the leadership of Haroun al Raschid, this Court wielded great power in Asia. Haroun al Raschid was a product of Arabian culture, a culture tinged with Muhammadanism. The secret of which I have spoke found its way to some of Haroun al Raschid's initiated Counselors—or to those who possessed at least a certain degree of knowledge—and the brilliance of his Court was due to the fact that it had come in touch with this secret. At this Court were concentrated all the treasures of wisdom, of art, of the truths of religious life to be found in the East—colored, of course, by Muhammadanism. In the days when, in Europe, at the Court of Charlemagne, who was a contemporary of Haroun al Raschid, peo-ple were still occupied in collating the first rudiments of grammar and everything was still in a state of semi-barbarism, there flour-ished in Baghdad that brilliant center of Oriental or, rather, western

19. See Rudolf Steiner, *Three Streams in Human Evolution.*

Asiatic spiritual life. Haroun al Raschid gathered around him men who were conversant with the great traditions of the Eastern Mysteries. And he had by his side one particular Counselor who had been an Initiate in earlier times and whose spiritual driving forces were still influenced by the previous incarnations. He was the organizer of all that was cultivated at the Court of Haroun al Raschid in the domains of geometry, chemistry, physics, music, architecture, and the other arts—above all, a distinguished art of poetry. In this renowned and scintillating assembly of sages, it was felt, more or less consciously: the earthly Intelligence that has come down from the heavens upon the earth must be placed in the service of Muhammadan spiritual life!

And now consider this: from the time of Muhammad and the early Caliphs onward, Arabian culture was carried from Asia across North Africa into Europe, where it spread as the result of warlike campaigns. And outstanding personalities came in the wake of those who by means of these campaigns spread Arabism as far as Spain and France and even, spiritually, the whole of western Europe. The wars waged by the Frankish kings against the Moors, against Arabism, are known to all of you...but that is the external aspect, that is what happens in outward history...much more important is to know how the spiritual streams flow perpetually within the evolution of humankind.

Haroun al Raschid and his wise Counselor passed through the gate of death. But they continued to pursue their earthly aims in remarkable ways after their life between death and rebirth. Their aim was to introduce Arabian modes of thinking into the European world with the help of the rudiments of the Intelligence now spreading in Europe. And so, after Haroun al Raschid had passed through the gate of death, while his soul was traversing spiritual, starry worlds, we see his gaze directed unswervingly from Baghdad across Asia Minor, to Greece, Rome, Spain, France, and then northwards to England. Throughout his life between death and rebirth his attention was directed to the South and West of Europe. And then Haroun al Raschid appeared again in a new incarnation—becoming Lord Bacon of Verulam. Bacon himself is the reincarnated Haroun al

Raschid, who in the intervening time between death and rebirth had worked as I have just described.

But the other, the one who had been his wise Counselor, chose a different direction—from Baghdad across the Black Sea, through Russia and then into Middle Europe. The two individualities took different paths and directions. Haroun al Raschid passed to his next earthly goal as Lord Bacon of Verulam; the wise Counselor during his life between death and a new birth did not divert his gaze from the sphere where influences from the East can be increasingly potent, and he appeared again as Amos Comenius (Komenski), the great educational reformer and author of *Pan-Sophia*. And from the interworking of these two individualities who had once been together at the Court in Baghdad there subsequently arose in Europe something which unfolded—more or less at a distance from Christianity—in the form of Arabism derived from influences of that past time when the Intelligence had first fallen away from Michael on the Sun.

What came outwardly and physically to expression in wars—in the Moorish invasion—was, as we know, repelled by the Frankish kings and the other European peoples. We see how the Arabian campaigns which with such a powerful initial impetus were responsible for the spread of Muhammadan culture, were broken and brought to a halt in the West; we see Muhammadanism disappearing from the West of Europe. Nevertheless, divested of the outer forms it had assumed and the external culture it had founded, this later Arabism became *modern natural science*, and also became the basis of what Amos Comenius achieved for the world in the domain of pedagogy. And in this way the earthly Intelligence, "garrisoned" as it were by Arabism, continued to spread right on into the seventeenth century.

Here we have indicated something that lies as substrata of the soil into which we today have to sow the seeds of Anthroposophy. We must ponder deeply over the inner and spiritual reality behind these things.

In Europe, while this stream was flowing over from Asia as the spiritual continuation of that illustrious Court of Baghdad, Christianity was also developing and spreading. But the spread of Arabism in

Europe was fraught with great difficulties. The natural science of Aristotle had been carried to Asia by the mighty deeds of Alexander and the impulses flowing from Hellenistic spiritual life, but it had been taken up by Arabism. In Europe, within the expanding Christian culture, Aristotelianism was at first known in a diluted form only. Then, in the manner which I have already indicated, it joined hands with Platonism—Platonism, which was based directly upon the ancient teachings of the Greek Mysteries.[20]

But at the very outset, Aristotelianism spread in Europe by slow degrees while Platonism took the lead and prompted the establishment of schools, one of the most important of which was the School of Chartres. At Chartres, in the twelfth century, the scholars of whom I spoke yesterday (Bernard Sylvestris, Bernard of Chartres, John of Salisbury and, foremost among them all, Alanus ab Insulis) were all working.[21] In this School people spoke very differently from those whose teachings were merely an echo of Arabism. The teachings given in the School of Chartres were pure, genuine Christianity, illumined by what still remained within human reach of the ancient Mystery Wisdom. Then something of immense significance took place. The leading teachers of Chartres, who had penetrated deeply into the secrets of Christianity with their Platonism and who had no part in Arabism, went through the gate of death. Then, for a brief period at the beginning of the thirteenth century, a great "heavenly conference'" took place. And when the most outstanding of the teachers—foremost among them, Alanus ab Insulis—had passed through death and were in the spiritual world, they united in a momentous cosmic deed with those who at that time were with them but who were destined in the very near future to come into earthly existence for the purpose of cultivating Aristotelianism in a new way. Among those preparing to descend were individualities who had participated with deep intensity of soul in the working of the Michael-Impulse during the time of Alexander. And at the turn of the twelfth century we may picture, for it is in keeping with the

20. See this volume, pp. 146 ff.
21. See this lecture, note 17.

truth, a gathering together of souls who had just arrived in the spiritual world from places of Christian Initiation—of which the School of Chartres was one—and souls who were on the point of descending to the earth. In the spiritual realms, these latter souls had preserved, not Platonism, but Aristotelianism, the *inner impulse of the Intelligence* deriving from the Michael Age in ancient times. Now, in the spiritual world, the souls gathered together ... among them, too, were souls who could say: We were with Michael and together with him we witnessed the Intelligence streaming down from the heavens upon the earth; we were united with him too in the mighty cosmopolitan Deed enacted in earlier times when the Intelligence was still administered from the Cosmos, when he was still the ruler and administrator of the Intelligence.

And now, for the time being, the teachers of Chartres handed over to the Aristotelians the administration and ordering of the affairs of spiritual life on earth. Those who were now to descend and were by nature fitted to direct the earthly, personal Intelligence, took over the guidance of spiritual life from the Platonists, who could work truly only when the Intelligence was being administered "from the heavens."

It was into the Dominican Order above all that those individualities in whose souls the Michael-Impulse was still echoing on from the previous Age of Michael, found their way. And from the Dominican Order issued that Scholasticism which wrestled through many a bitter but glorious battle to master the true nature and operation of the Intelligence within the human mind. Deeply rooted in the souls of those founders of Dominican Scholasticism in the thirteenth century was this great question: What is taking place in the domain of Michael?

There were some people, later known as nominalists, who said: Concepts and ideas are merely names, they have no reality. The Nominalists were under an Ahrimanic influence, for their real aim was to banish Michael's dominion from the earth. In asserting that ideas are only names and have no reality, their actual aim was to prevent Michael's dominion from prevailing on earth. And at that time the Ahrimanic spirits whispered to those who would lend their ear:

The Cosmic Intelligence has fallen away from Michael and is here, on the earth; we will not allow Michael to resume his rulership over the Intelligence! ... But in that heavenly conference—and precisely here lies its significance—Platonists and Aristotelians together formed a plan for the furtherance of the Michael-Impulses. In opposition to the Nominalists were the Realists of the Dominican Order, who maintained: Ideas and thoughts are spiritual realities contained within the phenomena of the world, they are not merely nominal.[22]

If one understands these things, one is often reminded of them in a really remarkable way. During my last years in Vienna, one of my acquaintances among other ordained priests was Vincent Knauer, the author of the work, *Haupt-probleme der Philosophie* (The Chief Problems of Philosophy), which I have often recommended.[23] In the nineteenth century he was still involved in this conflict between nominalism and realism. He was trying to make it clear that nominalism is fallacious, and he had chosen a very apt example to illustrate his arguments. It is also given in his books. But I remember with deep satisfaction a certain occasion when I was walking with him along the Währingstrasse in Vienna. We were speaking about nominalism and realism. With all his self-controlled enthusiasm—which had something remarkable about it, something of the quality of genuine philosophy in contrast to the philosophy of others who had more or less lost this quality—Knauer said: I always make it clear to my students that the ideas made manifest in the things of the world have reality—and I tell them to think of a lamb and a wolf. The nominalists would say: A lamb is muscle, bone, matter; a wolf is muscle, bone, matter. What receives objective existence in lamb—flesh as the form, the idea of the lamb— that is only a name. "Lamb" is a name there and not, as idea, a reality. Similarly, as idea, "wolf" is not anything real but only a name.

---

22. Cf. Steiner, *The Redemption of Thinking*.
23. Vincent Knauer, 1828–1894:"My old friend Vincent Knauer, the Benedectine monk, ... was, I might say, a saintly character."

But—Knauer went on—it is easy to refute the nominalists, for one need only say to them: Give a wolf nothing but lamb's flesh to eat for a time and no other food whatever. If the idea "lamb" contains no reality, is only a name, and if the lamb is nothing but matter, the wolf would gradually become a lamb. But it does not do so! On the contrary, it goes on being the reality "wolf." In what stands before us as the lamb, the idea "lamb" has, as it were, gathered the matter and cast it into the form. Similarly with the wolf: the idea "wolf" has gathered the matter and cast it into the form.

This was the fundamental issue in the conflict between the nominalists and the realists: the reality of what is apprehensible only by the intellect.

Thus we see that the task of the Dominicans was to work in advance, at the right time, for the next Michael rulership. And whereas in accordance with the decisions of that heavenly conference at the beginning of the thirteenth century, the Platonists—the teachers of Chartres, for example—remained in the spiritual world and had no incarnations of significance, the Aristotelians were to work at that time for the cultivation of the Intelligence on earth. And from Scholasticism—which only much later, in the modern age, was distorted, caricatured and made Ahrimanic by Rome—has proceeded all intellectual striving insofar as it has kept free from the influence of Arabism.

So at that time two streams of spiritual life are to be perceived in Middle and Western Europe; on the one side, there is the stream with which Bacon and Amos Comenius were connected; and, on the other side, there is the stream of Scholasticism that was and is *Christian Aristotelianism* and that takes its place in the evolution of civilization in order to prepare, as was its task, for the new Age of Michael. When, during the rulership of the preceding Archangels, the Scholastics looked up into the spiritual realms they said to themselves: Michael is yonder in the heights; his rulership must be awaited. But some preparation must be made for the time when he once again becomes the Regent of all that which, through the dispensation of cosmic evolution, fell away from him in the Cosmos. This time must be prepared for! ... And so a stream began to flow which, though diverted into a false channel through Ultramontanism, continued and carried with it the impulse of preparation proceeding from the thirteenth century.

It was a stream, therefore, whose source is Aristotelian and whose influence worked directly on the ordering of the Intelligence that was now in the earthly realm. With this stream is connected that of which I spoke yesterday, saying that one who had remained a little longer with Alanus ab Insulis in the spiritual world, came down as a Dominican and brought a message from Alanus ab Insulis to an older Dominican who had descended to the earth before him.[24]

An intense will was present in the spiritual life of Europe to *take a strong hold of thoughts*. In the realms above the earth these happenings led, at the beginning of the nineteenth century, to a great, far-reaching Act in the spiritual world, and what was later on to become *Anthroposophy* on the earth was cast into mighty Imaginations. In the first half of the nineteenth century, and even for a short period at the end of the eighteenth, those who had been Platonists under the teachers of Chartres, who were now living between death and rebirth, and those who had established Aristotelianism on earth and who had long ago passed through the gate of death—all of them were united in the heavenly realms in a great super-earthly Cult or Ritual. Through this Act all that in the twentieth century was to be spiritually established as the new Christianity after the beginning of the new Michael Age in the last third of the nineteenth century— all of this was cast into mighty Imaginations.

Many drops trickled through to the earth. Up above, in the spiritual world, in mighty, cosmic Imaginations, preparation was made for that creation of the Intelligence—an entirely spiritual creation—which was then to come forth as Anthroposophy. What trickled through made a very definite impression upon Goethe, coming to him in the form, as it were, of little reflected miniatures. The mighty pictures up above were not within Goethe's ken; he elaborated these little miniature pictures in his *Fairy Tale of the Green Snake and the Beautiful Lily*. Truly, it opens up a wonderful

---

24. See Steiner, *Karmic Relationships*, volume VI, lecture VII.

vista![25] The streams I have described flow on in such a way that they lead to those mighty Imaginations which take shape in the spiritual world under the guidance of Alanus ab Insulis and the others. Drops trickle through, and at the turn of the eighteenth century Goethe is inspired to write his Fairy Tale. It was, we might say, a first presentation of what had been cast in mighty Imaginations in the spiritual world at the beginning of the nineteenth, indeed by the end of the eighteenth century. In view of this great supersensible Cult during the first half of the nineteenth century, it will not surprise you that my first Mystery Play, *The Portal of Initiation*—which in a certain respect aimed at giving dramatic form to what had thus been enacted at the beginning of the nineteenth century—became in outer structure like what Goethe portrayed in his Fairy Tale. Having lived in the super-earthly realms in Imaginative form, Anthroposophy was to come down to the earth. Something came to pass in the super-earthly realms at that time. Numbers of souls who in many different epochs had been connected with Christianity came together with souls who had received its influences less directly. There were those who had lived on earth in the Age when the Mystery of Golgotha took place and also those who had lived on earth before it. The two groups of souls united in order that, in regions beyond the earth, Anthroposophy might be prepared. The individualities who, as I said, were around Alanus ab Insulis, and those who within the Dominican stream had established in Europe were united, too, with Brunetto Latini, the great teacher of Dante. And in this host of souls there were very many of those who, having again descended to the earth, are now coming together in the Anthroposophical Society. Those who feel the urge today to unite with one another in the Anthroposophical Society were together in supersensible regions at the beginning of the nineteenth century in order to participate in that mighty Imaginative Cult of which I have spoken.

---

25. *The Fairy Tale of the Green Snake and the Beautiful Lily* first appeared in 1795. It was then used as the conclusion of *The Conversations of German Emigrants*. These emigrants, uprooted by war, pass the time telling stories. There are several English editions.

This too is connected with the karma of the Anthroposophical Movement. It is something that one discovers, not from any rational observation of this Anthroposophical Movement in its external, earthly form only, but from observation of the threads that lead upwards into the spiritual realms. Then one perceives how this Anthroposophical Movement *descends*. At the end of the eighteenth and beginning of the nineteenth centuries it is, in very truth, a "heavenly" Anthroposophical Movement. What Goethe transformed into little miniature images in *The Fairy Tale of the Green Snake and the Beautiful Lily* were drops that had trickled through. But it was to come down in the real sense in the last third of the nineteenth century. Since then, Michael has been striving—moving downwards from the Sun to the earth—to take hold of the earthly Intelligence of men.

We know that since the Mystery of Golgotha Christ has been united with the earth—with humanity on earth. But, to begin with, Christ was not outwardly comprehended by human beings. We have seen also that in the age of Alexander the last phase of the rulership of Michael over the Cosmic Intelligence had descended to the earth. In accordance with the agreements reached with the Platonists, those who were connected with Michael undertook to prepare this earthly Intelligence in Scholastic realism in such a way that Michael would again be able to unite with it when, in the onward flow of civilization, he would assume his rulership at the end of the 1870s.

What matters now is that the Anthroposophical Society shall take up this, its inner task—this task which is: not to contest Michael's rulership of human thinking! Here there can be no question of fatalism. Here it can only be said that human beings must work together with the Gods. Michael inspires human beings with his own Being in order that there may appear on the earth a spirituality consonant with human personal Intelligence, in order that humans can be thinkers—and at the same time truly spiritual. This and this alone is what Michael's dominion means. This is what must be wrestled for in the Anthroposophical Movement. And then those who are working today for the Anthroposophical Movement will appear again on earth at the end of the twentieth century and will be united with the great teachers of Chartres. For according to the agreement reached in that heavenly conference at the beginning of the thirteenth century, the Aristotelians and the Platonists were to appear together, working for the ever-growing prosperity of the Anthroposophical Movement in the twentieth century, in order that at the end of this century, with Platonists and Aristotelians in unison, Anthroposophy may reach a certain culmination in earthly civilization. If it is possible to work in this way, in the way predestined by Michael, then Europe and modern civilization will emerge from decline.—but in no other way than this! The leading of civilization out of decline is bound up with an understanding of Michael.

I have now led you toward an understanding of the Michael Mystery reigning over the thinking and the spiritual striving of humankind. This means—as you can realize—that through Anthroposophy something must be introduced into the spiritual evolution of the earth, for all kinds of demonic, Ahrimanic powers are taking possession of humanity. The Ahrimanic powers in many human bodies exulted in their confidence that it would no longer be possible for Michael to take over his rulership of the Cosmic Intelligence that had fallen down to the earth. And this exultation was particularly strong in the middle of the nineteenth century, when Ahriman already believed: Michael will not recover his Cosmic Intelligence that made its way from the heavens to the earth. Truly great and mighty issues are now at stake! For this reason, it is not to be wondered at that those who stand in the midst of this battle have to go through many extraordinary experiences. . . .

This battle, more than any other, is laid in the *human heart.* There, within human hearts, it is and has been waged since the last third of the nineteenth century. Decisive indeed will be what human hearts do with this Michael Impulse in the world in the course of the twentieth century. And in the course of the twentieth century, when the first century after the close of *Kali Yuga* has ended, humanity will either stand at the grave of all civilization— or at the beginning of that Age when in the souls of human beings who unite Intelligence with Spirituality in their hearts, Michael's battle will be fought out to victory.

SIX

THE MICHAEL IMPULSE: TO READ
IN THE BOOK OF NATURE[26]
Dornach, August 1, 1924

...Now a great conflict arose in the Middle Ages between the leading personalities of the Dominican Order and those who, as a continuation of Asiatic Alexandrianism, found their way into Spain—
Averroes, for example.[27] What was the issue in this conflict? Averroes and those Muhammadan followers of Aristotle who sided with
him said, "Intelligence is universal, common to all." They spoke
only of a Pan-Intelligence—a universal Intelligence—not of an individual, human intelligence. To Averroes, individual human intelligence was only a kind of mirrored reflection of Intelligence in the
individual human head. In its reality, Intelligence had only general,
universal existence.

I will draw a mirror, thus, with nine parts (draws on blackboard). I
might equally well have drawn not only nine parts, but hundreds,
thousands, millions of parts. Over against the mirror is an object—
Intelligence—that will be reflected. Thus it was for Averroes, who
was so vigorously attacked by Thomas Aquinas.[28] For Averroes—in
the tradition of the old Michael epoch—Intelligence was Pan-Intelligence, a single Intelligence that several human heads reflected.
Once the human head ceased to work, the individual intelligence
ceased to be. But was this in fact true?

The truth is that what Averroes conceived *was* true until the end
of the Alexandrian age. Until the end of that age, it was simply a
cosmic and human fact. But Averroes held fast to it, while the
Dominicans received human evolution in themselves. Hence they

---

26. From: Rudolf Steiner, *Karmic Relationships (Esoteric Studies)*, vol. III, pp. 121–30.
27. Ibn Rushd (1126–1198). Islamic philosopher. Author of works on medicine,
religious law and philosophy, and above all Commentaries on Plato and Aristotle.
See also Steiner, *The Redemption of Thinking*, lecture II.
28. Thomas Aquinas, 1225–1274, *Doctor Angelicus*. Dominican religious philosopher and theologian. See also Rudolf Steiner, *The Redemption of Thinking*.

said, "It is not so." Of course, they might have said, "It was so once, but it is not so today." But they did not say this. They simply took as actual and true the condition of that time (the thirteenth century) which became even more so in the fourteenth and fifteenth centuries. They said, "Now everyone has their own intellect, their own intelligence."

This is what really happened. And to bring these matters to full clearness of understanding was the very task of the supersensible School I spoke of last Monday....[29]

Let us now enter a little into the more intimate details of the teachings of that supersensible School. For these teachings led to a knowledge of something, of which only a kind of shadowy reflection has existed in the human views of the world since ancient Hebrew times and in the Christian era. It exists, to this day (when a far deeper insight already ought to prevail) among most people only as a dim reflection of old traditions. I speak of the teaching concerning sin or the sinful human being—the being who was not predestined to descend so deeply into the material realm as actually occurred.

We can still find a good version of this teaching in Saint Martin, the "unknown Philosopher."[30] Saint Martin taught his pupils that originally, before earthly human evolution began, humanity stood at a certain height, from which it then sank down through a primeval sin, which Saint Martin describes as "Cosmic Adultery." By this primeval sin, humanity descended to that estate in which it finds itself today.

Saint Martin points here to something that is inherent in the doctrine of sin throughout human history and evolution; namely, the idea humanity does not stand at the high level at which it *could* be standing. All teachings about inherited or original sin are connected with this idea that humanity has descended from a height that was originally its own.

---

29. *Karmic Relationships*, vol. III, lecture VII.
30. Louis Claude de St. Martin, 1743–1803. Christian theosopher and philosopher. See also Rudolf Steiner, *Cosmic and Human Metamorphoses*, Lecture VII.

Now, following this idea to its conclusion, a conception of the world of a very definite shade or coloring gradually evolved. This kind of world view said in effect: "Human beings became sinful (and to become sinful means to fall from one's original height). And since they have in fact become sinful, they cannot see the world as they would have been able to see it in their sinless condition before the Fall. Thus they see the world darkly and dimly. They do not see it in its true form, but with many illusions and false fantasies. Above all, they do not see what they see in outer nature as it really is or with its true spiritual background. They see it in a material form which is not there in reality." Such was the meaning of the saying: Humanity is sinful. Such was its meaning in ancient times and is so still—in the traditions—often even to this day. Therefore upon earth too (and not only in the supersensible School), those who had kept the traditions of the Mysteries continued to teach that human beings cannot perceive the world, nor feel and act in it, as they would think and feel and act if they had not become sinful—if they had not descended from the height for which their Gods originally predestined them.

With this in mind, let us now turn our gaze to all the leading Spirits in the kingdom of the *Archangeloi* who follow one another in their rulerships, so that earthly dominion is exercised in turn through successive periods of 300–350 years. In the last three or four centuries it has been the dominion of Gabriel. Now it will be that of Michael, for 300 years to come. Let us therefore turn our gaze to the whole series of these Archangelic Beings: Gabriel, Raphael, Zachariel, Anael, Oriphiel, Samael, Michael. As we look to these Beings, we may characterize the relation that exists between them and the loftier Spirits of the Hierarchies somewhat as follows.

I beg you not to take these words too lightly or too easily. We have but human words to express these sublime realities. Simple as the words may sound, they are not meant lightly. Of all these Angels, the number of whom is seven, six have, to a very considerable extent, though not entirely—Gabriel most of all; but even Gabriel not completely—six, as I say, have to a very considerable extent resigned themselves to the fact that human beings face Maya, the great Illusion, because their quality no longer accords with their original predestination, because in fact they have descended from their original stature. Michael alone, Michael is the only one (again, I am forced to use banal expressions), Michael is the only one who would not give in. Michael, and with him even those who are the Michaelic spirits even among human beings, continues to take this stand: I am the ruler of the Intelligence. And the Intelligence must be so ruled that there shall not enter into it any illusion or false fantasy, nor anything that would restrict the human being to a dark, vague, cloudy vision of the world.

My dear friends: to see how Michael stands there as the greatest opponent in the ranks of the Archangels is an unspeakably uplifting sight—overpowering, magnificent. And each time a Michael Age returned, it happened upon earth not only that (as I have already said) intelligence as a means of knowledge became cosmopolitan, but also that intelligence became such that human beings were filled through and through with the consciousness: "After all, we *can* ascend to the Divinity."

This consciousness: "We can, after all, ascend to the Divine," played an immense part at the end of the last Michael Age, the Michael Age before our own. Starting in ancient Greece, the ancient Mystery places were everywhere in a state of discouragement; an atmosphere of discouragement came over them all. Discouraged, too, were those who lived on in Southern Italy and Sicily. The successors of the ancient Pythagorean School of the sixth century before Christ had been well-nigh extinguished. They were filled with discouragement. They saw how much materialistic illusion was spreading over the whole world.

Discouraged, too, were those who were the daughters and sons of ancient Egyptian Mysteries. Oh, these Egyptian Mysteries! When these Mysteries still handed down the deep old teachings, such as were expressed in the legend of Osiris or in the worship of Serapis, this was only like the slag from wonderful old veins of precious metal. And over in Asia, where were those mighty and courageous ascents to the spiritual world that had begun, for example, in the Mysteries of Artemis (Diana) at Ephesus? Even the Samothracian

Mysteries, the wisdom of the Kabiri, could now be deciphered only by those who bore deep within them the impulse of greatness to soar upward with might and main. By such souls alone could the clouds of smoke that ascended from Axieros, etc., from the Kabiri, be deciphered.[31]

Discouragement everywhere! Everywhere there was a feeling of what they sought to overcome in the ancient Mysteries when they turned to the secret of the Sun Mystery—which is in truth the secret of Michael. Everywhere a feeling: Humanity cannot, it is unable.

This Michael Age was an age of great trial and probation. Plato, after all, was but a kind of watery extract of the ancient Mysteries. The most intellectual element of this extract was then extracted again in Aristotelianism, and Alexander took it on his shoulders.

This was the word of Michael at that time: Humanity must reach the Pan-Intelligence, human beings must take hold of the Divine upon earth in sinless form. Radiating from the center of Alexandria, the best that has been achieved must be spread far and wide in all directions, through all the places of the Mysteries, discouraged as they are. This was the impulse of Michael. This is indeed the relation of Michael to the other *Archangeloi*. Michael has protested most strongly against the Fall.

This, too, was the most important content of his teaching, the teaching with which he instructed his own pupils in the supersensible School of which I have spoken. This teaching was as follows: Now that the Intelligence will be down among human beings on the earth, having fallen from the lap of Michael and from his hosts— now, in this new Age of Michael, human beings will have to become aware of the way of their salvation. They must not allow their Intelligence to be overcome by sinfulness; rather, they must use this age of Intelligence to ascend to the spiritual life in purity of Intelligence, free of all illusion.

Such is the mood and feeling on the side of Michael as against the side of Ahriman. I have characterized this great contrast. The very strongest efforts are already being made by Ahriman—and more

31. See Rudolf Steiner, *Mystery Knowledge and Mystery Centers.*

still will be made in the future—to acquire the Intelligence that has come into human hands. For if human beings once became possessed by Ahriman, Ahriman himself, in human heads, would possess the Intelligence intended for humanity.

My dear friends, we must learn to know this Ahriman, these hosts of Ahriman. It is not enough to find the name of Ahriman contemptible or to give the name of Ahriman to so many beings whom one despises. That is of no avail. The point is that in Ahriman a cosmic Being of the highest imaginable Intelligence stands before us, a cosmic Being who has already taken the Intelligence entirely into the individual, personal element. In every conceivable direction Ahriman is in the highest degree intelligent, over-intelligent. He has at his command a dazzling Intelligence, proceeding from the whole human being, with the single exception of the part of the human being which in the human forehead takes on a human form.

To reproduce Ahriman in human imagination we should have to give him a receding forehead, a frivolously cynical expression, for in him everything comes out of the lower forces, and yet from these lower forces the highest Intelligence proceeds. If ever we let ourselves in for a discussion with Ahriman, we would inevitably be shattered by the logical conclusiveness, the magnificent certainty of aim with which he manipulates his arguments. The really decisive question for the human world, in Ahriman's opinion, is this: Will cleverness or stupidity prevail? And Ahriman calls stupidity everything that does not contain Intelligence within it in full personal individuality. Every Ahriman-being is over-endowed with personal Intelligence in the way I have now described; critical to a degree in the repudiation of all things unlogical; scornful and contemptuous in thought.

When we have Ahriman before us in this way, then too we shall feel the great contrast between Ahriman and Michael. For Michael is not in the least concerned with the personal quality of Intelligence. It is only for humanity that the temptation is ever-present to make Intelligence personal after the patter of Ahriman. Truth to tell, Ahriman has a most contemptuous judgment of Michael. He thinks Michael foolish and stupid—stupid, needless to say, in relation to himself.

For Michael does not wish to seize the Intelligence and make it personally his own. Michael only wills, and *has* willed through the thousands of years, nay through the aeons, to administer the Pan-Intelligence. And now once more, now that human beings have the Intelligence, it should once again be administered by Michael as something belonging to all humankind—as the common and universal Intelligence that benefits all human beings alike.

We human beings shall indeed do rightly, my dear friends, if we say to ourselves: the idea that we can have cleverness only for ourselves is foolish. We cannot be clever only for ourselves. For if we want to prove anything logically to another person, the first thing we must presume is that the same logic holds good for him or her as for ourselves. And for a third party again it is the same logic. If anyone were able to have a personal logic it would be absurd for us to want to prove anything to that person by *our* logic. This after all is easy to realize; but it is essential in the present age of Michael that this realization also enters our deepest feelings.

Thus behind the scenes of existence is raging the battle of Michael against all that is of Ahriman. And this, as I have said, is among the tasks of the anthroposophists. They must have a feeling for the fact that these things are so at the present time. They must feel that the Cosmos is, as it were, in the very midst of this battle.

You see, this battle was already there in the Cosmos, but it became significant above all since the eighth or ninth century, when the Cosmic Intelligence gradually fell away from Michael and his hosts and came down to humanity on earth. It became acute only when the Spiritual or Consciousness Soul began to unfold in humanity at the beginning of the fifteenth century. In individual Spirits living on earth at that time, we see, even upon earth, some sort of reflection of what was taking place in the great supersensible School of which I spoke last Monday. We see something of it reflected in individual human beings on the earth.

In recent lectures, we have spoken much of heavenly reflections in earthly schools and institutions. We have spoke of the great School of Chartres, and others. But we can speak of this in relation to individual human beings too. Thus, at the very time when the

Consciousness Soul began to evolve in civilized humanity—when Rosicrucianism, genuine Rosicrucianism, was nurturing the early beginnings of the impulse to the Consciousness Soul—something of the impulse which was at work above the earth struck down like lightning upon a spirit living in that age. I mean Raimund of Sabunda.[32] What he taught at the beginning of the fifteenth century is almost like an earthly reflection of the great supersensible doctrine of Michael which I have characterized.

Raymond of Sabunda said: Human beings have fallen from the vantage-point that was originally given to them by their Gods. If they had remained at that point, they would have seen around them all that lives in the wondrous crystal shapes of the mineral kingdom, in the amorphous mineral kingdom, in the hundred-and-thousand fold forms of the plant kingdom, in the forms of the animal, all that lives and moves in water and air, in warmth and in the earthly realm. All this they would have seen as it really is, in its true nature.

Raymond de Sabunda called to mind how the Tree of Sephiroth and the Aristotelian categories[33] (those generalized concepts that look so strange to one who cannot understand them) contain what is meant to guide us through Intelligence, up into the universe. How dry, how appallingly dry do these categories seem when they are taught in the textbooks of Logic. Being, having, becoming, here, there—ten such categories, ten abstract concepts, and people say: it is too dreadful, it is appalling to have to learn such abstractions. Why should anyone grow warm with enthusiasm for ten generalized concepts such as being, having, becoming and so forth?

But it is just as though someone were to say: here is Goethe's *Faust*. Why do people make so much fuss of it? It only consists of letters. Nothing else is in the book, only letters in various combinations and permutations. Certainly someone who cannot read, and takes Goethe's *Faust* in hand, will not perceive the greatness contained in it. He or she will see only A, B, C, D... to Z. A person who does not know

---

32. Raimund de Sabunda (d.1436) Spanish theologian. Remembered for his *Theologia naturalis*, translated into French by Montaigne.
33. On categories, see, among others, Rudolf Steiner, *The Easter Festival in the Evolution of the Mysteries*, lecture IV.

how the letters are to be combined, who does not know how they are related to one another, cannot read Goethe's *Faust*.

So it is, too, with the Aristotelian categories. There are ten of them, not so many as the letters of the alphabet, but they are indeed the spiritual letters. And anyone who knows how to manipulate "being," "having," "becoming," etc., in the right way—just as we must know how to read the several letters so that they produce Goethe's *Faust*—anyone who knows how to do this, may still be able to divine what Aristotle for example said of these things in his instructions to Alexander.

Raymond of Sabunda was one who still drew attention to such things. He had knowledge of them. He said: Look, for instance, at what is still contained in Aristotelianism. There we find something that has still remained of that old standpoint from which humanity fell at the beginning of human evolution on earth. Originally, human beings still preserved some memory of it. It was *the reading in the Book of Nature*. But human beings have fallen; they can no longer truly read in the Book of Nature. Hence God, in His compassion, has given them the Bible, the Book of Revelation, in order that they may not entirely depart from what is Divine and Spiritual. Thus Raymond of Sabunda still taught, even in the fifteenth century, that the Book of Revelation exists for sinful humanity because it is no longer able to read in the Book of Nature. And in the way he taught these things, we can already perceive his idea that human beings must once again find the power to read in the great Book of Nature.

This is the impulse of Michael. Now that the Intelligence administered by him has come down to human beings, it is Michael's impulse to lead human beings to the point where they will read once more in the Book of Nature. The great Book of Nature will be opened again. Human beings will read in the Book of Nature again.

In reality, all those who are in the Anthroposophical Movement should feel that they can only understand their karma when they know that they personally are called to read again, spiritually, in the Book of Nature—to find the spiritual background of Nature, God having given His Revelation for the intervening time....

SEVEN

MICHAEL, SOPHIA, AND MARDUK [34]
Torquay, August 11, 1924

... In ancient Chaldea, the following was taught: human soul-forces reach their maximum potentiality when human beings direct their spiritual eye to the wonderful contrast between the life of sleep (when their consciousness is dimmed and they are oblivious of their environment) and the waking life (when they are clear-sighted, and aware of the world around them). These alternating states of sleep and waking were experienced differently thousands of years ago than they are today. Sleep was less unconscious, waking life not so fully conscious. In sleep, human beings were aware of powerful, ever-changing images, of the flux and movement of the life of worlds. They were in touch with the divine Ground, the essence, of the universe.

The dimming of consciousness during sleep is a consequence of human evolution. A few thousand years ago, waking life was not so clear and lucid as today. Objects had no clearly defined contours; they were blurred. They radiated spiritual realities in various forms. There was not the same abrupt transition from sleep to waking life. The people of that epoch were still able to distinguish these two states. The environment of their waking life was called *Apsu*; while the life of flux and movement experienced in sleep, the realm that blurred the clear distinction between the minerals, plants and animals of waking life, was called *Tiamat*.[35] Now, the teaching in the Chaldean Mystery Schools was that when human beings, in a state of sleep, shared the flux and movement of *Tiamat*, they were closer to truth and reality than when they lived their conscious life among minerals, plants and animals. *Tiamat* was nearer to the Ground of the world, more closely related to the human world than *Apsu*. *Apsu* was more remote. *Tiamat* represented something that lay nearer to

---

34. From: Rudolf Steiner, *True and False paths in Spiritual Investigation*, pp. 33–37.
35. For the whole story, see Alexander Heidel, *The Babylonian Genesis*.

humanity. But in the course of time *Tiamat* underwent changes and this was brought to the notice of the neophytes in the Mystery Schools. From the life of flux and movement of *Tiamat*, demoniacal forms emerged, equine shapes with human heads, leonine forms with the heads of angels. These demoniacal forms that became hostile to human beings arose out of the warp and woof of *Tiamat*.

Then there appeared in the world a powerful Being, *Ea*. Anyone today who has an ear for sounds can feel how the conjunction of these two vowels (E and A) points to that powerful Being who, according to these old Mystery teachings, stood at a person's side to help when the demons of *Tiamat* grew strong. *Ea* or *Ia*, later became—if one anticipates the prefix "Soph"—"Soph-Ea," *Sophia*. *Ea* means, approximately, abstract wisdom, wisdom that permeates all things. "Soph" is a particle that suggests (approximately) a state of being. Sophia, Sophea, Sopheia, the all-pervading, omnipresent wisdom sent to humanity her son, then known as *Marduk*, later called "Micha-el," the Micha-el who is invested with authority from the hierarchy of the Angels. He is the same Being as *Marduk*, the son of *Ea*, wisdom: Marduk-Micha-el.

According to the Mystery teachings, *Marduk-Micha-el* was great and powerful and all the demoniacal beings such as horses with human heads and leonine forms with angels' heads—all these surging, mobile, demoniacal forms, conjoined as the mighty *Tiamat*, were arrayed against him. *Marduk-Micha-el* was powerful enough to command the storm wind that sweeps through the world. All that *Tiamat* embodied was seen as a living reality, and rightly so, for that is how the Chaldeans experienced it. All these demons together were envisaged as the adversary—a powerful Dragon embodying all the demoniacal powers born of *Tiamat*, the night. And this Dragon-Being, breathing fire and fury, advanced upon *Marduk*. *Marduk-Micha-el* first smote it with various weapons and then drove the whole force of his storm-wind into the Dragon's entrails, so that *Tiamat* burst asunder and was scattered abroad.[36] And so *Marduk-Micha-el* was able to create out of the

---

36. The text says: "The North Wind bore (it) to places undisclosed."

Dragon the heavens above and the earth beneath. And thus arose the Above and the Below.

Such was the teaching of the Mysteries. The eldest son of *Ea*, wisdom, vanquished *Tiamat* and fashioned from one part of *Tiamat* the heavens above and from the other the earth below. And if, O human being, you lift your eyes to the stars, you will see one part of that which *Marduk-Micha-el* formed in the heavens out of the fearful abyss of *Tiamat* for the benefit of humankind. And if you look below, where the plants grow out of the mineralized earth, where minerals begin to take form, you will find the other part which the son of *Ea*, wisdom, has recreated for the benefit of humankind.

Thus the ancient Chaldeans looked back to the formative period of the world, to the forming from the formless; they saw into the workshop of creation and perceived a living reality. These demon forms of the night, all these nocturnal monsters, the weaving, surging beings of *Tiamat* had been transformed by *Marduk-Micha-el* into the stars above and the earth beneath. All the demons transformed by *Marduk-Micha-el* into shining stars, all that grows out of the earth, the transformed skin and tissue of *Tiamat*—this is the form in which people of ancient times pictured whatever came to them through the old attributes of the soul. Such information they accounted as knowledge....

EIGHT

MICHAEL, ARTHUR, AND THE GRAIL [37]
Torquay, August 21, 1924

... The lectures here have made it clear that in our own epoch the Impulse of the Being known in Christian terminology as the Archangel Michael is responsible for the spiritual guidance of

37. From: Rudolf Steiner, *Karmic Relationships (Esoteric Studies)*, vol. VIII, pp. 31–45.

civilization. This Michael rulership—if we may call it so—of spiritual life began in the 1870s and was preceded, as I have said, by that of Gabriel. I shall now say something about certain aspects of Michael's present rulership.

Whenever Michael sends his impulses into human earthly evolution, he is the bringer of Sun-Forces, the spiritual forces of the Sun. This is connected with the fact that during waking consciousness human beings receive these Sun-Forces into their physical and etheric bodies.

The present Michael rulership—which began not very long ago and will last from three to four centuries—means that the cosmic forces of the Sun penetrate right into human physical and etheric bodies. Here we must ask: What kind of forces, what kind of impulses, are these cosmic Sun-Forces?

Michael is essentially a Sun-Spirit. He is therefore the Spirit whose task in our epoch is to bring about a deeper, more esoteric understanding of the truths of Christianity.

Christ came from the Sun. Christ, the Sun-Being, dwelt on the earth in the body of Jesus and has lived since then in supersensible communion with the world of human beings. But before the whole Mystery connected with Christ can reveal itself to the soul, humanity must become sufficiently mature. This necessary deepening will to a great extent has to be achieved during the present Michael Age.

Now, whenever Sun-Forces work in upon the earth, they are always connected with an impulse that streams into earthly civilization as an in-pouring wave of intellectuality, for in our sphere of existence everything human beings and the world in general possess in the way of intellectuality or intelligence derives from the Sun. The Sun is the source of intellectual life that operates in the service of the Spirit.

Utterance of this truth may evoke a certain inner resistance today, for people rightly do not place too high a value upon the intellect in its present form. Those who have any real understanding of spiritual life will not set much store by the intellectuality prevailing in the modern age. It is abstract and formal, crowding the human mind with ideas and concepts that are utterly remote from living reality. Compared with the warm, radiant life pulsing through the world and humanity, it is cold, dry, and barren.

With respect to intelligence, however, this holds good only for the present time, since we are living in a very early period of the Michael Age and what we now possess as intelligence is only just beginning to unfold in general human consciousness. In time, this intelligence will have an altogether different character. In order to realize how the nature of intelligence changes during the course of human evolution, let us recall that in medieval Christian philosophy Thomas Aquinas still spoke of Beings, of "Intelligences" inhabiting the stars. In contrast to the materialistic views prevailing today, we ourselves also regard the stars as colonies of spiritual Beings. This seems strange and far-fetched to the ears of modern human beings who have not the remotest inkling that when they gaze at the stars they are gazing at Beings related in certain ways with their own lives and inhabiting the stars just as we ourselves inhabit the earth.

In the thirteenth century, when Thomas Aquinas spoke of Beings in the stars he assigned to each star a single Being in the sense that earthly humanity would be regarded as a single unit if the earth were to be observed from some distant heavenly body. We ourselves know that the stars are to be conceived as colonies of Beings in the cosmos. Thomas Aquinas did not speak of specific Beings or numbers of Beings inhabiting the stars, but when he referred to the "Intelligences" of the stars this authority of medieval Christian doctrine was continuing a tradition which at that time was already dying away. This is an indication that what is comprised today in the term "Intelligence" was once something altogether different.

In very ancient times human beings did not produce their thoughts from out of themselves; when they thought about the things of the world their thoughts were not the product of their own inner activity. The faculty of thinking, one's own activity in the forming of thoughts, has only fully unfolded since the fifteenth century, since the entry of the Consciousness Soul into the evolution of humanity. In older, pre-Christian times it would never have occurred to people to believe that they were producing their own thoughts out of themselves; they did not feel that they themselves were forming their thoughts, but rather that thoughts were revealed to them from the things of the world. They felt: Intelligence is universal, cosmic; it is contained in the things of the world; the intelligence-content, the thought-content of things is perceived, just as colors are perceived; the world is full of Intelligence, pervaded everywhere by Intelligence. In the course of evolution, humanity has acquired a drop of the Intelligence that is spread over the wide universe. Such was the conception in ancient times.

And so human beings were conscious all the time that their thoughts were revealed to them, were inspired into them. That is, people ascribed Intelligence only to the universe, not to themselves.

Throughout the ages, the Regent of Cosmic Intelligence, which streams like light over the whole world, has been the Spirit known by the name of *Michael.* Michael is the Ruler of Cosmic Intelligence. But after the Mystery of Golgotha something of deep significance took place in that Michael's dominion over Cosmic Intelligence gradually fell away from him. Since the earth began, Michael has administered Cosmic Intelligence. And in the time of Alexander and Aristotle when a human beings were aware of thoughts—that is to say, of the content of Intelligence within them—they did not regard these thoughts as their own, self-made thought: the felt that the thoughts were revealed to them through the power of Michael, although in that pagan era this Michael Being was known by a different name. This thought-content then gradually fell away from Michael. And if we look into the spiritual world we see that, by about the eighth century A.D., the descent of the Intelligence from the Sun to the earth had been accomplished. In the ninth century, people were already beginning, as forerunners of those who would come later, to unfold their own, personal intelligence. Intelligence began to take root within the souls of individual human beings. And so, looking down from the Sun to the earth, Michael and his hosts could say: What we have administered through aeons of time has fallen away from us, has streamed downward and may now be found in human souls on earth.

Such was the mood and feeling prevailing in the Michael-Community on the Sun. During the age of Alexander and for a few centuries before, Michael exercised his previous earthly dominion. By the time of the Mystery of Golgotha, however, Michael and his own were in the sphere of the Sun and from there they witnessed the departure of Christ from the Sun; they did not, as those who were below, witness Christ's arrival on earth. Michael and his hosts witnessed the departure of Christ from the Sun and at the same time they saw that their dominion over the Intelligence was gradually falling from their grasp.

Following the Mystery of Golgotha, therefore, the course of development is as follows. Christ came to earth and lived in union with it. Until the eighth or ninth century, the Intelligence gradually sank down to earth; and people began to ascribe what they called knowledge—what they unfolded in their thoughts—to their own, personal intelligence. Michael saw that what he had administered for aeons was now to be found in human souls. And so the Michael-Community realized: "During our next rulership—which will begin in the last third of the nineteenth century—when our impulses will pour once again through earthly civilization, we shall have to seek out on the earth the Intelligence that descended from the heavens, in order that we may once again administer—but now in human hearts and souls—what for aeons we administered from the Sun." In this way the Michael-Community prepared itself to find in human hearts what had fallen from its grasp and under the influence of the Mystery of Golgotha had also taken the path, although more gradually, from the heavens to the earth.

I will now indicate briefly how Michael and his hosts have striven in order that, beginning with this present Michael Age, they may once again take hold of the Intelligence that fell away from them in the heavens. From now on Michael, who has been striving from the Sun for those on earth who perceive the Spiritual in the cosmos, wishes to establish his citadel in the hearts and in the souls of earthly human beings. This is to begin in our present time. Christianity is to be guided into a realm of deeper truths, inasmuch as understanding of the Christ as a Sun Being is to arise within humanity with the help of Michael, the Sun Spirit, who has always ruled over the Intelligence, and who can now no longer administer it in the cosmos, but desires in future to administer it in and through the hearts of human beings.

In seeking to discover the origin and source of Intelligence in whatever form it may be revealed, people look today to the human head because, having descended from the heavens to the earth, the Intelligence weaves within the soul and manifests inwardly through the head. This was not always the case in times when human beings strove for Intelligence or the essence of the Intelligence as it revealed itself from the Cosmos. In earlier epochs people strove for Intelligence *not* by developing the faculties of the head, but by seeking for the Inspirations conveyed to them by cosmic forces.

An example of how in earlier times humanity sought cosmic Intelligence in a way in which it is no longer sought today, is to be found when one stands, as we were able to do last Sunday, at that place in Tintagel which was once the site of King Arthur's Castle and where Arthur and his twelve companions exercised a power of far-reaching significance for Europe.

From the accounts contained in historical documents it will not be easy to form a true conception of the tasks and the mission of King Arthur and his Round Table, as it is called. This becomes possible, however, when one stands on the actual site of the castle and gazes with the eye of the spirit over the stretch of sea which an intervening cliff seems to divide into two. There, in a comparatively short time, one can perceive a wonderful interplay between the light and the air, and also between the elemental spirits living in light and air. One can see spirit-beings streaming to the earth in the rays of the sun, one can see them mirrored in the glittering raindrops, one can see what comes under the sway of earthly gravity appearing in the air as the denser spirit-beings of the air. Again, when the rain stops and the rays of the sun stream through the clear air, one perceives the elemental spirits intermingling in quite a different way. There one witnesses how the Sun works in earthly substance, and seeing it all from a place such as this, one is filled with a kind of pagan "piety"—not Christian but pagan piety, which is something altogether different. Pagan piety is a surrender of heart and feeling to the manifold spirit-beings working in the processes of nature.

Amid the conditions of modern social life it is not, generally speaking, possible for people to give effect to the processes coming to expression in the play of nature-forces. These things can be penetrated only by Initiation-Knowledge. But you must understand that every spiritual attainment is dependent upon some essential and fundamental condition.

In the example I gave this morning to illustrate how the knowledge of material phenomena must be furthered and extended, I spoke of the interweaving, self-harmonizing karma of two human beings as a necessary factor.[38] And in the days of King Arthur and those around him, special conditions were required in order that the spirituality so wondrously revealed and borne in by the sea might flow into their mission and their tasks.

This interplay between the sunlit air and the rippling, foam-crested waves continues to this day. Over the sea and the rocky cliffs at this place, nature is still quick with spirit. But to take hold of the spirit-forces working in nature would have been beyond the power of *one* individual alone. A group was necessary, one of whom felt himself to be the representative of the Sun, at the center, and whose twelve companions were trained in such a way that in temperament, disposition and manner of acting, all of them together formed a twelvefold whole: twelve individuals grouped as the Zodiacal constellations are grouped around the Sun. Such was the Round Table: King Arthur at the center, surrounded by the Twelve, above each of whom a Zodiacal symbol was displayed, indicating the particular cosmic influence with which he was associated. Civilizing forces went out from this place to Europe. It was here that King Arthur and his Twelve Knights drew into themselves from the Sun the strength to set forth on their mighty expeditions through Europe to do battle with the wild, demonic powers still dominating large masses of the population, and drive them out of human beings. Under the guidance of King Arthur, these Twelve were battling for outer civilization.

---

38. See Steiner, *True and False Paths in Spiritual Investigation,* lecture X.

To understand what the Twelve felt about themselves and their mission, it must be remembered that in ancient times people did not claim a personal intelligence of their own. They did not say: I form my thoughts, my thoughts that are filled with Intelligence, myself. People experienced Intelligence as *revealed* Intelligence, and they sought for revelations by forming themselves into a group like the one I have described—a group of twelve or thirteen. There they imbibed the Intelligence which enabled them to give direction and definition to the impulses needed for civilization. And this group also felt that they performed their deeds in the service of the Power known in Christian-Hebraic terminology as Michael. The whole configuration of the castle at Tintagel indicates that the Twelve under the direction of King Arthur were essentially a Michael-Community, belonging to the age when Michael still administered the Cosmic Intelligence.

This was actually the community that worked longer than any other to ensure that Michael should retain his dominion over the Cosmic Intelligence. At the ruins of King Arthur's Castle today, the Akasha Chronicle still preserves the picture of the stones falling from those once mighty gates, and these falling stones become an image of the Cosmic Intelligence falling, sinking away from the hands of Michael into the minds and hearts of human beings.

Elsewhere, this Arthur-Michael stream has its polaric contrast in the Grail stream of which the Parsifal Legend tells.[39] This other stream comes into being in a place where a more inward form of Christianity had taken refuge. In the Grail stream, too, we have the Twelve around the One, but account is everywhere taken of the fact that the Intelligence—Intelligence-Filled Thoughts— no longer flows as revelation from the heavens to the earth. What now streams downward seems, when compared to earthly thoughts, like the "pure fool," Parsifal. Thus the Grail Stream realizes that Intelligence must now be sought within the earthly sphere alone.

---

39. See Rudolf Steiner, *Christ and the Spiritual Word. The Search for the Holy Grail.*

There, in the North, stands King Arthur's Castle, where human beings still turn to the Cosmic Intelligence, striving to instill the Intelligence belonging to the universe into earthly civilization. And further to the South stands that other castle, the Grail Castle, where Intelligence is no longer drawn from the heavens and where it is realized that what is wisdom before humanity is foolishness before God and what is wisdom before God is foolishness before human beings.[40] The impulse proceeding from this other Castle in the South strives to penetrate the Intelligence that is no longer the *Cosmic* Intelligence.

And so, in ancient times and continuing into the age when the Mystery of Golgotha took place in Asia, we find in the Arthur stream the intense striving to ensure Michael's dominion over the Intelligence, while in the Grail stream, which emerged from Spain, we find the striving in which account is taken of the fact that the Intelligence must in future be found on earth, since it no longer flows down from the heavens. The import of what I have just described to you breathes through the whole legend of the Grail.

Study of these two streams brings to light the great problem arising from the historical situation of that time. Human beings are confronted with the consequences—the after-effects—of both the Arthur-Principle and the Grail-Principle. The problem is: How does Michael himself, not a human being like Parsifal, but Michael himself, find the path leading from his Arthurian knights who strive to ensure his cosmic sovereignty, to his Grail knights who strive to prepare the way for him into the hearts and minds of human beings in order that therein he may again take hold of the Intelligence? Here the great problem of our own age takes definition: How can Michael's rulership bring about a deeper understanding of Christianity? Overwhelmingly this problem confronts us, marked by the contrast of the two castles: the one of which the ruins are to be seen to this day at Tintagel, and that other castle which will not easily be seen by human eyes, since in the spiritual realm it is surrounded, as it were, by a trackless forest, sixty leagues deep on every side.

---

40. Cf. I Corinthians 1:18–29.

Between these two castles looms the great question: How can Michael become the giver of the impulse that will lead to a deeper understanding of the truths of Christianity?

Now it would not be correct to say that the Knights of King Arthur were not battling for Christ and the true Christ-Impulse. It was simply that they bore within them the urge to seek for Christ *in the Sun* and would not abandon their conviction that the Sun is the fount of Christianity. Hence their feeling that they were bringing the heavens down to earth, that their Michael-battles were being waged for the Christ Who works from the rays of the Sun. But within the Grail stream, the Christ-Impulse is expressed in a different way. There people are conscious that the Christ-Impulse, having come down to the earth, must henceforth be made effective through human hearts. For they were convinced that the spiritual Essence of the Sun was now united with earthly evolution.

I have spoken in these lectures[41] of individuals who in the twelfth century taught and worked in the School of Chartres, where teachings still inspired by a lofty and sublime spirituality were given forth. I spoke of particular teachers in the School of Chartres, among them Bernardus Sylvestris, Bernard of Chartres, Alanus ab Insulis— and there were others, too, surrounded by a great company of pupils. Remembering what was especially characteristic of these teachers of Chartres, we may say: In some measure they still preserved within them the old traditions of nature teeming with life and being as opposed to an abstract, material nature. And this was why there still hovered over the School of Chartres elements of that Sun-Christianity that the heroes of Arthur's Round Table, as Knights of Michael, had striven to implant as an impulse in the world.

In a remarkable way the School of Chartres stands midway between the Arthur-Principle in the North and the Grail-Principle in the South. And like shadows cast by the castle of King Arthur and the castle of the Grail, the supersensible, invisible impulses made their way, not so much into the actual content of the teachings, as into the whole attitude and mood-of-soul of the pupils who gathered

41. See Rudolf Steiner, *True and False Paths in Spiritual Investigation*, lecture 4.

with glowing enthusiasm in the "lecture halls"—as we would call them today—of Chartres. These were times when in the Christianity presented by these teachers of Chartres, Christ was conceived as the sublime Sun-Spirit Who had appeared in Jesus of Nazareth. So that when these teachers spoke of the Christ they saw His Impulse at work in earthly evolution in the terms of the idea of the Grail and at the same time they also saw in Him the downpouring Impulse of the Sun.

What is revealed to spiritual observation as the essence and key-note of the teachings given at Chartres cannot be discovered from surviving literary texts attributable to individual teachers in the School of Chartres. To a modern student such writings seem scarcely more than glossaries of names. But in the brief sentences interspersed between the countless designations, names, defini-tions, those who read with spiritual penetration will discern the deep spirituality, the profound insight still possessed by these teach-ers of Chartres.

Toward the end of the twelfth century, these teachers passed through the gate of death into the spiritual world. And there they came together with that other stream, which was also linked with the Michael Age of ancient time, but in which full account was taken of the central truth of Christianity—namely that the Christ Impulse had come down from the heavens to the earth. In the spiri-tual world, the teachers of Chartres came into contact with all that the older Aristotelians had been able to achieve in preparation for Christianity as a result of Alexander's expeditions to Asia. But they also came together with Aristotle and Alexander themselves—who were then in the spiritual world. The impulse of which these two individualities were the bearers could not take effect on the earth at that time because it depended upon abandoning the old, nature-inspired Christianity that was still reflected in the teachings of Char-tres in which, as in Arthur's Round Table, a pagan, pre-Christian Christianity prevailed. In the days of Chartres it was not possible for the Aristotelians—for those who had established and promoted Alexandrianism—to be on the earth. Their time, beginning with the thirteenth century, came a little later.

In the intervening period something of great significance took place. When the teachers of Chartres and those who were associated with them passed through the gate of death into the spiritual world, they came together with souls who were preparing to descend to the physical world and who were eventually led by their karma to the Order which, above all, was connected with the cultivation of knowledge in the Aristotelian form—the Dominicans. The representatives of Chartres came together with these other souls who were preparing to descend.

Using trivial words of modern speech, I will now describe what then transpired. At the turning-point of the twelfth and thirteenth centuries—at the beginning of the thirteenth century—a kind of conference took place between the souls who had just arrived in the spiritual world and the souls who were about to descend. And the momentous agreement was reached, that Sun-Christianity as expressed, for example, in the Grail-Principle and also in the teachings of Chartres, should now be united with Aristotelianism. Those who descended to earth became the founders of Scholasticism, the spiritual significance of which has never been truly assessed and in which, to begin with, people could hope to win the day for their view of personal immortality in the Christian sense only by advocating it in the most radical, extreme way. The teachers of Chartres had laid less emphasis upon this principle of the personal human immortality. They still inclined to the view that having passed through the gate of death the soul returns to the bosom of the Divine. They spoke far less of personal, individual immortality than did the Dominican Scholastics.

Many significant happenings were connected with what was here taking place. For example: When one of the Scholastics had come down from the spiritual world to work for the spread of Christianity in an Aristotelian form, he had not, to begin with, been able fully to grasp the essential import of the Grail-Principle. Karma had willed it so. And here lies the reason for the comparatively late appearance of Wolfram von Eschenbach's version of the Grail story.[42] Another

---

42. Wolfram von Eschenbach, *Parzival.*

soul, who came down to the earth somewhat later than the first, brought with him the impulse that was necessary, and within the Dominican Order deliberations took place between an older and a younger Dominican as to how Aristotelianism might be united with the Christianity which, inspired more by nature and the workings of nature, had prevailed in King Arthur's Round Table.

Then the time came for those individualities who had been teachers in the Dominican Order also to return to the spiritual world. And now the great agreement was reached under the leadership of Michael himself who, looking down to the Intelligence that was now on the earth, gathered around him his own—spiritual Beings belonging to the supersensible worlds, a great host of elemental spirits, and many, many discarnate human souls who were longing for a renewal of Christianity. It was too early, *yet*, for this to take effect in the physical world. But a great and mighty supersensible School was instituted under the leadership of Michael, embracing all those souls in whom the impulses of paganism still echoed on, but who were nevertheless longing for Christianity, and those souls who had already lived on the earth during the early centuries of Christendom and who bore Christianity within them in the form it had then assumed. A Michael host gathered together in supersensible realms receiving in the spiritual world the teachings which had been imparted by the Michael Teachers in the time of Alexander, in the time of the Grail tradition, and which had also taken effect in impulses like that going out from Arthur's Round Table.

Christian souls of every type and quality felt drawn to this Michael-Community where, on the one side, deeply significant teaching was imparted concerning the ancient Mysteries and the spiritual impulses at work in olden days, while, on the other, a vista was opened into the future when, in the last third of the nineteenth century, Michael would again be working on earth and when all the teachings given forth in this heavenly School under Michael's own leadership in the fifteenth and sixteenth centuries were to be carried down to earth.

If you seek the souls who gathered around this School of Michael at that time, preparing for the later period on earth, you will find among them many who now feel the urge to come to the Anthroposophical Movement. Karma guided these souls. In the life between death and a new birth, they thronged around Michael, preparing to carry down once more a cosmic Christianity to the earth.

The karma of many souls who have come into the Anthroposophical Movement with real sincerity is connected with these preliminary conditions and antecedents. It is this that makes the Anthroposophical Movement into the true Michael Movement, the movement that is predestined to bring about the renewal of Christianity. This lies in the karma of the Anthroposophical Movement. It lies, too, in the karma of many individuals who have come with sincerity into that movement. To carry into the world the Michael-Impulse which may in this way be pictured in all its concrete reality, and which is betokened by many a sign on the earth today, and also comes strikingly to expression in the wonderful play of nature forces around the ruins of Arthur's Castle—this is the task of the Anthroposophical Movement in a very special sense. For, in the course of the centuries, the Michael-Impulse must find its way into the world of human beings if civilization is not to perish from the earth.

NINE

FROM RUDOLF STEINER'S LAST ADDRESS [43]
Dornach, September 28, Michaelmas Eve, 1924

When we read the *Fragments* of Novalis,[44] and give ourselves up to the life that flows so abundantly in them, we can discover the secret of the deep impression they make on us. Whatever we have before us in immediate sense-reality, whatever the eye can see and recognize as beautiful—all this, through the magic idealism that

---

43. From: Rudolf Steiner, *The Last Address*, pp.17–19.
44. Novalis (Friedrich von Hardenberg), 1772–1801, German Romantic poet and philosopher. See also Rudolf Steiner, *The Christmas Mystery: Novalis as Seer*; also Sergei Prokofieff, *Eternal Individuality: Towards a Karmic Biography of Novalis*.

lives in the soul of Novalis, appears in his poetry with a well-nigh heavenly splendor. The meanest and simplest material thing—with the magic idealism of his poetry he can make it live again in all its spiritual light and glory.

And so we see in Novalis a radiant and splendid forerunner of that Michael Stream which is now to lead you all, my dear friends, while you live; and then, after you have gone through the gate of death, you will find in the spiritual supersensible worlds all those others—among them also the being of whom I have been speaking to you today[45]—and all those with whom you are to prepare the work that shall be accomplished at the end of the century, and that shall lead humankind past the great crisis in which it is involved.

This work is: to let the Michael Power and the Michael Will penetrate the whole of life. The Michael Power and the Michael Will are none other than the Christ Will and the Christ Power, going before in order to implant the Power of the Christ in the right way into the earth. If this Michael Power is able verily to overcome all that is of the demon and the dragon (and you well know what that is), if you all, who have in this way received the Michael Thought in the light, have indeed received it with true and faithful heart and with tender love, and will endeavor to go forward from the Michael mood of this year, until not only is the Michael Thought *revealed* in your soul, but you are able also to make the Michael Thought *live* in your *deeds* in all its strength and all its power—if this is so, then will you be true servants of the Michael Thought, worthy helpers of what has now to enter earthly evolution through Anthroposophy, and take its place there in the meaning of Michael....

My strength is not sufficient for more today. May the words speak to your soul so that you receive the Michael Thought in the sense of what a faithful follower of Michael may feel when, clothed in the light rays of the Sun, Michael appears and points us to what must now take place. For it must even be so that this Michael garment, this garment of Light, shall become the Words of the Worlds, which are the Christ Words—the Words of the Worlds, which can

---

45. Rudolf Steiner is referring here to St. John the Evangelist.

transform the Logos of the Worlds into the Logos of Humankind.
Therefore let my words to you today be these:

> Sprung from solar powers,
> shining, world-blessing powers of spirit:
> divine thinking has predestined you
> to be Michael's coat of rays.

> He, the messenger of Christ, reveals in you,
> who bear humanity, the holy will of worlds;
> you, bright beings of the ether worlds,
> bear Christ's word to humankind.

> Thus the herald of Christ appears
> to waiting, thirsting souls;
> to them your word of light streams forth
> in the world age of the spiritual body.

> You, students and knowers of the spirit,
> take Michael's wise sign,
> practice taking into your soul's high purpose
> the word of love of the will of worlds.

TEN

FROM: *THE MICHAEL LETTERS* [46]

I

At the Dawn of the Age of Michael
August 17, 1924

Human beings enjoyed a different relationship to their thoughts
prior to the ninth century after the Mystery of Golgotha than they

---

46. From: Rudolf Steiner, *The Michael Mystery,* pp.1–7 and 33–43.

did later on. They did not feel the thoughts living in their souls were produced by them, but they regarded them rather as gifts given them by the spiritual world. Even such thoughts as they had about what they perceived with their senses seemed to them revelations of the Divine conveyed by objects in the sense world.

Anyone who can perceive the Spirit understands this feeling.

Those to whom a spiritual reality is manifested never feel that the spiritual percept is given and that they then form the concept to grasp it. Rather they actually *see* the thought contained in the percept. The thought is just as objectively present as is the percept itself.

During the ninth century—this is, of course, only an approximate time, to be understood as a median, for the transition took place gradually—individual personal intelligence began to illumine the souls of human beings. People got the feeling that *they formed* their thoughts. This thought-forming activity became the predominant feature of soul life, so that thinkers conceived of the human soul as expressing itself fundamentally in the application of intelligence. The previous conception of the soul had been an imaginative one. The soul's nature was seen as participating in the content of the spiritual world rather than as active thought-formation. Supersensible spiritual Beings were thought of as engaged in thinking and working on human beings, and sending their thoughts into them as well. This content of the supersensible spiritual world living in human beings was felt to be the soul.

We encounter concrete spiritual Beings immediately upon penetrating the spiritual realm with clairvoyant vision. In ancient teachings, the Being from whom the thoughts bound up with things flowing forth was called Michael. We can retain the name here. So it can be said that people once received the thoughts that came to them from Michael. Michael ruled over Cosmic Intelligence.

From the ninth century onward, human beings no longer felt that Michael was inspiring their thoughts. Thoughts had fallen away from his dominion; they had descended from the spiritual world into the individual souls of human beings.

From then on, humanity itself nurtured the life of thought. At first, uncertainty reigned as to what people were dealing with in the thoughts they had. Scholastic doctrine reflects this uncertainty. There were two categories of these philosophers: realists and nominalists.

The realists, led by Thomas Aquinas and his fellow thinkers, still sensed the ancient unity between thoughts and things. They saw in thought a reality living in the object; they conceived of a person's thoughts as realities that flowed out of things into the souls of those who perceived them.

The nominalists, on the other hand, were keenly aware that souls formed their own thoughts. They felt thoughts to be a purely subjective element that lived in the soul but had nothing to do with things themselves. In their view, thoughts were mere names that people made up for things. (They spoke not of "thoughts" but of "universals." However, this does not affect the principle they upheld, since thoughts always have a universal connotation in their relationship to things.)

We could say: The realists wanted to keep faith with Michael. Then, too, in view of the fact that thoughts had descended from Michael's realm into that of human beings, they wanted their thinking to serve him as the Lord of Cosmic Intelligence. The nominalists, however, on a subconscious soul level, carried the falling away from Michael to completion. They regarded the human being rather than Michael as the possessor of thoughts.

Nominalism gained ground and influence. This was the situation up to the last third of the nineteenth century, a period during which individuals able to perceive spiritual events in the universe felt that Michael remained connected with the stream of intellectual life. Michael seeks a new metamorphosis of his cosmic task. In earlier times, Michael allowed thoughts to stream from the external spiritual world into human souls. But beginning with the last third of the nineteenth century, it is his desire to live in human souls as thoughts are formed there. In that earlier age, human beings who were related to Michael perceived him carrying on his activity in the realm of the spirit. Now they realize that they must allow him to live in their hearts. Now they wish their thought-nourished spiritual life to be dedicated to him. In their independent individual life of thought, they let Michael teach them the paths their souls should be following.

Individuals who, in their former earthly lives, were recipients of inspired thoughts—individuals, in other words, who served Michael—felt themselves drawn to voluntary participation in the Michael-Community upon re-entering earthly incarnation at the end of the nineteenth century. From then on, they regarded the old inspirer of their thinking as their guide in higher thought activity.

A person alert to such matters could perceive what a transformation occurred in human thought life during the last third of the nineteenth century. Prior to that time, people could feel only that thoughts were formed by their own activity. Beginning with the period cited, people can rise above themselves and project their awareness into spiritual realms. There they encounter Michael, who reveals himself as linked from olden times with all thought activity. Michael frees thoughts from their restriction to the head region and opens a way for them to the heart. He sets inner enthusiasm glowing, enabling people to give themselves in soul devotion to everything that can be experienced in the light of thought. The Michael Age has arrived. Hearts are beginning to have thoughts. Enthusiasm is no longer generated by obscure mysticism, but by inner clarity supported by thoughts. To grasp this is to receive Michael into one's inner being. Thoughts that aim at understanding matters of the spirit in our time must spring from hearts devoted to Michael as the fiery Cosmic Lord of Thought.

II

The Human Soul State Prior to the Dawning of the Michael Age

August 31, 1924

The Age of Michael dawned in human evolution after a period in which, on the one hand, intellectual thought activity predominated, while, on the other, human beings focused their gaze on the external physical world of the senses.

The forming of thoughts is *not* intrinsically a development in the direction of materialism. The world of Ideas, which made itself known to humanity in earlier times in the form of inspiration, became an individual soul possession in the period prior to the Michael Age. No longer did souls receive Ideas "from above" as the content of the spiritual world. They now actively drew them forth from their own spirits. This step represents a maturing to the point where human beings became able to reflect on their own spiritual essence. Previously, they never penetrated to the depth of their own being. Rather, they regarded themselves as drops separated out of the sea of spiritual being for the period of their earthly lives, to return at its conclusion to that ocean.

The thought-forming activity taking place within human beings represents an advance in self-knowledge. From the supersensible point of view, matters stand as follows: the spiritual Powers to whom we may assign the name of Michael had dominion over Ideas in the spiritual universe. Human beings experienced these Ideas as they participated in the life of Michael's realm. Now they experience Ideas as their own, with the result that they have been separated for the time being from the Michaelic world. The inspired thoughts of earlier days also brought human beings the content of the spiritual world. But as inspiration ceased to flow and individuals began actively forming their own thoughts, human beings had to turn to sensory perception to find content for their thoughts. This meant temporarily filling with a material content the personal spirit to which they had attained. They fell into a materialistic way of looking at things in the epoch that brought their own spirit to a level higher than the one that preceded it.

The situation can easily be misunderstood. One may note only the fall into materialism and be saddened by it. But while the *outlook* of this period had to restrict itself to the external physical world, a *purified, independent human spirituality as experience* developed in the soul's depths. In the Michael Age, this spirituality may no longer remain unconscious *experience;* it must become conscious of its real nature, and that signifies the entrance of the Michael being into human souls. For a certain period of time, human beings filled their own spirit with material views of the natural world. Now they are to fill it again with a spirituality truly their own, as cosmic content.

For a time, thought-forming lost itself to material aspects of the cosmos. Now it must find itself again in the cosmic Spirit. Warmth and spirituality, permeated with essential being, can flow into the cold, abstract thought world. This characterizes the dawn of the Michael Age.

Only in separation from the thought being of the cosmos could a consciousness of freedom develop in the depths of human souls. What had its origin in the heights had to be discovered anew out of the depths. That is why the development of this consciousness of freedom had to be based temporarily on a natural science that focused its attention exclusively on externals. During the period in which human beings were unconsciously readying their spirit for pure Idea, their senses were focused outward on the material, a realm that did not impinge in any way on the delicate seed growing up within them.

But an experiencing of the spiritual and, coupled with it, spiritual perception itself, can enter again in a new way into the contemplation of external matter. The knowledge of nature acquired under the sign of materialism can be grasped in its spiritual aspect in the soul's inwardness. Michael, who once spoke "from above," can be heard speaking "from within," where he has taken up his new abode. We might say, to put it more imaginatively, that the Sun Element that humanity absorbed for so long only from the cosmos will begin shining in the soul itself. People will learn to speak of an "inner Sun." This will not cause human beings to feel less beings on the earth in their lives between birth and death, but they will know themselves to be *guided by the Sun* on their earthly course. They will come to feel how true it is that a Being illumines them inwardly with a Light that, though it shines upon earthly existence, is not lit there. As the Age of Michael dawns, it may seem as though all this were still remote from human experience. Spiritually, however, it is near; it needs only be "seen." It is immeasurably important that people's ideas should not stop at being merely "thoughts," but should go on to become "seeing" in the thinking of them.

III

The Michael-Christ Experience
November 9, 1924

Those who give themselves in a truly heartfelt way to inner contemplation of Michael's deeds and being will come to a real understanding of the way human beings must conceive a world that is no longer either Divine Being or its Revelation, nor yet an ongoing *effect*, but simply the Gods' wrought-work. To look into this world with insight is to have shapes and forms in view that everywhere speak plainly of Divinity, but in which a self-sustaining Divine Being is no longer to be found unless one gives oneself up to illusion. We should not restrict our insight to the merely knowable. The configuration of the world surrounding humanity today manifests itself most clearly to this view. But of far greater import for everyday life is the feeling, the will, the working in a world felt to be formed, indeed, in accordance with the Divine Image but not to be experienced as God-enlivened. To bring genuine moral life into a world of this kind requires the generating of ethical impulses such as are described in my *Philosophy of Freedom.*

Michael's being and present sphere of action can shine out in this wrought-work world for those of true feeling. Michael does not make an appearance in the physical realm; he restricts himself and all his activity to a supersensible region immediately bordering on the physical world as this exists in the present phase of cosmic evolution. This renders it impossible that the impression of Michael's being that we receive could mislead us into a fantastic view of nature, or make us try to share cultural-practical life in our God-wrought but not God-enlivened world as though we could be impelled to action by any but our own ethical-spiritual impulses. Whether thinking or willing, human beings will always have to approach Michael by transposing themselves into the spiritual realms.

In so doing, we will live spiritually in the following way. We will take knowledge and life as they have had to be taken since the fifteenth century. But we will hold fast to the Michaelic revelation, letting it shine like a light illumining our thoughts as we garner them from the world of nature; we will carry them in our hearts as warmth, even though we must live in accordance with the world of divine wrought-works. We will not only observe and experience the present-day world, but also that world mediated by Michael as well—a *past* state of the world, one brought by Michael's deeds and being into the present.

If it were otherwise, if Michael's activity were such that he brought his deeds into the world that we have to know and experience as physical, then we would presently be experiencing something of the world that really *was* once upon a time, but that *is* no longer. If such a thing were to come to pass, this illusory grasp of the world would lead man's soul away from reality suited to it and into another, Luciferic sphere.

Michael's way of making the past effective in our present experience is in keeping with the purposes of true spiritual world progress, in which nothing of a Luciferic nature has a part. It is important for human souls, in their conceiving of Michael's mission, to have a right picture of its avoidance of everything Luciferic.

This understanding of the Michaelic-Light making its appearance on the scene of human history provides the basis for finding the right approach to Christ as well.

Michael provides the proper orientation in those concerns where human beings approach the world around them in knowledge and action, whereas they will have to find an inner path to Christ.

Considering the form that our approach to nature has assumed during the last five centuries, it is thoroughly understandable that supersensible knowledge, too, should have become what it is today in our modern conceiving.

Nature has to be known and experienced as devoid of God. But, in this kind of relationship to the world, we are no longer able to experience ourselves. The relationship to nature that comes naturally to an individual as a self in this epoch gives us *no* understanding of ourselves as supersensible beings, and with only this relationship in view, we cannot live ethically in a way attuned to our humanity.

So it has come about that this way of living and experiencing is not allowed to come into contact with anything that has to do with our supersensible being, or, indeed, with the supersensible world. That realm is considered inaccessible to human knowing. An extra- or super-scientific realm of belief and revelation has to be postulated in addition to the scientifically knowable.

But the purely spiritual activity of Christ presents the opposite picture. Ever since the Mystery of Golgotha, it has been possible to reach Him. The relationship to Christ need not remain a vague, mystical one of unillumined feeling; it can become a fully concrete, deep, clear human experience.

From this communion with the Christ the human soul garners what it needs to know about its own supersensible nature. The revelation of faith must be felt to receive a constant influx of living experience of the Christ. To feel Him as the Being who mediates to the human soul the perception of its own supersensible nature leads to a thorough Christianizing of life.

The Michael experience and the Christ experience can thus stand side by side. Michael will guide us in the right way to a supersensible experience of nature, and this outlook on nature will be able to take its place, undistorted, alongside a spiritual view of the world and of the human being as a universal being.

Through a right relationship to Christ, humans will experience in living soul-intercourse with Him what they could otherwise receive only in the form of traditional revelations of faith. The inner world of the soul's experience can then be experienced as spiritually illumined and the outer world of nature as spiritually sustained.

If human beings were to try to attain insight into their own supersensible being without communion with the Christ, they would be seduced away from themselves and into the realm of Ahriman. Christ is the cosmically ordained carrier of humanity's impulses towards the future. For the human soul to unite with the Christ means receiving into itself, for cosmically intended nurturing, the seeds of its own future. Other beings whose present-day forms are such as the cosmos intends for humanity only in the future belong to the Ahrimanic sphere. Union with the Christ means protecting oneself properly from Ahrimanic influences.

Those individuals who insist on keeping traditional religious revelation free of any inclusion of human knowledge betray the fear that humanity may otherwise fall victim to Ahrimanic influences. We have to understand this fear. But it is necessary, on the other hand, to understand how it contributes to the knowing and acknowledging of Christ when the experience of Him is ascribed to the grace-filled flowing of the spiritual into human souls.

Thus the Michael experience and the Christ experience can stand side by side in future. This will enable human beings to travel their true path of freedom between seduction by Luciferic illusions in their thinking and living, and Ahrimanic enticement into a future shape of things that satisfies their conceit but does not rightly belong to *them* in the present epoch.

To fall victim to Luciferic illusions means to fall short of becoming fully human, that is, to fail to make the effort to progress to the stage of freedom, remaining content to stay at the earlier evolutionary divine-human level. To fall victim to Ahrimanic enticement means being unwilling to wait for the right cosmic moment to come to a certain stage of humanness and instead to take this stage prematurely.

In future, Michael-Christ will stand as path-indicators at the start of the route along which humanity, in keeping with cosmic goals, can advance between Lucifer and Ahriman and arrive at its world destination.

IV

Michael's Mission in the Cosmic Age of Human Freedom

November 16, 1924

If one approaches the study of Michael's contemporary mission, experiencing it spiritually, it becomes possible to see the cosmic nature of freedom in spiritual-scientific illumination.

This is not meant with reference to my *Philosophy of Freedom*, a work based on purely human cognitive powers, when they can be applied to the realm of the spirit. One does not need to commune with Beings of other worlds to attain the kind of insight dealt with there. But it might be said that *The Philosophy of Freedom* prepares the reader for an understanding of freedom that can become actual experience of spiritual communion with Michael. That experience may be described as follows.

If freedom is really to underlie human action, what is done in its light may not depend in any way whatsoever on the human physical and etheric organization. Free deeds can issue only from the I, and the astral body must be able to attune itself to this free I-activity in order to transmit it to the physical and etheric bodies. But this is only one aspect of the matter; the other becomes clear when we relate it to Michael's mission. What human beings experience in freedom may also not be allowed to influence their physical and etheric bodies in any way. If that were to happen, humanity would lose all connection with what it has become in its passage through the stages of its development influenced by divine-spiritual *being* and divine-spiritual *revelation*.

Human beings' experience of what remains the *mere wrought-work of their divine-spiritual surroundings* must not exert an influence on anything but the spirit (or ego) element in them. The only thing permitted to influence their physical and etheric organism is what began within the being and revelation of the divine-spiritual and continues on within a human being's own being, not what lies outside. What lies outside must not come in touch with what lives within in human nature as the element of freedom.

That this is possible derives solely from the fact that Michael carries over from a primeval period of evolution something that connects human beings with divine-spiritual reality without exercising any present effect on their physical and etheric structure. This provides the basis in Michael's mission for human communion with the spiritual world that takes place without involving natural processes.

It is elevating to witness how Michael lifts humanity's being into the sphere of the Spirit while its unconscious or subconscious aspects, developing below the level where freedom reigns, grow ever more deeply involved with matter.

Humanity's position in relationship to the being of the world will become an increasing puzzle to it if human beings do not rise to recognition of such matters as Michael's mission while still feeling their ties with nature's beings and processes. The ties with nature are learned as though from external perception; those with the spiritual world issue from something resembling an inner conversation with a form of being to which one gains access by opening oneself to a spiritual view of the universe.

In order for human beings to carry out impulses conceived in freedom, they must be able to keep certain workings of nature that act upon their being out of the cosmos from affecting them. This keeping at arm's length goes on in the subconscious when, on the conscious level, forces are active that support the I's life in freedom. Awareness of free action is a matter of inward perception for an individual; but for spiritual Beings, who relate to humans from other spheres of the world, the situation is different. The Being from the hierarchy of Angels who is charged with carrying over an individual's existence from one earthly life to another is at once aware, in witnessing free human action, that the human being involved is repelling cosmic forces that seek to go on shaping him or her, forces that are trying to continue giving the organization of the I such necessary physical support as they gave it before the Age of Michael set in.

As a Being of the rank of Archangel, Michael receives his impressions with the help of beings of the rank of Angels. He devotes himself, in the way described, to the task of conveying to human beings out of the spiritual realms of the cosmos the forces that can act as a replacement for suppressed natural forces.

Michael achieves this by bringing his activity into the most perfect attunement with the Mystery of Golgotha.

Christ's activity in our earthly evolution harbors the forces needed by human beings, when they act in freedom, to balance out the suppressed impulses that derive from nature. But they must then devote their souls truly to the inner communion with the

Christ that was spoken of in these communications on the subject of the Michael mission.

Human beings are aware that they are confronting reality when they confront the physical sun and receive its light and warmth. Just so must they live in relationship to Christ, the spiritual Sun, which has united its existence with that of earth, and take up livingly into their souls what corresponds in the spiritual world to warmth and light.

They will feel themselves permeated by "spiritual warmth" as they experience "Christ within them," and will say as they sense this permeation: "This warmth frees my humanity from cosmic ties by which it must not remain bound. Divine-spiritual Existence in primeval times had the task of bringing me to the attainment of freedom in regions in which it cannot now accompany me further, but in these regions it gave me the Christ in order that Christ's forces may now endow me as a free being with what was once supplied as a natural endowment by Divine-spiritual Existence in primeval times. Then, however, the way of nature and the way of the spirit were one. This warmth restores me to the Divine Element from which I sprang."

As human beings feel this, their experience in and with the Christ becomes one in innermost soul-warmth with the experience of true, genuine humanness. "Christ gives me my human nature." Such will be the profound sense suffusing the soul to its depths. And after one has experienced this feeling, one goes on further to experience oneself raised up by the Christ beyond mere earthly existence, becoming one with the starry surroundings that encompass the earth and with everything divine-spiritual to be met with there.

The same holds true of spiritual light. An individual can sense his humanity in fullness when he becomes aware of himself as a free agent. But a certain darkness accompanies this experience. Light's ancient divine-spiritual Source no longer shines. But the Light with which Christ endows the human I restores that primeval illumination. In communion of this kind with the Christ, one's whole soul can be irradiated by the Sun-like thought: "The glorious divine Light of ancient days lives again and shines out, though its luminosity is not the luminosity of nature." Today we can unite ourselves with spiritual-cosmic light-forces from a distant past in which we were not yet free individualities. Once we understand and unite our souls with Michael's mission, we can find in this illumination our guide for traveling the rightful human path.

This means that human beings will feel in spiritual warmth the impulse to carry them into the cosmic future in a way that enables them to remain true to the original gifts they received from the divine-spiritual beings even though, in their own realm as human beings, they have now evolved to the stage of free individuality. Human beings thus will sense in the spiritual Light the force to lead them, with ever higher and more inclusive perceptive conscious-ness, into the world in which they will find themselves together again, as free agents, with their original Gods.

If we were to shy away from a full experience of freedom and become fixed in our original state of existence, willing to continue on in the condition of primeval, naive divine grace that once pre-vailed, we would be led to Lucifer, whose desire it is to reject the world as it is today.

If we were to accept the present state of things, and be content to let only that universal rule of natural law conceived by a morally neutral intellect prevail, while restricting ourselves to a merely men-tal experience of freedom, we would be led—in this age, when evo-lution must continue into ever deeper regions of the soul in order to counterbalance those higher ones in which freedom reigns—to Ahriman, who would like to see the contemporary world turn into a purely intellectual cosmos.

These are the regions where security and certainty flourish in the souls and spirits of human beings who, looking outward in spirit see Michael and looking inward see the Christ. This certainty and secu-rity makes it possible for them to travel the cosmic path on which, never losing touch with their origin, they will find their rightful future perfecting.

APPENDIX

JOHANNES TRITHEMIUS
1462–1516
Abbot of Sponheim

A TREATISE ON THE SEVEN SECONDARY CAUSES, I.E.,
INTELLIGENCES, OR SPIRITS, WHO MOVE THE SPHERES
ACCORDING TO GOD

A Little Book or MYSTICAL CHRONOLOGY
*Containing within a Short Compass Marvellous Secrets
Worthy of Interest*[1]

To the august and pious Maximilian I, Emperor & Caesar by the
Grace of God:—

Most wise Emperor, this lower world, created and organized by
the First Intelligence, who is God, is ruled by Secondary Intelligences. Hermes, who gave us the science of the Magi, confirms this
view when he says that seven Spirits were assigned to the seven Planets from the beginning of the heavens and of the earth.

Each of these Spirits rules the universe in turn for a period of 354
years and 4 months. Many learned scholars, up to the present day,
have approved this assertion, which I do not guarantee, but only lay
before your Most Blessed Majesty.

---

1. *Johannis Trithemii abbatis spanheymensis, de septem secundeis, id est intelligentiis sive
spiritibus orbes post Deum moventibus libellus sive chronologia mystica multa scituque di-
gna, mira brevitate in se completens arcana* (1515). Written 1508. The present translation lays no claim to scholarliness or more than general accuracy. It was
translated by the editor for the interest of the reader: from the French, Jean
Trithème, *Traité des Causes Secondes*. Milan: Sebastiani (Archè), 1974.

The first Angel or Spirit, that of *Saturn*, is called *Oriphiel*. God confided the government of the world to him starting with the beginning of creation. *Oriphiel*'s reign began on March 15 and lasts 354 years and 4 months. The name *Oriphiel* was given to him on account of his spiritual office, not his nature. Under his rule, humans were crude and savage. Their customs recalled those of wild beasts of the wilderness. This requires no demonstration, for it is clearly evident from the Book of Genesis.

The second guiding Spirit of the world was *Anael*, the Spirit of *Venus*, who, following *Oriphiel*, began to emit stellar influence in the year of the world 354, on June 24. *Anael* ruled the world for 354 years and 4 months until the year of creation 708, as calculation shows. Under *Anael*'s rule, human beings began to be less crude. They built houses and cities, invented manual arts, and began the twin arts of the weaving and spinning of yarn. They also gave themselves up to the pleasures of the flesh and took wives. Forgetting God, they grew distant in many things from natural simplicity, invented games and songs, set themselves to playing the kithara and imagined all that had to do with *Venus* and her cult. This life of debauchery ended only with the deluge that was the punishment for their depravity.

The third ruler, *Zachariel*, the Angel of *Jupiter*, began to rule the world in the year 708 after the creation of the heavens and the earth, in the eighth month—that is, on October 26. *Zachariel* ruled the universe for 354 years and 4 months until the year 1060. Under *Zachariel*'s direction humans began to take turns usurping power. They began to hunt, to put up tents, to decorate their bodies with different kinds of clothes. The good were separated from the evil— the good invoked God, like Enoch who entered into Him, while the evil plunged into pleasures of the flesh. Under *Zachariel*, people began to live in society, to submit to laws imposed upon them by the strongest among them and, distancing themselves from their earlier barbarism, to civilize themselves. It was under *Zachariel*'s rule that Adam, the first human being, died, leaving to posterity the inevitability of death. Lastly, in these days, several human inventions occurred, curious arts, as historians tell us.

The fourth ruler of the world was *Raphael,* the Spirit of *Mercury,* whose rule began on February 24 of the year 1063 following the creation of the earth and the heavens, and lasted 354 years and 4 months. The invention of writing goes back to this period. To begin with, letters were imagined in the forms of trees and plants, later taking on more careful forms to be modified at will. Under *Raphael,* the use of musical instruments spread; commerce and trading were practiced, as well as long-distance navigation, and many other marvelous things.

The fifth ruler of the world was *Samael,* the Angel of *Mars,* who began to reign on June 26, 1417.

Samael ruled for 354 years and 4 months and impressed his influence strongly upon humanity. Under *Samael's* reign, in the year of the world 1656, the universal flood occurred, as the Book of Genesis clearly shows. It is a remarkable fact, as the ancient philosophers tell us, that each time *Samael,* the Genius of *Mars,* governs the world, a complete change occurs in some great monarchy: religions and castes are overturned; great persons and princes are exiled; laws are changed—as one can easily see in the historians. Such changes do not occur right at the beginning of *Samael's* reign, but only as it enters its second half. The the same is true for all the other planetary Spirits, as history shows. That is, the influence of the secondary powers reaches its height when the stars reach the zenith of their revolution.

The sixth ruler of the world was *Gabriel,* Angel of the *Moon. Gabriel* began his reign after that of *Samael,* the Spirit of *Mars,* on October 28, 1771 years after the creation of the world. *Gabriel's* rule lasted 354 years and 4 months until the year 2126. During this period human beings multiplied further and founded many new cities. It must be noted, too, that, according to the Hebrews, the Flood occurred under the rule of *Mars* in the year of the world 1656. Isidore and Beda, two interpreters of the Septuagint, on the other hand, claim that this cataclysm occurred in the year 2242— that is, under the rule of *Gabriel,* Spirit of the *Moon,* which by calculation seems to me closer to the truth, though this is not the place to prove it.

The seventh ruler of the world was *Michael,* the Angel of the *Sun,* whose rule began, according to ordinary calculation, on February 24 in the year 2126 after the creation, and finished 354 years and 4 months later in the year 2480. Under the rule of this Angel of the *Sun,* according to those historians most worthy of belief, Kings first began to appear among mortals, and among these was Nimrod, the first to use sovereign power to tyrannize his fellows who were devoured by passions. Thus human folly instituted the cult of the Gods. Humans began to worship the lower principles as Gods. At this time, too, humanity invented various arts: Mathematics, Astronomy, Magic. The cult of a single God was practiced by different creatures but, due to human superstition, knowledge of the true God was gradually forgotten. At this time, likewise, agriculture began to be practiced and human beings began to have more civilized customs and institutions.

In eighth place, *Oriphiel,* the Angel of *Saturn,* returned and ruled the universe again for 354 years and 4 months—from June 26, 2480 until September, 2834. Under this Angel's rule, nations multiplied, the earth was divided into regions, and many kingdoms were founded. The Tower of Babel was built and "the confusion of tongues" occurred. Thus humanity dispersed over the earth and human beings began energetically to work the soil and cultivate fields, to sow wheat and plant vines, to prune fruit trees and busy themselves with all that concerned food and clothing. From this moment on, the distinction of nobility began to manifest and those who excelled by their virtue and genius received the insignia they deserved from their princes. At this time, too, humanity began to gain a sense of the universe as a whole, as, after the multiplication of races and the founding of many kingdoms, different languages came into being.

Then, in ninth place, the Spirit of *Venus, Anael,* began to rule the world once more. This was on October 29 in the year 2834 after the creation of the heavens and the earth. *Anael* ruled for 354 years and 4 months until the year of the world 3189. During this period, human beings, forgetting God, began to create a cult of the Dead. They began to worship the Dead and their statues in place of God.

This was an error that lasted more than two thousand years. Fashion introduced the use of precious ornaments for the body and, with the help of different sorts of musical instruments, humanity abandoned itself once again to the passions and pleasures of the flesh, raising these up and even dedicating statues and temples to them. During this time Zoroaster, the first King of the Bactrians and other peoples, defeated in battle by Ninus, King of the Assyrians, discovered the mystery of incantations and curses.

In tenth place, *Zachariel*, the Angel of *Jupiter*, took up the direction of the world. This was on the last day of February in the year 3189 after the foundation of the heavens and the earth. *Zachariel* ruled for 354 years and 4 months, until the year 3543. This was a happy period, known with reason as the "Golden Age." The abundance of all the earth's goods led to the increase of the human species and the universe reached the height of its splendor. During this period, God gave Abraham the law of circumcision, promising for the first time the redemption of humanity by the incarnation of his only Son. Under *Zachariel's* rule, the Patriarchs, those founders of the spirit of justice, appeared. By their will and their works, the just were separated from the unjust. During this time, too, Jupiter, under the name of Lisanius, King and Son of Heaven and of God, was the first to give laws to the Arcadians, succeeding in civilizing them, building temples, instituting a priestly craft, and gaining many useful things for his people. This was why they gave him the name of Jupiter and, after his death, looked on him as a God. Yet he originated in the priestly caste of Heber, as history declares. It is also said that during this Angel's rule Prometheus, son of Atlantus, created humanity because, finding them coarse, he made them learned, human, good, and accomplished in manners and customs. He also invented the art of animating images. And it was he who first used the ring, the scepter, and the diadem, and invented royal insignia. At the same time, other sages of the race of Jupiter united men and women with the bonds of marriage, and brought humanity many other useful things. On account of their wisdom, after their death, these sages were raised into the ranks of the Gods. Of this kind were: Phoroneus, who was the first to give the Greeks laws and justice, Apollo, Minerva, Ceres, Serapis (among the Egyptians), and countless others.

In eleventh place, *Raphael*, the Spirit of *Mercury*, resumed the guidance of the world again on July 1, in the year of the world 3543, ruling 354 years and 4 months until the year 3897 from the creation of the world. During this period, as ancient historians clearly show, humanity yielded with ardor to the study of wisdom. Among the most illustrious of these devotees of wisdom were: Mercurius, Bacchus, Omogyrus, Isis, Inachus, Argus, Apollo, Cecrops, and many others who, by their discoveries, were useful to the world and to posterity. During this time, too, various superstitions arose in humankind, such as the cult of idols, incantations, and the art of producing diabolical prodigies. Everything generally attributable to the subtlety and genius of Mercury took on vast proportions. Moses, the most wise leader of the Hebrews, the expert in many sciences and in all the arts, priest of the sole and true God, delivered his people from the slavery in which the Egyptians had kept them. At this same time, Janus the First ruled over Italy; Saturn, who taught the manuring of fields and was taken for a God, succeeded him. About this time, too, Cadmus invented the Greek letters and Carmetis, daughter of Evander, Latin letters. It was also in the reign of *Raphael*, Angel of *Mercury*, that the All-Powerful gave his people by the intermediary of Moses, the Law to which the Incarnation of CHRIST gave a dazzling testimony. A prodigious variety of cults manifested in the world. There were then numerous Sibyls, Prophets, Augurs, Haruscipes, Magi, Diviners, not to mention the Sibyls of Erythrea, Delphi, and Phrygia.

In the twelfth epoch, *Samael*, Angel of *Mars*, became the world's ruler for a second time. This was on October 2 of the year of the world 3897. *Samael* ruled 354 years and 4 months until the year 4252. Under his reign, the great and celebrated destruction of Troy in Asia Minor occurred. Monarchies and many kingdoms fell and new ones were founded, such as Paris, Mainz, Carthage, Naples, and others. New kingdoms, too, arose, such as that of Lacedemon, Corinth, Jerusalem, etc.

During this period, long wars and great struggles of Kings and nations unfolded, as well as dynastic changes. The Venetians, for example, trace the origin of their people and the founding of their city to this period of the taking of Troy. More remarkably still, several nations of Europe and Asia lay claim to Trojan descent—but in the desire to glorify themselves, as if there had not existed famous people and nations in Europe before the ruin of Troy, the proofs they offer in support of the nobility of their origin are vain and deceptive.

Under the dominion of this same planet, *Mars*, Saul, the First, was chosen King of the Jews. After him came David, then his son Solomon, who built to the true God a Temple in Jerusalem that was famous throughout the world. Then the Divine Spirit, illuminating its prophets with the incomparable clarity of grace, gave them not only the gift of predicting the future incarnation of the Savior, but also many other things, as the Holy Scriptures attest. Among these prophets, we may cite Nathan, son of King David, Gad, Azaph, Achaias, Semeias, Azarias, Anan, and many others. The Greek poet Homer, singer of the Fall of Troy, the Phrygian Dares and the Cretan Dictis who witnessed and told of it, are also said to have lived at this time.

For the thirteenth period, *Gabriel*, the genius of the *Moon*, resumed the rulership of the world on January 30 of the year 4252 from the world's beginning. *Gabriel* ruled 354 years and 4 months, until the year 4606. During this period several great prophets shone among the Hebrews: Elisha, Micah, Abdiah, and others. Among the Hebrews, likewise, Kings succeeded each other with rapidity. Lycurgus gave the Spartans a code and laws. Capitus, Liberius, Romulus, and Procas Sylius, and Numitor—Italian Kings —flourished under this Spirit's reign. Under this same Lunar influence a number of other kingdoms arose, such as those of the Lydians, the Medes, the Macedonians, the Spartans, etc., while the Assyrian monarchy was ended by Sardanapalus. The Kingdom of Media also disappeared. At this time, many different kinds of laws were imposed upon humanity. Human beings neglected the worship of God. The cult of idols became widespread. In 4491, the 239th year of *Gabriel's* reign, the foundations of Rome were laid. The dominion of the Sylians ended in Italy, their place being taken

APPENDIX

by the Romans. Around this time, too, the Seven Sages appeared in Greece: Thales, Solon, Cheilon, Periander, Cleobulus, Bias of Priene, and Pittacus. From this moment on, philosophers and poets began to be held in high esteem. Romulus, founder of Rome, fratricide, and abettor of sedition, ruled the city for 37 years. His successor, Numa Pompilius, ruled for 42 years, developing the cult of the Gods and dying in the time of Ezechias, King of the Jews. Toward the end of *Gabriel's* rule, Nebuchadnezzar, King of Babylon, captured and destroyed Jerusalem and led King Sedecias and his people into captivity. The prophet Jeremiah foretold both this destruction and the end of this captivity.

Following *Gabriel,* on May 1 of the year of the world 4606, *Michael,* the Spirit of the *Sun,* took up the world's scepter for the second time. *Michael* ruled the universe for 354 years and 4 months, until the year 4960 of the world's foundation. During his period, Merodach, King of Babylon, gave the Hebrew people their liberty and their King. This was under the influence of *Michael,* who, as the book of Daniel tells, protected the Jews whom God had given him. At this time, too, the Persian monarchy arose whose first Kings, Darius and Cyrus, overturned the great Babylonian monarchy. This was in the reign of Balthasar, as Daniel and the prophets predicted. The Cumaean Sibyl was also famous then, because of the offer she made to King Tarquin the Elder to sell him at once, and at the same price, the nine books containing the series of predictions having to do with the Roman Republic. When the King refused to pay the price that was asked, the Sybil burnt the first three books before his eyes, and then demanded the same sum for the remaining six. Refused again, she threw three more books into the fire, and would have done the same for the last three, had not the King, persuaded by his Counsellors, saved these books from destruction by agreeing to pay the price asked in the beginning for the set of nine. These same Romans, after the expulsion of their Kings, designated two Consuls annually. This was the period when Phalaris, the tyrant, ruled in Sicily. Magic was held in great esteem at this time among the Kings of Persia. Pythagoras and other philosophers flourished in Greece. The city of Jerusalem and its Temple were reconstructed. The prophet Esdras restored from memory the Books of Moses, which had been burnt by the Chaldeans. This new text was called the Babylonian version. Xerxes, King of Persia, led an army against the Greeks, but without great effect. The Gauls captured, burned, and destroyed Rome, except for the Capitol which was saved by a goose who awoke the sleeping soldiers with his honking. The Athenians were then engaged in their famous wars and the philosophers Socrates and Plato gained their renown. Following the repeal of the Consuls, the Romans instituted the offices of the Tribunes and the Aediles. Meanwhile, a host of calamities assailed them.

Immediately following the end of *Michael's* dominion, Alexander the Great ruled in Macedonia; he overcame the Persian monarchy under Darius, and brought all Asia under his scepter, as well as a part of Europe. He died at the age of 33, after a reign of 12 years and 5 months. Many wars and ills followed his death and his empire was dismembered into four parts. Among the Hebrews, competitions were held for the High Priesthood for the first time. And the Kingdom of Syria was born.

After *Michael, Oriphiel,* the Spirit of *Saturn,* took up the government of the world for the third time (and the fifteenth period) on the last day of September in the year 4960 from the beginning of the world. He ruled for 354 years and 4 months, until the year 5315. Under his rule, the Punic Wars began between the Romans and the Carthaginians. The city of Rome was almost completely destroyed by fire and water. The Colossus, a bronze sculpture, 126 feet high, was toppled by an earthquake. After the Punic War, Rome, which had warred unceasingly for 440 years, enjoyed a year of peace. Jerusalem and its Temple were burnt and destroyed by Antiochus and Epiphanes. The Maccabees became famous for glorious battles. During this period, too, 606 years after the founding of Rome, Carthage was destroyed and burned for seventeen days. In Sicily, the revolt of the 70,000 slaves against their masters occurred. Great wonders took place at this time in Europe. Domestic animals fled into the woods, blood flowed, and an exploding ball of fire fell from the sky with a great din. Mithridates, King of Pontus and Armenia, waged a war against Rome for 40 years. The Kingdom of the

Hebrews was restored, after a hiatus lasting 575 years—from Zede-
chias to Aristobulus. The Germans and the Teutons invaded Italy
and were defeated after many battles, losing 160,000 men, not
counting the considerable number of those who perished with their
families under Caius and Manlius, after having treacherously killed
many Romans. Finally, 40 years of civil war desolated Italy. Three
suns appeared in Rome, melting, after a short time, into one. A few
years later, Julius Caesar usurped the supreme power, and following
him Augustus extended his power into Asia and Africa, uniting
these under a single rule. Augustus ruled for 36 years, during which
God gave the world peace.

   In the year of the world 5199, the 751st year of Rome's foundation,
the 42nd year of Octavius Caesar Augustus, 245 years into the reign
of *Oriphiel*, the Spirit of *Saturn*, the eighth month, on December 25,
Jesus Christ, the Son of God, was born of the Virgin Mary, in Bethle-
hem, in Judea. Note that by the admirable ordering of divine Providence, the universe was created in the first rulership of *Oriphiel* or
Saturn and was saved, restored, and renewed by his mercy during his
third administration—a harmonious agreement which sufficiently
proves the influence of the seven planets on the government of the
universe. Indeed, during Oriphiel's first rulership, the whole world
formed but a single, vast monarchy, which, during his second rulership, subdivided into a multitude of little kingdoms—as we have
shown above—which themselves were brought into unity once again
under his third rulership. This notwithstanding, it is clear to those
with clairvoyant eyes that the second period of *Oriphiel* also saw a single monarchy with the building of the Tower of Babel. During this
third reign of *Oriphiel* the Kingdom of the Jews was scattered and the
perpetual sacrifice of victims was suspended. And freedom will not
be given to the Jews again until the third period of *Michael* in August
1880 of the Christian Era, which is the year of the world 7170. In the
year 299 of the Angel *Oriphiel*'s rulership, Peter transferred the great
Office of the Pontiff of the Universal Christian Church from Judea
to Rome. Many Jews and Gentiles embraced the Christian religion
on account of the preaching of sermons of great simplicity and unso-
phistication, illuminated not by human knowledge but by the Spirit

of God. The world at this moment returned to the innocence and simplicity of the first age. In both, *Oriphiel*, Spirit of *Saturn*, presided. The heavens were united with the earth. Two scepters were given to humanity to rule the world: a higher one, for spiritual things, was given to the Pope; another, for temporal things, was given to the Emperor. Many Christians, persecuted by the princes of this world, perished for their faith. Toward the end of *Oriphiel's* reign, the Romans destroyed Jerusalem, and the Jews were scattered over all the earth: 110,000 were killed; 80,000 were sold; and the rest fled. In this way, Rome completely destroyed Judea.

In sixteenth place, after Oriphiel, *Anael*, Spirit of *Venus*, took up the direction of the universe for the third time on the last day of January, 5315 years from the foundation of the heavens and the earth, 109 years after Christ's Nativity—to rule for 354 years and 4 months to the year of the world 5669 and 4 months, which is the year 463 of the Lord's incarnation. We may note that, during almost this entire reign of the Angel of *Venus*, the Christian Church increased amidst persecutions, and finally prevailed after thousands were murdered for their faith in Christ. Numerous heresies then arose in the bosom of the Church—heresies that were extinguished from the blood of the virtuous only with great trouble and after much time. At that time, too, numerous people arose who were celebrated in all branches of knowledge: theologians, astronomers, doctors, orators, historians—not only among the gentiles but also among Christians. The faithless finally stopped persecuting the Church after Constantine the Great was baptized in the year of the world 5539—when the Angel of *Venus*, *Anael*, had passed the culminating point of its cycle of dominion. After this there were still some troubles caused by impious people, but the Church generally lived in peace. During this period, the human race which, since the time of King Ninus had been miserably lost in the cult of idols for 2,300 years, was mercifully brought back to knowledge of the one God. Many subtle arts grew up and, in agreement with the nature of *Venus*, developed and embellished themselves. For human manners change with the times and things below correspond with things above, and receive their influence. The soul, besides, is free, and not under the influence of the stars, unless it becomes stained, being too attached to the body, and allows itself to be guided by the latter. For the Angels, engines of the orbs, can neither destroy nor alter anything established by nature. A huge comet announced the death of Constantine. The Arian heresy troubled the Holy Church in many places. Toward the end of *Anael's* rule, in the time of the Emperor Julian, crosses appeared on the linen robes of certain persons. In Asia and Palestine, wars, plagues, and famines followed the apparitions in which these crosses were seen. In these days, too, around the year 360 of the Christian Era, the Franks came out of Germany and invaded, occupied, and conquered Gaul, to which they gave their name. France was great and large, and its capital was Mainz (Herbipolis). Bavarians, Swabians, Saxons, Thuringians, the inhabitants of the Rhine, and the tribes surrounding the Papal Kingdom occupied the greater part of what was then France and which today includes Germany. 280 years into this reign of *Anael*, the Roman Empire began its decline. Its capital, Rome, was captured and burned by the Goths. This was after Constantine had moved the seat of the Empire to Byzantium, a fatal deed that caused the decadence of the entire monarchy. Indeed, toward the end of *Anael's* rule, there appeared, as historians tell, Radagif, Alaric, and Athaulfe, Kings of the Goths, who were soon followed by Ganseric, King of the Vandals, and Attila, King of the Huns—all of whom invaded the whole of Europe and cut the Empire into pieces.

Following *Anael*, and in seventeenth place, *Zachariel*, Spirit of *Jupiter*, took up the direction of the world for the third time on June 1 of the year of the world 5669, which is the year 463 after the Birth of the Saviour. He ruled for 354 years and 4 months, to the year of the world 6023, which is the year of the Savior 817. During these days, many people gave themselves passionately to the study of Christian philosophy. Many wonders occurred: comets, earthquakes, rainfalls of blood.

Merlin, who was born in Caledonia at the beginning of *Zachariel's* rule, made astonishing predictions. Arcturus, commonly called Arthur, most famous King of Britain, overcame the barbarians, brought peace to the Church, triumphed in many battles, spread abroad the Christian faith, and brought all of Gaul, Norway, Dacia, as well as several provinces, under his rule. Arthur was the most glorious prince of his time; after accomplishing many high deeds, he suddenly disappeared, and for many years the Britons awaited his return. Many poets sang of his prodigious exploits; under his rule, England flourished and commanded three times ten kingdoms.

In these days, the monastic Orders began to multiply in God's Church. Theodoric, King of the Arian Goths, conquered Italy. The Empire and the Church were in trouble. Zeno and Anastasius, the Emperor of the East, Theodoric and his successors in Italy, Honorius, King of the Vandals in Africa—all these exercised an unequaled tyranny. Clovis, King of the Franks of Gaul, was baptized, overcame the Goths, and imposed peace, though not in the whole world. This was in the time of St. Benedict, around the year 500 of the Christian Era, toward the opening of the reign of *Zachariel*, the Angel of *Jupiter*, whose influence led to changes of dynasties and kingdoms, as the historians repeatedly affirm. What this Angel cannot do himself, he leaves to his successor *Raphael*, Angel of *Mercury*, who put Charlemagne on the throne of France. Indeed, during *Zachariel*'s 350 years many empires crumbled, including those of the Goths, the Vandals, the Burgundians, the Lombards, the Thuringians, the Germans, the Bavarians, and many others. The Emperor Justinian was the first to give the Republic a coherent set of laws. Several eminent people gained renown under *Zachariel*. Justinian built the basilica of *Sancta Sophia* in Constantinople. The Empire, divided, was in trouble and confusion. Many omens appeared, as history tells. Kusro, King of the Persians, took Jerusalem. Later, he was assassinated by Heracles. At this time, around the year 600 of the Christian Era, the Arab Mohammed founded the sect of the Saracens. This would soon completely supplant the Roman Empire in Asia. Dagobert, King of France, conquered and destroyed the English, then called the "Saxons."

It must be noted that soon afterward the Christian faith began to weaken in Asia and Africa, while the sect of the Saracens gradually penetrated everywhere, soon covering the whole world, with the exception of Europe, where the Order of St. Benedict spread the

Christian religion. Toward the year of our Lord 774, crosses appeared on some people's clothing and, a little later, the Roman Empire was divided, one part passing into Frankish hands under Charlemagne. This prince restored the Church and fought many wars. After his victories, the name "Western Gaul" was given to the Saxon territory.

In eighteenth place, following *Zachariel* (the Angel of *Jupiter*) *Raphael* (the Spirit of *Mercury*) assumed the government of the world for the third time on November 2, 6023 years after the world's foundation, which is the year 817 of the Savior's birth. *Raphael* ruled the universe for 354 years and 4 months, until the year of the world 6378, which is the year of our Lord 1171. At the beginning of this period of *Mercury*, as we have said, the Roman Empire passed into the hands of Charlemagne. After him, his son Louis reigned for 25 years; after his death his sons fought against each other, thus weakening the Empire yet again. The Normans devastated Gaul. Twice, Rome was sacked by the Saracens. It rained blood for three days under Louis II. In Saxony, a whole town, with all its buildings and inhabitants, was swallowed up in a terrible abyss opened up by an earthquake. Toward the year of our Lord 910 great troubles arose in Italy, which left the Frankish Empire and chose its own Kings. The first was Berenger, Prince of Friuli, who was followed by seven Kings in a space of about fifty years—when the Empire passed to the Germans. The first Emperor was Otto I, who undertook to reconstruct the monarchy.

Otto II, his son, and Otto III, his nephew, the successors on the imperial throne, converted the Hungarian people to the Christian faith. In the year 1000 of the Christian Era, Otto III, who died without progeny, established the Electors of the Empire, as has been conserved even to our own days. The Saracens took Jerusalem again.

Many omens were seen in the sky, the air, on the earth, the sea, and in the waters. Following the death of Otto III, Henry I was elected by the princes to succeed him. Henry I reigned 20 years and founded the Church of Bamberg. At the same time, Kunegund, his wife, died a virgin, famous for her miracles. After Henry, Konrad I was elected Emperor. He reigned 20 years. At this time also Godefroy, Count of

Bouillon, dispersed the infidels from Jerusalem and the Holy Land. Before the end of *Raphael*'s rule, many omens and numerous signs were seen; and, a little later, the Tartar race left its frontiers and inflicted great evils on the Roman Empire. Famines, plagues, earthquakes, and other calamities befell the Empire. In the year of our Lord 1153, Frederick I, called Barbarossa, assumed the scepter. He reigned for 33 years beginning in the 336th year of *Raphael*'s rulership and accomplished many admirable things. He increased the power of his Empire and successfully undertook many wars. Under his reign, the Egians and the Lithunians embraced Christianity.

In nineteenth place, *Samael,* the Angel of *Mars,* took up for the third time the governance of the world on March 3 of the year of the world 6378. He ruled 354 years and 4 months, until the year of the world 6732, or the year of the Lord 1525. Under his rulership there were many wars in the world; thousands of people perished, and several kingdoms lost their borders. The Emperor Frederick I had many differences with the Princes of Italy; he waged great wars against them in which they perished in the thousands. He ravaged Milan from top to bottom. Liège was destroyed. Jerusalem was taken again by the Saracens.

The Empire of the Tartars grew greatly on the face of the earth. This was a true calamity for the world—and continues still today. After Frederick, his son Henry was elected Emperor. And on Henry's death a schism between Philip and Otto divided the Empire, causing great troubles. Many battles were fought on the German borders—at Argentine, Cologne, Leiden, Spires in Wurtemburg and throughout the kingdom. The Order of Mendicants was founded during this epoch, in the fortieth year or so of *Samael,* which shows that all things are providential. In Asia and Africa, the Saracens fought the Christians in numerous places. Constantinople was taken by the Germans, and Baudoin, Count of Flanders, was raised to imperial dignity. More than 20,000 German children, seduced by lying speeches into trying to reconquer the Holy Land, were carried off by pirates on the open sea. A group of shepherds from Spain approached Paris, seizing the property of the clergy, much to the delight of the people—but when they sought to seize the possessions of lay people, they were massacred. In 1212 (of the Christian Era), Frederick II was elected Emperor; he reigned 33 years and did many things against the Church. In 1238, there was an eclipse and continuous earthquakes destroyed thousands of people. Frisia was almost completely submerged and more than 100,000 people drowned. The Tartars devastated Hungary and Poland, and conquered Armenia and several other countries. In the year1244 of the Christian Era, a Jew, digging in the ground near Toledo, found a book in which it was written that Christ would be born of the Virgin Mary in the third world and would suffer for the salvation of humanity; he converted immediately and was baptized. The third world, i.e., the third period of the Spirit of *Saturn*, was, as we have shown, when Christ was born of a Virgin. During this period of *Samael*, the Roman pontiffs, deposing the Emperor Frederick, left the imperial throne empty for 28 years until the election of Rudolf, Count of Hamburg, who was chosen in favor of the other princely candidates: Henry, Count of Schwarzenburg in Thuringia; William, Count of Holland; Konrad, Frederick's son; Alphonzo, King of Castille; and Richard, Count of Cornwall, brother of the King of England. Ills multiplied upon the earth. Then, around the year of our Savior 1260, the Swiss Confederation was born, a small country that was to grow with time. Because its people were warlike, it attacked other nations and thus extended its borders. This made all Germany know of the existence of this new republic. Then, in the year 1273 of the Christian Era, the Assembly of Imperial Princes elected Rudolf of Hapsburg. He ruled for 18 years, prudent and wise in many things. All the Dukes of Austria descend from him. The Tartars invaded the Christian lands, seizing Constantinople and Greece, and causing much damage. The Saracens took several cities in Asia, killing more than 400 Christians. Upon the death of Rudolf, Adolf of Nassau was elected Emperor and ruled for 6 years. Albert, Rudolf's son, defeated him at Worms and, after killing him, was elected in his place in 1298. After ruling 10 years, he was himself killed by his brother's son. The Order of the Templars was destroyed on the orders of Pope Clement V. The island of Rhodes was taken by the Saracens following an uninterrupted siege lasting 4 years. After the assassination of Albert by his nephew, Henry VIII, Count of Luxemburg, was named Emperor and ruled 5 years. After him, Louis IV of Bavaria was Emperor for 32 years, beginning in 1315. The Roman Cardinals gave him the crown. Frederick, Duke of Austria, opposed them, but he was defeated. Then Charles IV, King of Bohemia, was Emperor for 31 years. He raised the Bishopric of Prague to an Archbishopric. There were great earthquakes....

In 1453, Constantinople was taken by the Turks on account of the treachery of a certain Janvens. Soon the whole of Greece abandoned Christianity. For, in a short time, several Christian principalities and kingdoms were taken and ravaged by the Turks. In these days, many serious wars broke out among the Christians—in Gaul, in England, in Saxony, in Westphalia, in Prussia, in Flanders, in Sweden, as well as in other countries. At this time, too, the art of printing, which was an admirable discovery, a divine gift, occurred at Mainz, the capital of Germany. In the year 1456 of the Christian Era, the Turks, massacred in Hungary by the faithful, perished in great numbers. An admirable pilgrimage of children came to Saint-Michel. There were earthquakes in the Kingdom of Naples which caused more than 40,000 people to perish....

In the year 1486 of the Christian Era, Maximilian, son of Frederick, was consecrated King of the Romans in Frankfurt and hailed as Holy Roman Emperor by Pope Julius II in 1508. He founded the military order of St. George against the heretics and the Turks. He vanquished the Swiss, reduced the Sicambrians, and triumphed over all rebels. The King of France, pursuing the imperial Crown according to his custom, hatched plots against the Empire; but the All-Powerful maintained what had been organized by *Samael.* In 1508, the Venetians, revolting against the authority of the Emperor, were punished by banishment and death. Stubbornness will be punished, wise submission rewarded. Toward the end of this third period of Samael, an important change, returning things to their original, first state, will lead to the destruction of many worlds. In fact, if by the will of God, the "gamma point" is brought to face the North, a great change will occur in some monarchy or great kingdom. A great religious sect will rise up to replace the ancient cults.

It is to be feared that the fourth beast of the Apocalypse could lose a head. During the first period of *Samael, Mars* announced the flood; during the second, the fall of Troy; toward the end of the third, there will be a break in unity. Indeed, based upon the precedents, one might infer the following: This third period of *Mars* will not conclude without this prophecy being fulfilled and a new religion being instituted. Now, only 17 years remain between the present year of the Christian Era (1508) and the end of *Samael*'s reign in 1525. Omens of ill fortune will be seen. For, before the year 1525 of the Christian Era, the crosses seen these last 10 years on people's clothes will have their consequences....

For the twentieth period, *Gabriel,* Angel of the *Moon,* will take up the direction of the world again on June 4 of the year of creation 6732, which is the year 1525^2 of the Christian Era. *Gabriel* will govern the world for 354 years and 4 months until the year of the world 7086, the eighth month, or the year of the Lord 1879. It would require a prophecy for the series of future events. I do not guarantee the things I have written, most wise Caesar, but one can reasonably believe in them without damage to one's faith. There are some who believe that these periods correspond to lunar months; if such is your opinion, I could agree, but then it would be necessary to change what I have written.

For the rest, I bear witness with my hand and confess with my mouth that in all things I believe and admit only what the Catholic Church has approved by the authority of its Doctors; all else I thrust aside as vain and superstitious fiction.

---

2. Cf. Rudolf Steiner in *True and False Paths in Spiritual Investigation,* p.139: "In a note book of Rudolf Steiner, under the date of 18th August, 1924 ('Morning Lecture, Torquay') the following entry was made in connection with the Archangel epochs—"

1879–1510	Gabriel	Moon
1510–1190	Samael	Mars
1190– 850	Raphael	Mercury
850– 500	Zachariel	Jupiter
500– 150	Anael	Venus
150– 200	Oriphiel	Saturn

BIBLIOGRAPHY

Books by Rudolf Steiner:

Anthroposophical Leading Thoughts. London: Rudolf Steiner Press, 1973.

The Apocalypse of St. John. Hudson, NY: Anthroposophic Press, 1993.

Behind the Scenes of External Happenings. London and New York: Rudolf Steiner Press and Anthroposophic Press, 1947.

The Bible and Wisdom. North Vancouver, Canada: Steiner Book Centre, 1986.

Boundaries of Natural Science. Spring Valley, NY: Anthroposophic Press, 1983.

The Case for Anthroposophy. London: Rudolf Steiner Press, 1970.

Christ and the Spiritual Word. The Search for the Holy Grail. London: Rudolf Steiner Press, 1963.

The Christmas Conference (for the Foundation of the General Anthroposophical Society 1923/24). Hudson, NY: Anthroposophic Press, 1990.

Christianity as Mystical Fact. London: Rudolf Steiner Press, 1992.

The Christmas Mystery: Novalis as Seer. Spring Valley, NY: Mercury Press, 1985.

Community Life, Inner Development, Sexuality, and the Spiritual Teacher. Hudson, NY: Anthroposophic Press, 1991.

Cosmic and Human Metamorphoses. London: Anthroposophical Publishing Co., 1926.

The Cycle of the Year as Breathing-Process of the Earth. Hudson, NY: Anthroposophic Press, 1984.

The Easter Festival in the Evolution of the Mysteries. Hudson, NY: Anthroposophic Press, 1988.

The Effects of Spiritual Development. London: Rudolf Steiner Press, 1978.

Esoteric Christianity and the Mission of Christian Rosenkreutz. London: Rudolf Steiner Press, 1984.

The Fall of the Spirits of Darkness. Rudolf Steiner Press: Bristol, England, 1993.

The Festivals and their Meaning. London: Rudolf Steiner Press, 1981.

The Four Mystery Plays. London: Rudolf Steiner Press, 1982.

The Four Seasons and the Archangels. London: Rudolf Steiner Press, 1968.

Foundations of Esotericism. London: Rudolf Steiner Press, 1983.

Goethean Science. Spring Valley, NY: Mercury Press, 1988.

Goethe's World View. Spring Valley, NY: Mercury Press, 1985.

Goethe's Standard of the Soul (as Illustrated in Faust and in the Fairy Story of the Green Snake and the Beautiful Lily). Translated by D.S. Osmond. London: Anthroposophical Publishing Co., 1925.

Guidance in Esoteric Training. London: Rudolf Steiner Press, 1977.

How To Know Higher Worlds. Hudson, NY: Anthroposophic Press, 1994.

Ideas for a New Europe, Crisis and Opportunity for the West. Sussex, England: Rudolf Steiner Press, 1992.

The Influences of Lucifer and Ahriman. revised trans. Hudson, NY: Anthroposophic Press, 1993.

The Inner Nature of Man and Our Life Between Death and Rebirth. London: Rudolf Steiner Press, 1994.

Karmic Relationships (Esoteric Studies), vols. III, VI, VIII. London: Rudolf Steiner Press.

The Last Address. London: Rudolf Steiner Press, 1967.

Man and the World of Stars. New York: Anthroposophic Press, 1963.

Man in the Light of Occultism, Theosophy, and Philosophy. London: Rudolf Steiner Press, 1964.

The Michael Mystery. Spring Valley, NY: St. George Publications, 1984.

Michaelmas and the Soul Forces of Man. Spring Valley, NY: Anthroposophic Press, 1946.

The Mission of the Individual Folk Souls. 2nd ed. London: Rudolf Steiner Press, 1970.

Mystery Knowledge and Mystery Centers. 2nd ed. London: Rudolf Steiner Press, 1973.

Mysticism at the Dawn of the Modern Age. The Occult Movement in the Nineteenth Century. 2nd edition. Blauvelt, NY: Rudolf Steiner Publications, 1980.

Occult Physiology. 3rd revised edition. London: Rudolf Steiner Press, 1983.

Occult Science & Occult Development. Christ at the Time of the Mystery of Golgotha & Christ in the Twentieth Century. London: Rudolf Steiner Press, 1966.

Occult Research into Life Between Death and a New birth. New York: Anthroposophic Press, 1949.

An Outline of Occult Science. Hudson, NY: Anthroposophic Press, 1972.

The Philosophy of Freedom (The Philosophy of Spiritual Activity). Hudson, NY: Anthroposophic Press, 1986.

Preparing for the Sixth Epoch. Spring Valley, NY: Anthroposophic Press, 1957.

Psychoanalysis and Spiritual Psychology. Hudson, NY: Anthroposophic Press, 1990.

The Reappearance of Christ in the Etheric. Spring Valley, NY: Anthroposophic Press, 1983.

The Redemption of Thinking. Spring Valley, NY: Anthroposophic Press, 1983.

The Riddles of Philosophy. Spring Valley, NY: Anthroposophic Press, 1973.

Rosicrucianism and Modern Initiation. 3rd revised ed. London: Rudolf Steiner Press, 1982.

Rudolf Steiner: An Autobiography. 2nd ed. Blauvelt, NY: Rudolf Steiner Publications, 1977.

The Science of Knowing. Spring Valley, NY: Mercury Press, 1988.

Spiritual Beings in the Heavenly Bodies and in the Kingdoms of Nature. Hudson, NY: Anthroposophic Press, 1992.

The Spiritual Foundations of Morality. Hudson, NY: Anthroposophic Press (new edition forthcoming, 1995).

The Spiritual Guidance of the Individual and Humanity. Hudson, NY: Anthroposophic Press, 1992.

The Spiritual Hierarchies and Their Reflection in the Physical World. Hudson, NY: Anthroposophic Press, 1987.

The Stages of Higher Knowledge. Hudson, NY: Anthroposophic Press, 1967.

The Temple Legend. London: Rudolf Steiner Press, 1985.

Theosophy of the Rosicrucian. 2nd ed. London: Rudolf Steiner Press, 1966.

Towards Social Renewal. 3rd ed. London: Rudolf Steiner Press, 1977.

Three Streams in Human Evolution. London: Rudolf Steiner Press, 1965.

True and False Paths in Spiritual Investigation. 3rd ed. Hudson, NY: Anthroposophic Press, 1985.

Verses and Meditations. Bristol, England: Rudolf Steiner Press, 1993.

Ways to a New Style in Architecture. New York: Anthroposophical Publishing Co., 1927.

The Wisdom of Man, of the Soul, and of the Spirit: Anthroposophy, Psychosophy, Pneumatosophy. New York: Anthroposophic Press, 1971.

Books by Other Authors:

Adams, George. "Rudolf Steiner in England," in *A Man Before Others: Rudolf Steiner Remembered.* Bristol: Rudolf Steiner Press, 1993.

Aharon, Jesaiah Ben. *The Spiritual Event of the Twentieth Century: An Imagination.* London: Temple Lodge Publishing, 1993.

Allen, Paul, editor. Revised 3rd ed. *A Christian Rosenkreutz Anthology.* Blauvelt, NY: Rudolf Steiner Publications, 1981.

Biesantz, Hagen and Klingborg, Arne. *The Goetheanum: Rudolf Steiner's Architectural Impulse.* London: Rudolf Steiner Press, 1979.

Easton, Stewart. *And Another Strong Angel.* Phoenixville, PA: Rudolf Steiner Institute, 1979.

Harrison, C. G. *The Transcendental Universe.* Hudson, NY: Lindisfarne Press, 1993.

McDermott, Robert A. *The Essential Steiner.* San Francisco: HarperCollinsPublishers, 1984.

Pfeiffer, Ehrenfried. *The Task of the Archangel Michael.* Spring Valley, NY: Mercury Press, 1985.

Prokofieff, Sergei. *Eternal Individuality: Towards a Karmic Biography of Novalis.* London: Temple Lodge Press, 1992.

—— *The Twelve Holy Nights and the Spiritual Hierarchies.* 2nd rev. ed. Temple Lodge Publishing, 1993.

—— *The Cycle of the Year as a Path of Initiation.* London: Temple Lodge Press, 1991.

Querido, René and Glas, Werner. *Michael's Struggle with the Dragon: Facing Evil in Our Time.* Fair Oaks, CA: Anthroposophical Society in America/Rudolf Steiner College Publications, 1989.

Schroff, Lois. *The Archangel Michael.* Herndon, VA: Newlight Books, 1990.

Unger, Carl. *The Language of the Consciousness Soul.* Spring Valley, NY: St. George Publications, 1983.

Wegman, Ita. *Esoteric Studies: The Michael Impulse.* London: Temple Lodge Publishing, 1993.

RUDOLF STEINER (1861–1925) was the founder of Anthroposophy, a modern spiritual path or science. Out of his spiritual researches, he was able to provide indications for the renewal of many human activities, including education (Waldorf schools), agriculture (Biodynamics), medicine (Anthroposophical medicine), special education (the Camphill Movement), economics, philosophy, religion, and the arts. In 1924, he founded the General Anthroposophical Society, which today has branches throughout the world.